MICHII

Six hundred brand-new, fascinating, amusing, informative, surprising and entertaining lists provide more laughs, surprises and incredible data about Michigan people, places, phenomena, oddities and events.

by
Gary W. Barfknecht

Friede Publications

Friede Publications
2339 Venezia Drive
Davison, Michigan 48423

Printed in the United States of America

ISBN 0-9608588-3-0

CONTENTS

vi

12. MICHTAKES

FOREWORD

When I shared *Michillaneous* with you in 1982, I didn't know how you would receive my unique offering. I only hoped that you would have as much fun reading the "Michigan Book of Lists" as much as I had researching and writing it.

You did. In Michigan alone, at least 50,000 people have read *Michillaneous*, leading *Publishers Weekly* to call it a regional best-seller. Some 40 newspapers and other publications reviewed the book — all of them positively — including the *Detroit News*, which used excerpts in their Sunday *Michigan* magazine for several months. Partly as a result of interest generated by a national AP wire-service story and partly as a result of gift-giving by friends and relatives, *Michillaneous* has also been sent to former Michigan residents in just about all 50 states as well as more than a dozen foreign countries.

But even before I knew how you would receive *Michillaneous*, I had planned to do *Michillaneous II*. I had to, because the research process hadn't really been completed — only temporarily interrupted so that *Michillaneous* could make its way into print. After publication of *Michillaneous*, I resumed my search for more entertaining, informative, and offbeat facts about Michigan people, places, and events.

Michillaneous II, then, is not a revision or an update of *Michillaneous* but, rather, is a continuation. Though most of the chapter titles and even some of the list titles are the same, the items within the nearly 600 lists, are all new.

I also created, or perhaps I should say the material I found created, three new chapters: *Michtakes*, which lists fellow Michiganians who have hit their figurative thumbs with figurative hammers in such a way that our little daily foul-ups pale by comparison; *Michigan Electives*, which chronicles both ordinary and extraordinary events from our state's political past; and *On the Move*, an enlightening and sometimes amusing look at Michigan's involvement with automobiles, ships, railroads, airplanes, and anything else that moves.

But the biggest surprise that resulted from the creation of *Michillaneous II* is that it is not the end of Michigan life in lists — there will be a *Michillaneous III*. Again, there almost has to be because a great deal of entertaining and informative material that, for editorial reasons and space limitations, didn't fit particularly well in either *Michillaneous* or *Michillaneous II* is too good to file forever. Also, there are still many dark, dusty research corners that I haven't had a chance to clean out. And even as you read this, our fellow Michigan residents, by living their daily lives, continue to provide a wealth of offbeat anecdotes that are truly stranger than fiction.

But perhaps the most limitless source of information for *Michillaneous III* is that lurking in the memories and minds of you, the reader. After publication of *Michillaneous*, we received hundreds of letters filled with compliments, challenges, constructive criticism, and most importantly, contributions of valuable ideas, items or even entire lists.

I hope the same will be true of *Michillaneous II* and, again, invite you to participate. Please tell me what you know that I don't know. If you have come across some unusual information, have thought of a list idea, have compiled an entire list, or have found any mistakes — please pass them along. Just as in *Michillaneous II*, we will certainly give you all the credit.

Please join the fun. Send contributions, clippings, or criticisms to: Gary Barfknecht, Friede Publications, 2339 Venezia Drive, Davison, Michigan 48423.

1

JUSTICE FOR ALL

7 NUDE CRIMES AND MISDEMEANORS

1. BARE FACTS (Detroit) — October 1983

A 24-year-old woman who had pleaded guilty to two counts of accosting and soliciting was taken to a cell while officials made a routine check on her background. When she returned to the courtroom for sentencing a few minutes later, she was wearing handcuffs, high heels, a wig — and nothing else. The shocked judge managed to keep his composure, however, and calmly sentenced her to 90 days.

2. OVEREXPOSED FILM (Kalamazoo) — August 1982

A woman who brought a roll of film containing 30 nude photos of herself to a K-mart for processing charged, in a lawsuit, that a male clerk had made copies of the pictures then distributed them and her phone number to his friends.

3. RELIGIOUSLY SKINNY DIPPING (Madison Heights) — July 1982

When the pastor of the Apostolic Church arrived to prepare for evening services, he found a man frolicking naked in the baptismal font. Police blessed the man, who had also eaten almost all of a supply of chocolate candy bought for Sunday-school children, with breaking-and-entering charges.

4. CHEEKS RED FROM EMBARASSMENT (Lansing) — July 1982

When a 32-year-old man pulled down his pants outside a restaurant to "moon" friends inside, two motorcycle patrolmen, who were also inside eating breakfast, were not amused and arrested the practical joker for disorderly conduct.

5. BARE HUNTING (Mio) — November 1984

Two young southern-Michigan men who were carrying rifles as they strolled down a main road — while wearing only tennis shoes — were arrested and charged with disorderly conduct.

6. AN ARRESTING REVIEW (Ann Arbor) — January 1969

Ann Arbor police officers arrested six actors and four actresses who had stripped naked during a play at the University of Michigan. The members of the New York company had performed in *Dionysus 69,* a three-hour play which included two 15-minute nude scenes.

7. NAKED CAME THE STRANGER (Saginaw) — May 1982

A resident called police and reported that a naked stranger was wandering around inside his home. By the time officers arrived, the intruder had dressed himself in a shirt and trousers taken from the home but shed the stolen clothes as he fled. A few minutes later, police caught the man, who was again totally naked, and escorted him to their patrol car in front of a large crowd that had gathered.

7 COMMON CRIMES

The number of criminal offenses, by type, in Michigan in 1982.

1.	LARCENY AND THEFT	326,283
2.	BURGLARY	162,457
3.	MOTOR-VEHICLE THEFT	61,252
4.	AGGRAVATED ASSAULT	28,952
5.	ROBBERY	24,470
6.	RAPE	4,083
7.	MURDER AND NONNEGLIGENT MANSLAUGHTER	870

4 MOST DANGEROUS COUNTIES

Based on the total number of criminal offenses (murder, non-negligent manslaughter, rape, robbery, aggravated assault, burglary, larceny, and motor-vehicle theft) per 1,000 residents as reported in 1981. State average = 68.

1.	LAKE	100
2.	WAYNE	94
3.	CRAWFORD	93
4.	MACKINAC	90

5 SAFEST COUNTIES

Based on the total number of criminal offenses (murder, non-negligent manslaughter, rape, robbery, aggravated assault, burglary, larceny, and motor-vehicle theft) per 1,000 residents as reported in 1981. State average = 68.

1.	LEELANAU	21
2.	HOUGHTON	24
3.	CLINTON	25
4.	ONTONAGON	25
5.	PRESQUE ISLE	25

4 CRIMES WITH AND AGAINST NATURE

1. NOTHING TO CROW ABOUT (Pontiac) — December 1981

A woman who gave a "minister" $200 cash and a $1,000 diamond ring to remove "evil spirits" that were leading her toward a nervous breakdown was told by the 47-year-old man to buy a live rooster and keep it until her next appointment. When she returned a week later, the reverend had her hold the rooster by the feet while he bit it on the neck then smeared its blood on the woman's neck and nose.

The woman evidently felt she didn't get her money's worth, however, and reported the incident to Oakland County authorities, who charged the man with practicing medicine without a license.

2. DOG DECLARED DANGEROUS WEAPON (Escanaba) — February 1982

Two grocery-store employees chased a man, whom they suspected of stealing two steaks, to his van. At the van, the suspect slid open the door and said, "Get 'em Bear," whereupon a German shepherd lunged at one of the pursuers, knocking off the young man's glasses but not seriously injuring him.

A jury later found the dog-owner not guilty of shoplifting but, in the first such ruling in Michigan judicial history, convicted him on one count of assault with a deadly weapon — his dog.

3. FRAT RATS (Ann Arbor) — December 1979

When their house cat didn't use its litter box, five University of Michigan fraternity members chopped off its paws, hung it from a tree, and set it on fire. The young men, who pleaded no contest to a charge of cruelty to animals, were fined $360 and ordered to do 200 hours of community service work.

4. NO RED NOSE FOR RUDLOPH

A Michigan law prohibits displaying or advertising wine with a picture of a reindeer.

2 DOG DINNERS
It's a Man-Eat-Dog World

1. IMLAY TOWNSHIP (Lapeer County) — November 1982

Animal-control officers, who were investigating the disappearance of a 60-pound Doberman, entered the house of an impoverished 59-year-old recluse and found him cooking dog-meat stew and escalloped potatoes with dog liver. The man, whose house lacked heat, electricity, and running water, pleaded guilty to animal cruelty and was sentenced to 90 days in jail.

2. BENTON HARBOR (July 1983)

A 32-year-old Vietnam veteran was arrested for cruelty to animals after police officers, who were investigating a gunshot, found a shotgun, a dish containing dried dog blood, three small dog bones, and an empty bottle of barbecue sauce near a makeshift grill at the man's home.

3 BARNYARD OFFENSES

1. RUSTLING (1979-81)

As food prices rose and unemployment lines grew longer in recession-plagued Michigan, many hungry city-dwellers rented trucks, opened farm fences at night, and helped themselves to cows, sheep, and even horses, often butchering the animals right in the field.

Livestock losses to rustlers became so great — $614,000 in 1980, a 50% increase over 1979 — that some farmers, particularly in hard-hit south-central Michigan, patrolled their fields at night, armed with bright lights and shotguns.

2. CONTENTED COWS (Ypsilanti) — June 1983

A 66-year-old farmer who grew marijuana to mix with his cattle feed was arrested as he was harvesting the weed behind his home. The man, who pleaded no contest to manufacturing marijuana, said he fed the unusual mixture to his five cows because he had read it would make them, "either lay down after eating or get the munchies and eat more, thus making them beautiful."

3. CASTING SILVER BEFORE SWINE (Fort Geiger, North Carolina) — July 1980

An 18-year-old Marine from Port Huron was ordered to go to a nearby farm and search for silverware accidentally thrown away with leftover mess hall food that was purchased by the farm-owner to feed to his pigs.

The Marine, however, refused, saying it was unhealthy, and, as a result, was sentenced to 30 days at hard labor and a reduction in rank.

2 PROMINENT POACHING BUSTS

1. The largest poaching ring in state and possibly U.S. history was broken January 20, 1979, when a force of 125 state conservation officers, 30 special U.S. agents, and other state conservation personnel arrested 54 people throughout Jackson, Wayne, Ingham, Eaton, Clare, and Kent counties. The arrests climaxed a 15-month intensive investigation of a multi-million-dollar operation that had illegally killed and marketed nearly 300 deer, 1,700 squirrels, 4,400 ducks, more than 11,000 snowshoe and cottontail rabbits, and thousands of raccoons, red fox, pheasants, geese, and fish.

2. As a game warden and his keen-nosed bird dog stepped onto the loading platform at the Fleetwood (Dickinson County) train station on November 28, 1909, the dog suddenly dashed to a coffin being loaded onto the train and began barking. The dog made such a fuss that the officer removed the coffin lid and, instead of finding a man who had supposedly died in a hunting accident, discovered 500 dead partridges illegal market hunters had planned to smuggle to Milwaukee.

5 FANTASTIC FRAUDS

1. AN EARLY VICTOR-VICTORIA (1861-63)

Shortly after the outbreak of the Civil War, Sarah Emma Edmonds disguised herself as a man and in 1861 enlisted in the Union Army at Flint under the name of Franklin Thompson. For the next two years, "Thompson" took part in several battles as a member of the Second Michigan Infantry and, on several occasions, even served as a spy, usually choosing as a disguise that of a woman.

Edmonds finally revealed her true identity in 1882 when she applied for a federal pension, which, after a special congressional investigation, was granted. Edmonds was also accepted into membership in the Grand Army of the Republic — the only woman ever received into full membership by that organization.

2. BORROWED BACKGROUND (Detroit) — Fall 1964

Daniel West, a quiet, distinguished, gray-haired, 55-year-old Black Democrat, who, according to the official *Michigan Manual*, was a graduate of Swarthmore College and Yale Law School, Phi Beta Kappa, easily won re-election to a second term in the Michigan House as the representative from Detroit's 24th District.

But a disgruntled primary-election loser began an investigation that revealed that West had guaranteed his victory by asking acquaintances to file false voter registrations and had committed or encouraged other acts of voter fraud. Shocked investigators also discovered that West was, in reality, an ex-convict who had stolen the background of a deceased New York attorney with the same name.

At the same time, the IRS, which had been conducting an independent investigation, arrested West for tax fraud, charging that he had made up fake spouses and dependents for as many as 1,500 legitimate filers so that they and he could split sizeable refunds.

As a result, West's colleagues barred him from taking his seat in the House, and in July 1965, after being scheduled to go on trial on 117 counts of income-tax fraud, the man with the borrowed background permanently disappeared.

3. THE SOPER FRAUDS (1890s)

In 1891, Daniel E. Soper, who, while serving as Michigan's Secretary of State, was accused of improperly using state funds, resigned and moved to Arizona. Shortly after, however, Soper returned to Michigan and participated in the "discovery" of a variety of artifacts — cups, tables, copper coins, and tablets which contained pictures of sphinxes, pyramids, and the tower of Babylon — which he purported to prove that descendants of Biblical tribes once lived in Michigan.

Every expert and scholar who examined the artifacts, however, quickly judged the "discoveries" as obvious and not very skillful fakes and speculated that Soper and accomplices had crudely manufactured the items, buried them, then "discovered" them in an attempt to profit by their sale to unsuspecting individuals and museums.

Soper denied the charges and continued to "discover" the biblical artifacts as late as 1920. Though the "finds" stopped with Soper's death in 1923, to this day some still search Michigan in the belief that what became known as the "Soper frauds" were genuine.

4. THE WIZARD OF LESLIE (1973)

Michigan inventor Floyd Wallace (Leslie) made national headlines when he demonstrated a device that he claimed could turn low-grade coal, tires, and household garbage into crude oil. The "wizard of Leslie," as he came to be known, then reportedly sold five million dollars worth of $30,000 limited partnerships in his remarkable garbage-to-gasoline process.

Investigators, however, concluded that a 25-gallon drum, pre-filled with oil and hidden inside the "converter," was the source of the "produced" oil and in 1984 arrested Wallace and five others for fraud.

5. OVER THEIR CREDIT LIMIT (Battle Creek) — October 7, 1982

In the biggest single case of credit-card fraud ever uncovered in the United States, two out-of-state men were arrested in Pennfield Township with 90 counterfeit credit cards, 90 false drivers licenses, and $41,000 in cash.

3 FAKE PHYSICIANS

1. THOMAS NOVAK (Detroit) — 1960-64

The high school graduate, who had attended a few medical classes at the University of Michigan and Wayne State University, purchased the office of a retiring physician for $15,000 in 1960 then, in what Attorney General Frank Kelley called "one of the most fantastic stories of deception in the state's history," made $120,000 while posing as a physician for the next four years.

But in 1964, when Novaks applied for a special insurance policy available only to physicians, a routine background check exposed his charade, and he was sentenced to a year in prison for practicing medicine without a license.

2. LEE OTIS PENIX (1980-82)

The former Detroiter, who may not have even acquired a high-school degree, affected a Nigerian accent, posed as a physician, and duped officials at three Chicago teaching hospitals into hiring him as a research assistant. The 30-year-old ex-convict then used his position, according to charges brought by Chicago police, to steal $80,000 in laboratory equipment.

3. WILLIAM DOUGLAS STREET JR. (July-September 1975)

Detroit's self-described "Great Imposter" is very effective at fooling people, including Detroit Tiger officials, who in 1971 gave him a plane ticket for a Florida tryout after he had convinced them that he was a professional football star, Jerry Levias, who wanted to switch to baseball.

In 1975, Street, who had been sent to prison as a result of many of his frequent charades, passed himself off as a medical resident and assisted during 16 surgeries — including mastectomies, appendectomies, stomach operations, and a hemorrhoid operation — at a Chicago hospital before being discovered.

5 MEDICAL MALADIES

1. NO APPOINTMENT NECESSARY (Grosse Pointe Woods) — February 8, 1985

A 15-year-old boy with braces on his teeth walked into an orthodontist's office unannounced and asked the man to remove them. When the dentist refused because the boy did not have the permission of his parents and his regular orthodontist, the youth pulled a .45-caliber automatic pistol from his pocket, pointed it at the dentist, cocked it, and said, "Would this make you change your mind?"

As the doctor immediately escorted the boy to a dental chair, his assistant, who had overheard the conversation, called police, who arrived moments later and subdued the over-anxious patient.

2. DEPORTED TO THE U.P. (October 1979)

A Grand Rapids physician who was discovered to be an illegal alien avoided deportation to Hong Kong by agreeing to practice medicine for three years in Mackinac County, which had experienced a severe shortage of doctors.

3. MOST SUED (1983)

According to an eight-year study completed by the Physicians Insurance Company of Michigan, obstetricians and gynecologists are sued for malpractice more often than any other medical-specialty group practicing in Michigan.

4. AMERICA'S DRUG-DEALING CAPITAL

As of 1984, according to the FBI, Michigan led the nation in purchases of dispensed, abused, controlled substances such as amphetamines, commonly prescribed to control obesity; Diluadid, a synthetic morphine; codeine; Preludin; and the stimulant Ritalin. Though almost all of the addictive prescription drugs were legitimately purchased by Michigan doctors and pharmacists, drug-enforcement officials believed that most of the substances were diverted to the illicit market and sold in other states.

To help control this massive abuse, the Michigan State Board of Medicine in February 1985 banned the prescription of all amphetamines in Michigan.

5. HOME BIRTH DEATH (Midland) — 1983

In the first case of its kind in the state, a 40-year-old lay midwife was charged with involuntary manslaughter after a baby girl had died during a home birth the woman had attended. The prosecution claimed that the midwife was negligent and failed to provide adequate care, but the jury accepted the defense's argument that the child was stillborn and found the woman not guilty.

2 BOTTLE-RETURN PROBLEMS

1. FIRST TO BE CANNED (Southfield) — February 7, 1979

Three months after a new state bottle-return law had taken effect, a Southfield party-store operator and his employee/sister became the first in the state to be arrested for selling non-returnable throwaway cans and bottles. A judge dismissed the charges, however, ruling that the law provided for enforcement by the Liquor Control Commission, not the courts.

2. CONS' CANS CORRECTED (January 1984)

Acting on a protest by the Michigan United Conservation Clubs, Michigan Corrections Director Perry M. Johnson ordered a halt to the sale of beverages in throwaway containers at all Michigan correctional facilities. Though clearly prohibited by law since November 1978, drinks in nonreturnable containers had still inexplicably been sold to prisoners at several state correctional facilities.

3 RARE OFFENSES

1. MAN ATTACKS CAR (Romulus) — May 13, 1982

A retired auto worker, upset over the loss of American jobs because of the influx of imported cars, grabbed a .357-magnum revolver and shot at a Japanese-made Datsun that had cut sharply in front of him on west-bound I-94. As the import and its driver fled at 90 m.p.h., the 56-year-old Ypsilanti man chased them in his van and fired three more hollow-point bullets, all of which missed.

Police, who stopped both cars for speeding, arrested the assailant, who was later found not guilty of assault with attempt to commit murder on grounds of insanity.

2. SLAVERY (Ann Arbor) — Fall 1983

Mike Kozminski, a 60-year-old dairy farmer, and his 56-year-old wife, Margarethe, were arrested on charges that they had held two retarded farmhands against their will for more than 10 years.

State labor department investigators, who testified in Michigan's first slavery trial in more than half a century, said that "Bob and Louie" had worked on the farm 112 hours a week, 52 weeks a year without pay because they apparently believed they would be hunted and put in jail if they fled. Washtenaw County sheriff's deputies added that they had found the two farmhands living in an unheated, vermin-infested trailer "unfit for human habitation," and health department officials said the pair had been fed a diet of garbage, "moldy bread, and maggot-ridden poultry."

In February 1984 a U.S. District Court jury found the Kozminskis guilty on two counts of involuntary servitude and one count of conspiracy to violate the farmhands' civil rights. A sentencing judge later handed down 20-year suspended sentences and ordered the Kozminskis to pay $42,000 in fines and back wages.

3. WAR CRIMES (1982)

Valerian Trifa, head of the 35,000-member Romanian Orthodox Episcopate of America, headquartered at Detroit, appeared in court to face U.S. Justice Department charges that, during World War II, he had led an anti-Semitic group in Rumania and had incited riots that led to the death of hundreds of Christians and Jews.

But in the midst of the deportation trial, the Justice Department abruptly dropped charges that Trifa had persecuted Jews. In return, the 68-year-old archbishop admitted that he had been a member of the fascist Iron Guard organization and "voluntarily" agreed to leave the U.S.

4 UNUSUAL THEFTS

1. MAN'S LINGERIE LOOTED (Saginaw) — April 1, 1983

A 25-year-old man who liked to wear women's clothing reported to police that a robber had twisted his arm behind his back, snatched $40 from his bra, and fled.

2. BRIDGE BRIGANDAGE (1984)

When prices for scrap aluminum reached 40 to 45 cents a pound, amateur thieves began dismantling freeway aluminum bridge railings and selling them. The railings from 16 bridges over freeways in the Detroit area alone were decimated in one four-month period, including three that were carted off in their entirety.

3. ONE GARAGE TO GO (Bay City) — September 1984

Three men with a pickup truck and a flatbed trailer arrived at a piece of property that had been repossessed by a bank, dismantled a new 20-by-28-foot garage from its foundation, and stole it.

4. PAID BACK WITH INTEREST (Dewitt)

As Kelly Terrell shopped at a mall in December 1983, a thief stole his 1975 Chevrolet pickup truck from the parking lot. Two months later, Terrell received a phone call from a stranger, who lectured him about leaving his keys in the truck and scolded him for not properly caring for the vehicle. The caller then told Terrell that he could retrieve his truck in the same parking lot where it had been stolen.

Terrell arrived at the mall and found, inside his truck, a three-page list of repairs the thief had made, including extensive body work and a new paint job.

5 MOST BURGLARIZED COUNTIES

Five counties with the most reported burglaries per 1,000 residents in 1981. State average = 18.5.

1. LAKE	61
2. CLARE	37
3. ROSCOMMON	34
4. CRAWFORD	32
5. KALKASKA	30

3 LEAST BURGLARIZED COUNTIES

Three counties with the fewest reported burglaries per 1,000 population in 1981. State average = 18.5.

1.	CLINTON	5.9
2.	LEELANAU	5.9
3.	DICKINSON	6.2

3 LARGEST BANK ROBBERIES

1. ECORSE (June 9, 1982)

A lone gunman, armed with a long-barreled revolver, escaped with about $500,000 in cash from the Security Bank & Trust shortly after an armored car had made its morning delivery.

2. DETROIT (January 1981)

A bandit, who used a chemical spray to disable armored-car drivers in front of the Bank of the Commonwealth's main branch, escaped with more than $500,000 in cash and checks.

3. YPSILANTI (January 16, 1980)

A 19-year-old bank-vault teller stole $421,000 from the National Bank of Ypsilanti where he worked.

4 COUNTIES WITH THE HIGHEST AUTOMOBILE-THEFT RATES

Based on the number of stolen cars per 1,000 registered vehicles in 1981. State average = 8.5.

1.	WAYNE	25.1
2.	MACOMB	7.9
3.	OAKLAND	6.7
4.	WASHTENAW	6.4

5 COUNTIES WITH THE LOWEST AUTOMOBILE-THEFT RATES

Based on the number of stolen cars per 1,000 registered vehicles in 1981. State average = 8.5.

1.	MONTMORENCY	.38
2.	MISSAUKEE	.71
3.	ALCONA	.76
4.	PRESQUE ISLE	.80
5.	OSCODA	.96

4 PROMINENT GOVERNMENT OFFICIALS WHOSE CARS WERE STOLEN

1. WILLIAM HART, Detroit Police Chief (Detroit) — August 14, 1980

Hart's official vehicle, a 1980 dark-green Plymouth Fury, was stolen from the driveway of his home. Later in the day, the unmarked, city-owned car — stripped of its wheels, telephone, police radio, hood, trunk, doors, dashboard, and seats — was found behind a vacant house.

2. FRANK KELLEY, Michigan Attorney General (Ferndale) — November 12, 1984

The private car of Michigan's top law-enforcement officer was stolen from a municipal parking lot while Kelley shopped in a nearby store. Fourteen years earlier, another one of Kelley's cars had been stolen in Southfield.

3. CARL LEVIN, U.S. Senator (Detroit) — January 21, 1984

As Levin sat in his aide's car outside the Book Cadillac Hotel, he glanced up to see his own car, which he had parked across the street, drive away. Levin and his aide took off after the car, trailed it for about 15 minutes to an east-side residence, and watched as the thief punched out the trunk lock and searched the car.

Levin flagged down a passing taxi, had the driver call police, and, when they arrived, pointed out the thief, who was still standing near the stolen car.

4. WILLIAM G. MILLIKEN, Governor (Romulus) — July 13, 1980

Milliken's 1980 black Lincoln Continental Mark VI limousine — equipped with a state-police radio and a riot gun — was stolen from a hotel parking lot during the national Republican convention. Two days later, the car — minus the gun — was found abandoned near Joe Louis Arena (Detroit).

Five years earlier, a group of youths had stolen Milliken's new $8,900 official limousine in Lansing then abandoned it in Detroit.

5 BAD DRIVERS

1. On October 26, 1972, a 34-year-old Detroit phonograph salesman, called the worst driver in Michigan history, had his license revoked — for 21 years. The man, who was also sentenced to 90 days in jail, had amassed more than 100 driving points in four years (12 points in two years means automatic loss of license), the most in state history, according to the Secretary of State.

2. The death of a Detroit man, who was killed in November 1967 while attempting to collect an unpaid gambling debt, brought to an end one of the state's worst driving records. At the time of his death the 36-year-old man:

— had had his license revoked until 1994.
— owed $874 from two collisions he was involved in.
— had been convicted of 47 moving violations, including five for reckless

driving, from 1958 to 1967.

— had accumulated 45 points from 1965 to 1967.

— had served at least 235 days in jail and paid at least $765 in fines and costs because of traffic convictions.

— used six aliases and drove autos registered to other people to keep driving while suspended.

3. A 22-year-old Sparta man, whose car had run out of gas on April 8, 1982, smashed a window at the Algoma Township firehall, opened the garage door, and crashed through part of a wall as he took off in the township's fire truck. As the truck roared down the wrong side of the highway near Rockford, the man, who reportedly had been drinking, passed out and fell off the moving vehicle, which then ran off the road and smashed into a tree.

4. In 1981, after Detroit had begun cracking down on people who had not paid traffic tickets, one of the first cases heard by one traffic court judge was that of a woman who had not paid 300 tickets worth $7000 in fines. The judge, who said he had never seen such a total in his 28 years on the bench, sentenced the woman to pay $100 a month until all fines were paid.

5. In separate incidents during 1984, one Cadillac policewoman reportedly ran into a garage wall with a patrol car, collided with a fire truck, failed to stop for an unloading school bus, and accidentally shot a computer with her pistol in the station house. City officials fired the woman, but the Civil Service Commission overruled their action, stating that none of the alleged infractions was cause for dismissal.

5 BUNGLED GETAWAYS

1. ELIMINATING THE EVIDENCE (Ann Arbor) — May 24, 1983

A 32-year-old man bolted from a jewelry store with two stolen diamond rings and sped off in a waiting taxi but was captured by state police officers after traveling only 15 miles. The man admitted to the theft and said he had stomped the rings, worth $7000, into the dirt at the spot of the arrest.

Metal detectors, however, turned up nothing, so suspicious police investigators got a search warrant and ordered x-rays, which revealed that the man had swallowed the gems. As hospital personnel prepared to administer an enema to retrieve the evidence, the man said that, if they would allow nature to take its course, he would cooperate, then asked for a magazine, a cigarette, and a little time.

2. FAIRY TRAIL (Detroit) — July 14, 1983

Two men broke into St. Andrew's Catholic Church and stole, among other things, a tabernacle full of communion wheat wafers, which fell onto the street as they fled. Police followed the Hansel-and-Gretel-like trail to a nearby house where they arrested the men.

12

3. DEAD BATTERY (Detroit)

According to *The Oops Book — The Complete Book of Blunders*, a man who fled after robbing a grocery store returned seconds later and forced the clerk to help start the getaway car with jumper cables.

4. NOT YOUR STANDARD FARE (Kalamazoo) — July 20, 1982

At 4 a.m. a 56-year-old cab driver answered a call in his standard-sized Plymouth to find three suspicious-looking men standing in a residential driveway. When the men said they needed a much bigger cab because they had a lot to haul, the driver radioed for a more spacious Checker Cab — and the police, who arrived as the men piled two televisions, a microwave oven, three suitcases, and other stolen items onto the driveway.

5. FLOWER POWER (Ann Arbor) — May 24, 1983

A Pittsfield Township police officer, who was investigating the theft of $300 worth of flowers from a country market, arrested two suspects after following a trail of flower petals almost half a mile to the front door of their condominium.

4 UNUSUAL CATCHES

1. A TRUE BELIEVER (Detroit) — October 1982

On the day Martha Jean "The Queen" Steinberg's car was stolen, she threatened the wrath of the Almighty on anyone in the listening audience of her popular radio gospel program who so much as saw the car without calling police. Evidently the thief was listening, for when Steinberg returned to her Home of Love Church, she found her car parked in its usual place — with the gas tank filled.

2. SMASHED ON BEER (Grand Rapids) — March 1982

An armed man was foiled in an attempt to rob a party store when a quick-thinking customer smacked him over the head with a full case of beer.

3. THREE FOR ONE (Detroit) — March 28, 1984

When two police officers arrested the four occupants of a stolen 1984 Buick Regal that had crashed into a garage after running nine stop signs, they discovered that a 1981 Oldsmobile Toronado parked inside the garage was also stolen.

Then, as the officers returned to their precinct with the suspects, they spotted a third vehicle, a 1982 Oldsmobile that also was reported stolen, chased it, and arrested the driver.

4. LARGEST POT SEIZURE — August 1984

An estimated $8.75 million worth of marijuana was confiscated from a Flushing Township home and from a rented truck that was stopped near Ypsilanti. The separate busts netted more than eight tons of baled marijuana, the largest seizure ever made in Michigan.

6 FIRST LAW ENFORCERS

1. GEORGE GRADY (Dowagiac) on August 16, 1965, became Michigan's first black chief of police.

2. On August 18, 1967, JACK HALL (Benton Township) was sworn in as Michigan's first black state trooper.

3. RONALD J. MUSCHONG (Warren), who broke his spine in a 1972 trail-bike accident, was appointed as the head of his city's police department in April 1985 and became the first police chief in Michigan history to run his department from a wheelchair.

4. In May 1985, SANDRA THOMPSON (Detroit) became the first black female sergeant in the Michigan State Police.

5. KAY E. WHITFIELD (Pontiac) and 6. NOREEN E. HILLARY (Grand Rapids) were sworn in as Michigan's first female state-police officers on May 26, 1967.

4 UNIQUE LAW ENFORCERS

1. For two years during the late 1970s, MICHAEL CALLAHAN served simultaneously as a St. Clair County assistant prosecutor and as a priest at Our Lady of Guadalupe Parish in Port Huron.

2. ROY CASE (Donaldson) is the only county sheriff in Michigan who is also a practicing minister. The 56-year-old associate pastor of a Presbyterian church has been Chippewa County's sheriff since 1956, and his 30-year-old son Rod, who attended the Detroit Bible College, is a deputy in the 25-member department.

3. DEPUTY DOG

In September 1981 the Clinton County Sheriffs Department officially deputized an 18-month-old German shepherd.

4. RON LEONARD (Flint) runs Extradition Transport Service, Michigan's only private, fugitive-transfer airline. Leonard hires former cops as pilots and flight attendants to fly prisoners, most of them handcuffed, from the location of their capture to the place where they will be prosecuted.

WOMEN IN THE LAW
6 MILESTONES

1. 1871

Sara Killgore was admitted to the bar and became the first woman to practice law in Michigan.

2. 1941

Lila Neuenfelt (Dearborn) became the first female circuit court judge in Michigan history. Neuenfelt served on the Wayne County Circuit Court until her retirement in 1966.

3. 1967

Geraldine Bledsoe Ford took the bench as a Detroit Recorders Court judge and became the first black woman to serve in the Michigan judiciary.

4. 1969

Cornelia Kennedy was appointed to the U.S. District Court of the Eastern District of Michigan and became the first Michigan woman to serve on a federal bench.

5. 1972

Mary Coleman became the first woman elected to the Michigan Supreme Court.

6. 1978

Mary Coleman was elected by her colleagues as the first female Chief Justice of the Michigan Supreme Court.

9 JUDICIAL MILESTONES

1. July 24, 1788

The Canadian Council, in creating several North American judicial districts, included Detroit in the District of Hesse and sent Judge William Dunmore Powell to conduct the first non-military court proceedings ever held in Michigan.

2. July 29, 1805

The Supreme Court of the Michigan Territory was organized.

3. July 1, 1836

The first Circuit United States Court for the state of Michigan was provided for by congressional act.

4. July 1836

The first Michigan State Supreme Court, a traveling panel composed of three judges, began conducting sessions.

5. January 15, 1919

When all-male juries twice were unable to determine the guilt or innocence of a Flint man charged with being intoxicated, the judge, defense attorney, and prosecutor all agreed to pick Michigan's first all-woman jury. The six women quickly agreed on a guilty verdict.

6. July 11, 1923

A 13-member jury, the first in Michigan judicial history, heard evidence at a Hart murder trial. The extra juror was impaneled to fill in if one of the regular 12 couldn't complete the lengthy trial.

7. October 1961

Judge Otis Smith became Michigan's first and only black supreme court justice. Smith, who was re-elected in 1963, served until 1967.

8. January 2, 1969

District judges, all of whom were required to be attorneys, replaced all municipal judges and justices of the peace throughout Michigan, and for the first time in 100 years all justice in Michigan was in the hands of professionals.

9. May 8, 1972

Miss Lee Whitman (Tawas City) became the first 18-year-old appointed to a Michigan county jury board.

2 NOTABLE LEGAL SCHOOLS

1. THE UNIVERSITY OF MICHIGAN started the state's first law school in October 1859.

2. MICHIGAN STATE UNIVERSITY in 1982 opened the nation's first and only school exclusively for the study of lie detectors.

3 LETTERS OF THE LAW

1. POSTAGE DUE (December 1984)

When the postal service discovered that a Brighton mailman had put Christmas cards without stamps into the mailboxes of each of his 540 patrons, they fired the 29-year veteran, who was only seven years away from retirement.

But five days later, after thousands of people — including members of the U.S. Congress — and newspaper, radio, and television editorials nationwide had protested the punishment, the service reduced their sentence to a five-day suspension and an order to pay the $70.20 postage due.

2. POST NOT HASTE (July 1979)

A 32-year-old Coldwater postman who had dumped over 10,000 pieces of mail in his garage because, he said, he was overburdened and didn't have time to deliver them, was convicted of obstructing the mails.

3. SUBPOENAS BY MAIL (April 1983)

The Michigan Supreme Court authorized use of first-class mail, instead of hand-delivered subpoenas, as a money-saving means of calling witnesses in criminal proceedings to court.

2 PUNISHING SENTENCES

1. FIRST JAILED JOURNALIST (March 5, 1829)

The Michigan Territorial Supreme Court fined John P. Sheldon, editor of the *Detroit Gazette*, for printing editorials critical of their decisions and, when Sheldon refused to pay, jailed him for contempt of court. Angry Detroit citizens, however, collected and paid Sheldon's fine then held a festive reception upon his release.

2. FORMER PRESIDENT SUES MICHIGAN NEWSPAPER (May 1913)

Theodore Roosevelt sued Ishpeming's *Iron Ore* mining journal for libel after an editorial had charged that the former president was habitually drunk. Roosevelt traveled to Marquette to testify in person, and, after he had also produced a parade of character witnesses that attested to his temperance, the jury awarded the former president six cents in damages and ordered George A. Newett, the paper's editor, to print a public retraction.

3 DISCRIMINATING DECISIONS

1. The state Civil Rights Commission in September 1982 awarded $400,000, the largest amount in the commission's history, to a 27-year-old Wyoming, Michigan woman whom they ruled had been discriminated against by an apartment landlord. The award, the commission said, was "for damages relating to mental anguish" suffered when the landlord, who was also a Wyoming city councilman, sent the woman a notice intended for Wyoming District Court that read: "Her apartment is filthy and she has a nigger living with her."

2. When the U.S. Supreme Court ruled that women must be allowed to join all-male civic groups, the 23-member Zilwaukee Jaycees, after burning their banners, by-laws, jackets, and shirts in an August 1984 bonfire, became the first and only Jaycee chapter in the country to disband their group rather than admit women.

A new Zilwaukee chapter, however — composed of 12 men and 12 women — formed a short time later.

3. In September 1984 the Army ended a controversy which had depicted them as being prejudiced against tall women when they allowed Teresa Young, a 19-year-old Kalkaska woman who had previously been rejected because of her 6' 3" height, to enlist for a three-year hitch.

2 FALSE CLAIMS

1. HIS CASE LACKED TEETH (Flint) — February 1983

A sewage-treatment-plant employee whose upper denture plate had fallen out and into a moving line of sewage was denied a $295 damage claim he filed against the city.

2. A HAIRY ISSUE (Lawrence) — 1981

A male instructor whose hairpiece was singed by a flash fire in a skills-center classroom filed a claim with the Van Buren County Intermediate School District asking that they pay for the damage. After a year of discussions and negotiations, the board agreed to pay one half of the $200 repairs.

4 GRIEVOUS TOILETS

1. BUT CAN WE STILL REFER TO IT AS *THE JOHN*? (March 1984)

The owner of a Utica toilet firm was ordered by a federal judge to pay entertainer Johnny Carson for "all profits and unjust enrichment" from the firm's unauthorized use of the phrase *Here's Johnny* in marketing a line of portable toilets (also advertised as "The World's Foremost Commodian"). The familiar phrase had been used since 1962 to introduce the popular host of television's *Tonight* show.

2. DOWN THE DRAIN (June 1983)

A 44-year-old Berrien County woman got so angry that her 18-year-old son had married without her permission that she took $7,000 of his money and flushed the cash down the toilet. Her son filed a formal complaint, and as a result, the woman was sentenced to five years' probation and ordered to repay the money.

3. FLUSHED WITH MONEY (1982)

Because a gas-fired incinerator toilet at Grand Haven's M-31 Bascule Bridge regularly broke down and often took weeks to repair, four bridge tenders filed a grievance with the Michigan Highway Department demanding a better facility. As a result, a new comfort station — with a suspended, insulated pipe running under the bridge to a 300-gallon holding tank on the banks of the Grand River — was constructed in the bridge tower at a cost of $20,000.

4. FLUSHED OUT (1978)

An Amish-Mennonite family, whose religion forbade the use of modern conveniences, received permission from state and county health officials to construct and use an outhouse on a 20-acre plot they had purchased at Central Lake. But the village council unanimously upheld their town's 1962 ordinance banning outhouses, so the family, though they had offers of free attorney service to fight the ruling, moved back to Pennsylvania.

3 UNUSUAL WORKMAN'S COMPENSATION AWARDS

1. 1980

A state Administrative Law judge awarded $83,500 in death benefits to the widow of a Southfield man who died on a business trip after he had had sex with one of his company's secretaries.

2. 1923

A janitor, who had injured his inner ear while working at an Alpena school, cut his throat while, according to doctors, he was in a "delirium" brought on by his injury. The department of labor ruled that, since the suicide resulted from his on-the-job injury, the janitor's family was entitled to compensation.

3. September 1984

The State Accident Fund, which administers Workers Compensation claims, granted a $90,000 lump-sum settlement to the estate of Michigan Supreme Court Justice Blair Moody, who died of a heart attack in 1982 at age 54. The award resulted from a claim by Moody's family that occupational stress and long working hours had contributed to his death.

5 FAMILY DECISIONS

1. After a long, emotional legal battle, a 12-year-old Kalamazoo girl, who had become pregnant in 1981 after being repeatedly raped by her mother's boyfriend, was forbidden by a juvenile-court judge from obtaining an abortion. In 1982, a few months after the girl had given birth to a healthy baby, another judge ruled that she was not a fit mother and ordered the baby placed in a foster home.

2. In 1982 a New York City man paid a Lansing woman $10,000 to be artificially inseminated with his sperm and bear a child, which he agreed to take at birth. But when the baby boy was born with a birth defect, the New York man first ordered Sparrow Hospital to withhold medical treatment from the infant then argued that the baby was not his.

National attention was further focused on legal and moral questions surrounding the growing surrogate birth "industry" when the results of complicated blood tests, demanded by the New York man to prove he was not the father, were announced live on the *Phil Donahue* television show. When the announcement was made that the woman's husband conclusively was the father, the couple agreed to raise the child.

3. Citing "potential emotional interference with job performance, collusion in grievance disputes, favoritism, morale probems resulting from the appearance of favoritism, and conflicts of interest that arise if an employee is required to supervise the employee's spouse," the Michigan Supreme Court in January 1985 upheld employment rules that bar married couples from working for the same employer.

4. In a first-of-its-kind ruling for Michigan, the state Appeals Court said in September 1984 that a father must support a child conceived against his wishes by a woman who falsely tells him she is taking contraceptives.

5. The state Court of Appeals ruled in May 1982 that a Monroe public hospital could not ban a man from their delivery room simply because he was not married to the woman who was bearing his child.

6 UNUSUAL DIVORCES

1. TIL DEATH DO US PART (Detroit) — April 1981

Willie Nance shot his wife Elizabeth to death shortly after a Wayne County Circuit Court judge had dissolved their 24-year marriage. But, because the order had not been committed to writing, Nance, who was later convicted of second-degree murder, asked that the divorce be set aside. The state Court of Appeals, however, said, "no," ruling that allowing a murder to stop a divorce would "set a terrible precedent."

2. DIVORCED AFTER DEATH (March 1983)

In 1980, 91-year-old Mina Smith (Mio), who had begun to get senile, left her husband to live with a married daughter in Bloomfield Hills. When Frank Smith then refused to help provide support for his wife of 19 years, the daughter became her mother's legal guardian and began divorce proceedings.

In January 1983, Mina Smith died, but her attorney allowed the divorce proceedings to continue to settle the underlying legal issue of whether or not a mentally incompetent spouse could get a divorce through a legal guardian. Two months later, Mina Smith, though deceased, won the right to sue her husband for divorce.

3. TWO FOR ONE (Warren) — August 1982

In 1979 a 27-year-old woman got married, lived with her husband for two weeks, then called it quits. About a year later, she married a second man, and that marriage lasted five months. When filing for her second divorce, however, the woman discovered that there was no official record of her first divorce, so she filed papers against both men.

4. LIVING SEPARATELY TOGETHER (Lake Leelanau) — October 1982

A couple who were granted a divorce were also ordered by the judge to continue to live under the same roof — but not at the same time. The judge, reasoning that it would be best for the couple's two children, directed the youngsters to remain in the family's home and the parents to take alternating one-month turns living there.

5. CLOSE ENCOUNTERS OF THE WORST KIND (Grosse Pointe Woods) — 1983

A Wayne County circuit judge granted a divorce but also ordered the couple to continue living together in their home until their twin 15-year-old sons became legal adults.

6. FIRST-DEGREE DIVORCE (June 7, 1983)

The Michigan Court of Appeals (Lansing) ruled that a woman who was

ivorced after helping pay for her husband's schooling owned part of his law
degree and ordered the man to pay his ex-wife $2,000 a year for ten years. The
case was the nation's first in which a higher court had ruled that a professional
degree was marital property.

3 UNUSUAL DIRECTIVES

1. TAKE ME TO YOUR LEADER (October 1973)

The Detroit Police Department issued a seven-point memorandum that out-
lined appropriate action to take in case visitors arrived from outer space.

2. THIS WON'T HURT (May 1975)

The state dental board ruled that dentists have the right to slap an unruly or
uncooperative child or use other "behavioral management techniques" that
involve force for treating youthful patients. The ruling came after the board had
dismissed charges against an East Lansing children's dentist who was accused of
inflicting bruises and cuts to the eye, nose, ear, and leg of an 11-year-old girl.

3. EAR TODAY OR GONE TOMORROW (September 1974)

The seven-member Alger County Board of Commissioners ordered their
county dog catcher to cut off the ears of stray dogs he had destroyed to verify the
$3-per-dog fee he was paid. When the Munising man refused and offered to take
pictures of the dead animals instead, the board voted unanimously to fire him.

3 CONFLICTING SENTENCES

After analyzing more than 56,000 criminal sentences over a three-year period ending in 1983, the *Detroit News* concluded that:

1. More than eight out of 10 times, white judges imposed longer sentences than
   did black judges in similar cases.

2. Two out of three times, male judges gave longer sentences than female judges
   did.

3. Three out of four times, judges sentencing in their home counties gave longer
   sentences than visiting judges.

2 UNUSUAL SENTENCES

1. An heir to the Upjohn pharmaceutical fortune, who had pleaded no contest to
a charge of first-degree criminal sexual conduct for repeatedly raping his step-
daughter, was sentenced in October 1983 to pay up to $2 million for an incest-
treatment center instead of serving a long prison term. Public outrage, however,
forced a resentencing, and the man was then ordered to take an experimental
drug that would purportedly reduce his sex drive. When the Michigan Supreme

Court ruled that the chemical castration was illegal, the man received a third sentence — five to 15 years in prison.

2. Exasperated with an epidemic of wild driving that plagued Detroit in 1922 Judge Charles L. Bartlett took 30 convicted reckless drivers to a nearby hospital, forced them to visit with maimed children and other auto-accident victims then sent them to jail for two to 30 days. The judge later expanded his unique rehabilitative program by forcing convicted speeders to visit the morgue and ordering public mental tests to determine their sanity.

2 PERFECT LAW-AND-ORDER TIMES
What if you built a jail and nobody came?

1. June 24, 1824

Not one person in the entire Michigan Territory, which then included the present states of Michigan and Wisconsin, was in prison for crime or debt. As a later observer said, "either the officials were very lax or the inhabitants were a remarkably law-abiding people.

2. July 7, 1916

The Michigan attorney general reported that Oscoda County had issued no arrest warrants nor prosecuted anyone for the first six months of 1916, a record never before set by any Michigan county.

7 MAJOR PRISON MILESTONES

1. January 1839

At Jackson, the state of Michigan's first prison, a plank building surrounded by a high fence of tamarack poles, received its first inmate. Stone walls were erected in 1841, and in the 1880s, a massive medieval-like structure was built. The present facility, the world's largest walled prison, was constructed during the 1930s.

2. July 16, 1861

The Detroit House of Correction opened at Detroit. Counties other than Wayne who sent prisoners to the institution were charged an average of $1.25 a week per prisoner, and, until 1885, the federal government also used the facility to hold prisoners and criminals from other territories.

3. August 1, 1861

A women's wing in the Detroit House of Correction opened. Until then the State Prison at Jackson, exclusively designed for male inmates, had held Michigan's relatively few female prisoners.

4. 1885

The Ionia State Hospital for mentally insane criminals opened.

5. 1889

Construction began on the state's second maximum-security facility, the Northern State Prison, located at Marquette.

6. November 14, 1977

The $10.5-million Huron Valley Women's Facility, Michigan's first prison built exclusively for female felons, was formally dedicated near Ypsilanti.

7. August 20, 1981

The Huron Valley Men's Facility, the state's third maximum-security prison, opened near Ypsilanti.

2 UNIQUE PRISONS

1. KINROSS CORRECTIONAL FACILITY (Sault Ste. Marie)

After nearly 25 years of military presence to defend the Soo locks, Kincheloe Air Force Base closed in 1977 and was converted to the medium-security state prison.

2. The MICHIGAN DUNES CORRECTIONAL FACILITY (Saugatuck)

The medium-security prison was formerly St. Augustine Seminary, which was purchased by the state in 1978 for $4 million and converted at a cost of another $2.3 million.

20 POW CAMPS

During World War II, nearly 5,000 German and Italian prisoners of war worked in Michigan's fields, food processing centers, and lumber camps. Between 1943 and 1946, the following Michigan cities had prisoner-of-war camps operating in their area:

1. ALLEGAN
2. AUTRAIN
3. BATTLE CREEK (Fort Custer)
4. BLISSFIELD
5. COLOMA
6. DETROIT (State fairgrounds)
7. DUNDEE
8. EVELYN
9. FREELAND
10. FREMONT
11. GRANT
12. GROSSE ISLE
13. HART
14. ODESSA
15. OWOSSO
16. PORT
17. RACO
18. ROMULUS
19. SAWYER
20. WATERLOO

2 SPECIAL FIRST WARDENS

1. CHARLES E. ANDERSON became the first black warden in Michigan prison history when he was appointed as the head of Southern Michigan Prison (Jackson) on March 16, 1977.

2. PAMELA WINTHROW became the first woman to head a full-fledged men's prison in Michigan when in February 1983 she took over as the superintendent of the Michigan Dunes Correctional Facility (Saugatuck).

6 TYPICAL INMATES

After a three-year study of every prisoner who had been sent to a Michigan correctional facility through March 1983, the *Detroit News* reported the following prisoner breakdown:

1.	BLACK MALES	16,991
2.	WHITE MALES	13,117
3.	BLACK FEMALES	1,272
4.	WHITE FEMALES	542
5.	OTHER MALES	450
6.	OTHER FEMALES	24

7 UNIQUE PRISON INMATES

1. RACQUEL (RICARDO) ELLINGTON (May 1982)

The 25-year-old genetic male who had almost completed a sex-change created a judicial quandry over what type of prison — men's or women's — (s)he should be incarcerated in. After two months of medical and psychiatric examination and testimony, Ellington, who had been sentenced to a one-to-five-term for stealing women's clothing, was sent to the Huron Valley Correctional Facility for women.

2. DEAN LANGWORTHY (September 1983)

The 28-year-old Ionia State Reformatory inmate became the first prisoner in the country to legally demand smoking and non-smoking incarceration areas. Langworthy, who is serving 60 to 90 years for shooting a friend in the head, hauling his body to a field, dousing it with gasoline, and setting it on fire, unsucessfully charged in a class-action suit that his incarceration with heavy smokers constituted "cruel and inhuman punishment."

3. JOHN MCINTYRE (Jackson) — January 12, 1838

The Wayne County resident, who had been convicted of larceny, arrived at Jackson as the first inmate of Michigan's first prison (see page 22).

4. CASTRA NOVA (1914)

The 21-year-old man began serving a life sentence for the first-degree murder of a Detroit police officer. Nearly 56 years later, Governor William G. Milliken commuted Nova's sentence, and he was released after spending more time behind bars than any other prisoner in Michigan history.

5. DANIEL TAYLOR (1982)

The Flint man, who was serving time in a Colorado prison for nearly killing a man in 1977, became the first Vietnam veteran in the country ever to be released from prison to be treated for "post-traumatic stress syndrome" — the psychiatric term describing the mental wreckage that so many U.S. soldiers brought home from southeast Asia.

6. A man phoned the Mundy Township Police Department from the Genesee County jail in November 1984, told an officer that he was going to be away for some time, and asked that a vacation check be put on his home. The man, who was awaiting trial on a breaking and entering charge, also told the officer he wanted anyone who broke into his house prosecuted.

7. On January 18, 1968, Governor George Romney approved a pardon that wiped out all traces of the prison record of an Ypsilanti man who had served two years in prison for conspiring to violate gambling laws. The pardon was the first under new "clean-the-slate" guidelines for former prisoners who had demonstrated six years of exemplary conduct after returning to their communities.

2

DEATH SENTENCES

2 UNUSUAL FUNERALS

1. DETROIT (1876)

Seventeen-year-old Minnie Keusch, who had contracted typhoid fever, was certified dead and placed in her coffin. Shortly before the coffin was to be sealed for burial, a bereaved sister bent down, and, as she placed a final kiss on Minnie's forehead, the "dead" girl, according to *The Book of Lists III*, opened her eyes. Minnie, who decided on that day to become a nun, died in 1958, just three months short of her 100th birthday.

2. SAUGATUCK (April 18, 1905)

An undertaker dropped dead of a heart attack while conducting the funeral of a man who had died of a heart attack.

2 UNUSUAL INTERMENTS

1. TICKET TO THE HEAVENS (April 1985)

The R.G. and G.R. Harris Funeral Homes Inc. (Livonia, Detroit, and Garden City) became the first Michigan burial facility to sell space on a special satellite that is scheduled to carry the ashes of 10,300 deceased Americans to an outer-space interment in 1987. According to the Florida group that is organizing the launch, the funereal space capsule will orbit Earth indefinitely and will be coated with a highly reflective material so that it can be seen passing overhead on clear nights.

2. DOUBLING UP (Detroit) — September 1984

The Woodmere Cemetery became the first Michigan graveyard to advertise cost-cutting two-for-one burials — interments in which one casket is stacked "piggy-back" on top of another in the same grave.

3 CONSPICUOUS CREMATIONS

1. A BURNING DESIRE (Hancock) — August 1984

Violet Cliff, a secretly wealthy schoolteacher who died November 23, 1983, at the age of 83, directed in her will that her home and all possessions, valued at $260,000, be "put to the torch." Nine months later, 60 volunteeer firemen, under order from a Houghton County probate judge, threw gasoline on Cliff's antique-filled five-room house and on a barn where her near-mint-condition 1937 Ford coupe was kept, then carried out the terms of her will.

2. DEAD CHEAP (Kalamazoo) — January 1985

Funeral director John Avink opened Michigan's first, and the nation's sixth, nationally franchised crematorium, a no-frills facility that offers only one service — quick, cheap, and immediate body disposal.

3. FIRST CREMATION (Detroit) — December 10, 1887

The first cremation of a dead body in Michigan took place at the Detroit Crematorium, the first such facility in Michigan and only the fifth in the country.

2 DEATHLY ASSOCIATIONS

1. JACKSON (January 14, 1879)

Twenty-six undertakers met and formed the Undertaker's Association of Michigan, the first such organization in the nation.

2. DETROIT (August 27, 1913)

Representatives of crematories from all over the United States assembled at the chapel of the Detroit Crematorium and founded the Cremation Association of America.

What's A Body To Do?
2 INSTANCES OF USEFUL BODIES

1. SHORTAGE OF FOOD (Detroit) — 1770

An English newspaper reported that food was so scarce in Michigan that Detroit residents ". . . have been obliged to keep two human bodies, that they had found unburied upon the shore, in order to collect and kill the ravens and eagles that come to feed on them, for their subsistence."

2. SURPLUS OF BODIES (Detroit) — 1982

Wayne State University, with more than 20,000 wills on file from people planning to donate their bodies after death, has the largest cadaver-donation program of any medical school in the nation. The school receives so many cadavers — as many as 350 per year, which are shrouded in plastic then set side by side on aluminum shelves in a warehouse-size room — that they are one of the few institutions able to supply bodies to other medical schools.

5 UNUSUAL MEDICAL MALADIES

1. HILLSDALE COUNTY (February 1983)

A five-year-old girl who had hurt her arm while ice skating became ill a few days later and was taken to Hillsdale Hospital, where she was treated for a possible bone infection due to the injury. When her physical condition continued to mysteriously deteriorate, she was transferred to the University of Michigan Hospital, where she lapsed into a coma from what was diagnosed, too late, as rabies.

On March 9, 1983, the girl, who may have been bitten by a bat several months before, became the first Michigan resident to die from rabies in more than 35 years.

2. LANSING (1974)

Because technological advances had rendered traditional criteria — no heartbeat and lack of breathing — meaningless as a criteria of death, a group of religious, medical, legal, and legislative leaders met to establish a new definition of death in Michigan. Their recommendation — no brain waves showing on encephalographs taken twice within a 24-hour period — became law in 1975.

3. GRAND RAPIDS (1978)

Grand Rapids led the nation's 100 largest cities in cardiovascular-disease death rate, with 55.82% of all adult deaths in the city in 1978 attributable to heart disease.

4. KALAMAZOO (March 23, 1982)

A 14-year-old Mendon boy died as the only known Michigan victim of Eastern Equine Encephalitis, a deadly disease that is generally restricted to horses but can be transmitted to humans by mosquito bites.

5. BEAVERTON (October 22, 1979)

A 23-year-old cancer patient who was the first person in Michigan to admit smoking marijuana to ease the pain of his treatment died only hours before a state law was signed which allowed the use of the illegal drug for medical purposes.

4 DEADLIEST SMOKING DISTRICTS

According to a University of Michigan department of epidemiology study, 11,903 Michigan residents died in 1982 as a direct result of smoking tobacco. The department chairman sent the study, along with a breakdown of smoking deaths by state senatorial district, to all state legislators with the message, "Smoking is Killing Your Constituents."

The four Michigan senate districts that experienced the most preventable smoking deaths, according to the study, were:

1. DISTRICT 36 (Alcona, Alpena, Benzie, Crawford, Iosco, Kalkaska, Lake, Leelanau, Manistee, Missaukee, Montmorency, Ogemaw, Oscoda, Presque Isle, Roscommon, and Wexford counties)

    468

2. DISTRICT 4 (Detroit)

    432

3. DISTRICT 1 (East side of Detroit, all of the Grosse Pointes, and Harper Woods)

    431

4. DISTRICT 2 (Hamtramck, Highland Park, and part of Detroit)

    422

2 SHOCKING DEATHS

1. HOLLY (October 31, 1923)

A 15-year-old boy, in an attempt to plunge Holly into darkness as a Halloween prank, climbed to the top of a utility pole and reached for the power-feed line leading to the village. As the boy cut through the wire with pliers, he was hurled to the ground unconscious by a high-voltage electric shock and died the next day.

2. CINCINNATI, OHIO (June 22, 1983)

At a suburban hotel, someone ran a cord from a poolside radio through a metal-framed doorway to an inside outlet. When the door was shut, the cord was partly cut, which electrically charged the door and electrocuted an 11-year-old Grand Haven girl as she tried to open it.

4 DEADLY DIVERSIONS

1. TAYLOR TOWNSHIP (April 24, 1965)

At a carnival in a shopping-center parking lot, five laughing children were riding in a "Flying Comet," a mechanical "maypole" whose arms and attached buckets whirled in circles 10-to-12 feet above the ground. Suddenly, the arm holding their bucket collapsed, and the children were dragged around the center pole until the operator shut off the motor. Two died and three were critically injured in the tragedy which prompted the legislature to enact a safety-inspection law for such thrill rides.

2. BESSEMER (February 4, 1984)

A 33-year-old chair-lift operator at the Big Powderhorn Mountain ski resort was pulled between a cable and a large pulley when the lift accidentally started after he had shut it off. Simultaneously, the cable came off the pulley and a heavy counterweight fell, sending shock waves along the cable that launched skiers from their chairs and pitched them to the snowy ground 10-to-35 feet below. The workman was crushed to death, and eight skiers suffered rib and back fractures, broken wrists, facial lacerations, and sprains in the freak accident.

3. BRIDGMAN (August 11, 1983)

As an Indiana man, who was staying at the Warren Dunes State Park, swallowed a drink of beer, a bee, which apparently had flown into the can, stung him on the inside of his throat. Within minutes, the 60-year-old camper's throat passages swelled shut, and he suffocated to death.

4. DETROIT (May 7, 1922)

A 65-year-old spectator, overcome with the excitement of the moment according to doctors, died of heart failure at the moment Detroit Tiger Ty Cobb hit a seventh-inning home run with two on in a home game against the Chicago White Sox.

2 UNATTENDED BABIES

1. On a 95-degree July 16, 1983, a 22-year-old Mt. Clemens woman left her 13-month-old daughter in the back of a small hatchback car while she and her boyfriend drank and fished along the Belle River in St. Clair County. Two to four hours later, as the temperature inside the car approached 140 degrees, the baby died, her body 40 percent covered by second-degree burns and so dehydrated that her blood was drying in her veins.

The woman, whose blood-alcohol content at the time of the dehydration death was 2 1/2 times the level at which a driver is considered legally drunk, was convicted of involuntary manslaughter and sentenced to 30 days in jail.

2. On July 19, 1983, a five-month-old Benton Harbor girl, whose body temperature reached 108 degrees after she was left in a car for two hours while her parents picked blueberries near Watervliet, died from a cerebral hemorrhage caused by the high temperatures.

7 ATHLETIC VICTIMS

1. BILL ADAMS (April 2, 1981)

During a routine batting practice, the veteran Lansing Waverly High School baseball coach was hit in the right temple by a line drive and died two days later.

2. REGGIE HARDING

Immediately after his 1964 graduation from Detroit Eastern High School, Harding signed with the Detroit Pistons and became the only player ever to go straight from high school into the National Basketball Association.

But from that high point, Harding's pro career and his life steadily declined. In 1965 the NBA suspended him for a conviction of assault and battery on a policeman; in 1967 the Pistons traded him to Chicago; and in September 1969 he was sent to Southern Michigan Prison for parole violations. Finally, on September 1, 1972, during an argument at an east-side Detroit residence, 30-year-old Harding was shot twice in the head and died the next day.

3. DAVID and 4. DANIEL HELWIG (November 9, 1983)

The two Marquette brothers, who were roller skating from Boston to Los Angeles to promote Mattel Toys' "Baby Skates" doll, were killed when a semi-trailer rig slammed into their motor home near Fort Worth, Texas. One brother was skating in front of the motor home and the other was inside when the truck struck them from behind.

5. WIN MERCER (January 12, 1903)

Shortly after being named the Detroit Tiger manager for the 1903 season, the 28-year-old former Tiger pitcher wrote a cryptic note that referred to the evils of women and gambling then committed suicide in a San Francisco hotel room by inhaling gas.

6. BILL MUNCEY (October 18, 1971)

The 52-year-old Royal Oak native and hydroplane racing's all-time victory leader died of head injuries when his boat flipped backwards at about 170 m.p.h. during a championship race at Acapulco, Mexico.

7. KELLY PINTAL (April 14, 1982)

The 11-year-old Bath girl, who had won physical-fitness certificates for five consecutive years, died of a heart attack while jogging with classmates in preparation for the Presidential Physical Fitness Awards.

UNTIMELY DEATHS OF 5 PROMINENT MICHIGANIANS

1. DOUGLASS HOUGHTON (October 14, 1845)

Michigan's first state geologist, who surveyed and mapped much of the Lower and Upper peninsulas, drowned, at age 36, near Eagle River during a Lake Superior storm.

2. FRANK D. FITZGERALD (March 16, 1939)

After serving only two-and-a-half months of his second term, 54-year-old Fitzgerald suffered a heart attack and became the first and only Michigan governor to die while in office.

31

3. FATHER JACQUES MARQUETTE (May 18, 1675)

The 37-year-old missionary-explorer, who founded Michigan's oldest settlement, Sault Ste. Marie, in 1668, died of a lingering illness after returning from an exploration of the Mississippi River.

Two French companions buried Marquette near either Frankfort or Ludington (the exact location of Marquette's death has long been a subject of controversey), but, two years later, Christian Indians removed his remains and reburied them at his St. Ignace mission.

4. STEVENS T. MASON (January 4, 1843)

Mason, who became acting Michigan territorial governor at age 19 and the state of Michigan's first governor at age 24 (see page 251), died of pneumonia at the age of 31.

5. FATHER GABRIEL RICHARD (September 13, 1832)

After his selfless and ceaseless treatment of Detroit victims of Michigan's first cholera epidemic, the 64-year-old priest, educator, and civic leader, known as the "patron saint of Detroit," died of exhaustion.

2 PROMINENT MICHIGANANIANS WHO DIED IN PLANE CRASHES

1. WALTER P. REUTHER (May 9, 1970)

The UAW president, his wife, and four other persons were all killed when their chartered plane clipped treetops, crashed, and exploded as it approached the Pellston airport.

2. KIM SIGLER (December 1, 1953)

The former governor and three companions were killed when Sigler's personal airplane crashed into a radio tower near Battle Creek. Six-and-a-half years earlier, Sigler had received his private pilot's license and had become Michigan's first flying governor.

2 WHOSE PARACHUTES DIDN'T OPEN

1. CLEM STONE (Paris, France) — 1937

In 1933, Clement A. "Clem" Sohn, a parachutist from Fowler, Michigan, constructed an outfit made of sailcloth and steel tubing, which he then used during delayed-parachute jumps at air shows. Billed as the "Human Bat," Sohn would jump from a plane and, using the visually sensational rigging to maneuver during a free-fall, drop to a breathtaking 1,000 feet before opening his parachute and drifting to the ground.

But when 26-year-old Sohn jumped at the 1937 Paris Air Show, both of his parachutes, probably damaged during the long the transatlantic voyage, failed to open, and the Human Bat died.

2. JACK WALLACE (Tecumseh) — October 20, 1963

The 36-year-old veteran skydiver from Ypsilanti died when an improperly altered parachute, which he had received in a trade with a novice shortly before a jump, failed to open and he plunged into high-tension wires.

3 FATAL FALLS

1. During an August 29, 1891 balloon ascension at the Detroit Exposition, stunt man John Hogan (Jackson) lost his grip on a trapeze bar and fell 1,000 feet to his death.

2. One year after Hogan's death (see previous item), also at the Detroit Exposition, Gertie Carmo, the first Michigan woman to fly, struggled unsuccessfully against rain and gusting winds to fully inflate her hot-air balloon. At showtime, Carmo lifted off in the half-inflated balloon which, because it did not gain altitude rapidly enough, struck a tower on one of the Exposition buildings and flipped Carmo out of the gondola to her death.

3. On October 3, 1913, a 27-year-old Laingsburg stunt man rose in a balloon over the Alpena County Fairgrounds, parachuted out, but became entangled in the chute's ropes and drowned after landing in the Thunder Bay River.

3 PLUNGING SURVIVALS

1. DOWAGIAC (September 16, 1963)

A 31-year-old Vandalia sports parachutist, who had jumped from an altitude of 3,100 feet over Dowagiac, struggled frantically to open his reserve chute which had become tangled in the silk of his unopened main chute. The man hit the roof of a building but, because the reserve chute had partially opened and the building's roof had flexed enough to break his fall, lived.

2. DETROIT (September 27, 1963)

A Warren maintenance worker, who was helping install an elevator at an apartment building, slipped and plunged 20 floors down an empty shaft. But because he partially broke his fall by grabbing at a rope that hung in the shaft, the 39-year-old man suffered only a fractured ankle and hand cuts.

3. DEARBORN (December 25, 1982)

A five-month-old boy, who was being held by his aunt near a second-level shopping-mall railing, suddenly arched his back, threw himself out of her arms over the railing, and though he fell 30 feet to the level below, suffered only a slight skull fracture.

3 SHOCKED SURVIVORS

1. GREGORY BLEVINS JR. (Pontiac) — July 2, 1981

The seven-year-old, while playing with his four-year-old brother behind a shopping center, opened an unlocked door to a Consumers Power high-voltage transformer, reached in, and received a shock that set his clothes on fire and caused third-degree burns over 41 percent of his body. As a result of his injuries, Blevins underwent several operations and faced continued skin grafts until he finished growing.

Two years after the incident, in a consent judgment, the owners of the shopping center agreed to make annual payments that would total $22 million if the boy lives to the age of 65.

2. JOANNE FLATT (Olympia, Washington) — June 1982

The 24-year-old construction worker from Flint concentrated on blueprints at a job near Olympia, Washington, as a nearby crane operated close to a high-voltage power line. Suddenly, the crane struck the overhead wires, and 115,000 volts of electricity surged through Flatt's body. The jolt, which caused a momentary power outage in an entire county and parts of another, knocked her to the ground unconscious and reduced her blueprints to ashes.

Though Flatt lost part of a leg and the toes from her other foot and suffered severe burns to her shoulder and legs as a result of the accident, stunned doctors termed her very survival a miracle.

3. JOHN K. KULHANJIAN (Walled Lake) — July 1971

While pulling shingles from the roof of a building, the 18-year-old youth backed into an uninsulated, live wire, which sent 15,000 volts of electricity through his body. A Wayne County circuit-court jury later ordered Detroit Edison to pay Kulhanjian, who survived but suffered severe burns and brain damage, $1 million.

2 INCREDIBLE SHOOTING SURVIVALS

1. Michael Farhat (Kalamazoo), who was shot five times in the mouth and jaw area during an August 29, 1982 robbery, survived serious injury or death, doctors said, because the bullets from the robber's small-caliber handgun struck the 57-year-old victim's dental bridgework.

2. On June 20, 1982, a pair of young robbers shot 47-year-old Flint cabdriver James Pollock three times in the back of the head at point blank range then climbed over the front seat and kicked him onto the street. As the pair drove away with the cab, Pollock, who never lost consciousness, walked down the street and flagged down a police car, which took him to a hospital, where he recovered.

2 WHO COUGHED UP BULLETS

1. GEORGE ADAMS (Detroit) — June 20, 1982

In 1913 a stray bullet hit the 16-year-old Albanian immigrant during a 4th of July celebration. While eating a Father's Day lunch 69 years later, Adams felt something scratchy in his throat, coughed, and expelled the bullet doctors had dared not remove because it had lodged too near his heart and lungs.

2. JOHN EATON (Port Huron) — March 22, 1907

In 1867 a hunting companion's gun accidentally discharged and sent a load of buckshot into the back of 30-year-old Eaton's neck. Forty years later, during a coughing spell, Eaton spit out one of the pellets.

3 MIRACULOUS CAR-ACCIDENT SURVIVALS

1. In the predawn hours of Christmas Eve 1978, a car driven by George Sinadino (Lansing) left the road and crashed into a cyclone fence, sending a two-inch-wide pipe through the cafe owner's windshield. The pipe then pierced Sinadino's midsection, passed within an inch of his heart and spine, skewered him to the car seat, and finally lodged against the rear fender of his car.

Though it took police, fire fighters, and paramedics two hours to cut the pipe in front of and in back of Sinadino to remove him from the car, he survived to earn a place in *Ripley's Believe It or Not.*

2. Three-year-old Tina Castillo (Kent City), a passenger in a car that was struck by a speeding freight train March 3, 1982, was thrown 80 feet through the air onto the railroad tracks then run over by two diesel engines and 16 railroad cars. When the train stopped, rescuers found the tot under a tanker car, suffering from a broken hip and head injuries as a result of the initial crash but somehow untouched by the train.

3. Sharolyn Whitaker (Scottsville) reached for a tissue while driving along M-22 on May 26, 1984, lost control of her car, drove off the road, hit a ditch, flew into the air, and plunged 200 feet over the edge of a bluff. As a result of the spectacular accident, which left her pinned in her car for $17^{1}/_{2}$ hours before being found, Whitaker received only minor injuries and a ticket for careless driving.

3 DEADLIEST DRIVING COUNTIES

Three counties with the most motor-vehicle-traffic fatalities per 10,000 population based on 1982 statistics. A total of 1,417, or an average of 1.5 of every 10,000 Michigan residents, died as a result of traffic accidents in 1982.

1. KALKASKA		6.4
2. ONTONAGON		6.1
3. ROSCOMMON		6.1

4 SAFEST DRIVING COUNTIES

Four counties with the fewest motor-vehicle-traffic fatalities per 10,000 population based on 1982 statistics. State average = 1.5.

1. IRON   0.0
2. DICKINSON   0.4
3. ROSCOMMON   0.6
4. OTTAWA   0.9

3 FREAK AUTO FATALITIES

1. GENOA TOWNSHIP (Livingston County) — March 24, 1984

A 21-year-old Brighton man, who had leaned over the running engine of his girlfriend's car to try to determine the cause of a strange noise, bled to death when the car's fan flew off and sliced his neck.

2. OSCODA (February 18, 1984)

The left-front wheel flew off a car driven on southbound US-23, hit a curb, became airborne, and struck and killed a 64-year-old man as he left a store.

3. BATTLE CREEK (January 3, 1933)

A 22-year-old man who forgot to take his car out of gear was killed when he crank-started the vehicle and it lurched forward, pinning him to his house.

2 SAFEST LABOR-DAY WEEKENDS

The two lowest traffic-death tolls for Labor Day holiday weekends since the Automobile Club of Michigan began keeping records in 1957.

1. 1958   12 deaths
2. 1984   16 deaths

3 CYCLIC DEATH STATISTICS

1. In 1966 Michigan motorcyclists were not required to wear helmets. **122** bikers died that year.

2. In 1967 Michigan passed a mandatory helmet law. Only **84** cyclists died.

3. The 1967 law was ruled unconstitutional, so in 1968 bikers again did not wear helmets. **124** died. In 1969 Michigan passed a constitutionally correct, mandatory helmet law which has been in effect ever since.

5 MACKINAC BRIDGE CONSTRUCTION DEATHS

It took 85,000 blueprints, 42,000 miles of wire, 20-million man-hours of labor, and three-and-a-half years to complete the $100-million Mackinac Bridge. The bridge also took the lives of five of the 2,500 workers who built it.

1. ROBERT ABBOTT (St.Ignace), a 40-year-old laborer, suffered a heart attack and fell to his death.

2. JACK BARKER, 28, (Colorado) and 3. ROBERT KOPPEN, 27, (Plymouth) — July 6, 1956

On their first day of work, the two ironworkers fell 525 feet to their deaths when winds snapped the moorings of a catwalk.

4. JAMES LASARGE, 26, (Manistee), an ironworker, fell to his death.

5. FRANK PEPPER (California)

The 46-year-old diver died of the "bends" while working near Pier 19.

2 UNUSUAL INDUSTRIAL DEATHS

1. On June, 25, 1984, a 28-year-old Royal Oak man fell into a 600-gallon vat of hot gravy at the Elias Brothers Restaurants Inc. (Warren) commissary and died.

2. When a Dearborn Heights auto worker climbed into a bin on January 25, 1979, to retrieve parts that a robot, which was programmed for the job, wasn't getting fast enough, the robot smashed the man's head, killing him instantly.

2 UNUSUAL POISONINGS

1. EAST LANSING (1873)

While researching the mysterious toxic poisoning of residents of some of Michigan's older homes, Robert Clark Kedzie, a chemistry professor at the Michigan Agricultural College, found that the principal ingredient of certain types of wallpaper sold in Michigan contained arsenic. After the paper was installed, the dust from the "Paris Green" coloring often settled out of the paper and infected anyone nearby.

The coloring was eventually removed from production, but not until Kedzie had obtained dozens of samples of arsenic-contaminated wallpaper, bound them into large books, and sent 100 copies to libraries around the state under the title, *Shadows from the Walls of Death.*

2. JACKSON (May 20, 1979)

Three Southern Michigan Prison inmates stole three gallons of copy-machine fluid from a supply room and sold it to 150 fellow inmates as moonshine. Two of the inmates who drank the fluid, which contained methyl alcohol, died, and several others suffered stomach cramps and temporary blindness.

3 FATAL FAITHS

1. BLACK HEBREW ISREALITES (Allegan) — July 4, 1983

Twelve-year-old John Yarbough, who, according to court testimony, had been whipped, placed in homemade wooden stocks, then beaten by his mother at the House of Judah religious camp, died. Medical examiners also testified that the boy's body was covered with many bruises and scars from previous beatings at the Black Hebrew Israelite Jewish camp, whose leader, "Prophet" William A. Lewis, advocated strict corporal discipline.

Ellen Yarbough was convicted of involuntary manslaughter in the death of her son and sentenced to four to 15 years in prison. Two other camp members, who pleaded no contest to child-cruelty charges, were sentenced to one-year jail terms.

2. FAITH ASSEMBLY (1983)

Five Michigan residents were among 52 people nationwide who died while they or their parents were following the teachings of the Faith Assembly, a new, rapidly growing church that teaches members to avoid doctors. The five Michigan victims included four adult diabetics, who died after they stopped taking insulin, and a 13-day-old Charlotte girl, who died when her parents withheld medical treatment.

3. PEOPLE'S TEMPLE (Guyana) — November 18, 1978

Martha Hickes (Detroit), who joined the "People's Temple" commune in 1976, was one of 913 people who died when the cult's leader, Rev. Jim Jones, ordered his followers to commit mass suicide by drinking cyanide-laced Kool-Aid.

5 WHO DIED BECAUSE OF THEIR PRINCIPLES

1. RABBI MORRIS ADLER — (Southfield) February 12, 1966

As the 56-year-old nationally known Jewish leader conducted an ecumenical service at Shaarey Zedek Synagogue, 23-year-old Richard Wishnetsky rose from his seat and, while screaming that the rabbi and congregation were hypocritical, walked to the front of the building, shot Adler in the head, then fired another bullet into his own brain. Both men died — the assassin four days later and Adler on March 11, 1966.

2. JERRY BUCKLEY (Detroit) — July 22, 1930

During 1929, the popular radio commentator had built a large listening audience and made many enemies by emotionally attacking illegal gambling, gang warfare, corrupt politicians, and other local evils that flourished in Detroit during the prohibition era. In July 1930, Buckley made even more enemies by supporting the recall of Mayor Charles Bowles, whom many Detroit residents blamed for the lawlessness and corruption.

At one a.m. on July 22, shortly after Buckley had told his listeners that Bowles had just become the first large-city mayor ever to be recalled (see page 255), three men shot and killed him. The killers were never identified or caught.

3. PAUL L. CABELL JR. (Flint) — February 24, 1972

In the early morning hours, the 26-year-old black assistant principal at Beecher High School penned a note that eloquently pleaded for an end to the racial antagonisms and violence that had plagued his school. Cabell ended the message with, "It seems that there is no other way for me to get your attention," then committed suicide.

4. STATE SENATOR WARREN G. HOOPER (Springport) — January 11, 1945

Hooper was shot to death one day before he was scheduled to testify as a key witness in a grand-jury inquiry into legislative bribery and political corruption. Hooper's murder all but ended the special investigation, and his killer or killers were never found.

5. VIOLA LIUZZO (Detroit) — March 24, 1965

On a road from Selma to Montgomery, Alabama, four members of the Ku Klux Klan killed Liuzzo, a white civil-rights worker who had marched in a protest to demand equal voting rights for the state's blacks. The Klansmen were later convicted of violating Mrs. Liuzzo's civil rights.

4 SUICIDE STATISTICS

Of the 1,103 people in Michigan who took their own lives in 1982:

1. 843 (76.4%) were male.
2. 556 (50.4%) were ages 20 to 44.
3. 168 (15.2%) were senior citizens, age 65 and over.
4. 86 (7.8%) were teenagers.

4 MURDER FACTS

Based on 1982 statistics:

1. A Michigan resident is murdered an average of once every nine-and-a-half hours.

2. Three-fourths of all murder victims are male.
3. More than three-fourths of murder victims were 44 years of age or younger.
4. More Michigan residents (1,103) commited suicide than were murdered (936).

4 MOST MURDEROUS COUNTIES

Based on the murder rate per 100,000 population for 1981. State average = 9.3.

1.	WAYNE	25
2.	MACKINAC	20
3.	LUCE	15
4.	PRESQUE ISLE	14

4 NASTY NEIGHBORHOODS

1. DETROIT (September 9, 1925)

A mob of 700 screaming, rock-throwing whites charged the house of a black family who had moved into the white neighborhood, while the owner, Dr. Ossian Sweet, his family, and several armed friends huddled inside.

Suddenly, a shot rang out from an upstairs window. The crowd scattered as 10 more shots quickly cracked and popped then abruptly stopped. Across the street, a man, who had watched the mob from a friend's porch, lay dead with a bullet in his back, and the Sweet family was charged with his murder.

But, using the Seul Choix precedent (see number 4), famous defense attorney Clarence Darrow argued that Sweet was ". . . justified in defending himself when he apprehended that his life was in danger," and in an open-housing and civil-rights milestone, all were found innocent.

2. PONTIAC (May 15, 1982)

At 5:30 a.m., as four people slept in a homemade tent they had pitched in their yard, their neighbor, according to a lawsuit, fired a projectile through the tent with a homemade cannon.

3. ST. CLAIR SHORES (1961)

Two neighbors argued, sometimes passionately, for months about what type of grass they should grow in a strip of lawn between their homes. One man finally settled the disagreement by getting a deer rifle and, in broad daylight, shooting and killing his neighbor.

4. SEUL CHOIX (June 18, 1859)

Just before dawn, three men walked onto fisherman Gus Pond's property, beat up a hired hand, then began tearing down Pond's net house. Pond, who had been punched, threatened, and harrassed by the three men for months, threatened to shoot them if they didn't leave. When the men continued to rip off shingles, Pond reluctantly raised his shotgun, jerked the trigger, and killed one of the intruders with a barrel of "pigeon shot."

Pond was convicted of manslaughter, but in a decision that changed America's legal concept of self defense, the Michigan Supreme Court reversed the conviction stating, "a man assaulted in his dwelling is not obliged to retreat, but may use such means as are absolutely necessary to repel the assailant from his house . . ."

4 MURDERED GAME WARDENS

1. ARVID ERICKSON and 2. EMIL SKOGLUND (Gwinn) — September 29, 1926

Minutes after Erickson and Skoglund had caught 46-year-old Roy Nunn deer hunting out of season, the ex-convict shot and killed them, brought their bodies to Marquette, weighted them down with bricks, and dumped them into Lake Superior.

A month later, Nunn confessed and, after being convicted of the murders of the first two Michigan game wardens ever killed in the line of duty, spent the remaining 22 years of his life in prison.

3. ANDREW SCHMELTZ (Negaunee) — October 20, 1936

When Schmeltz tried to take a .22-caliber rifle from Raymond Kivela, who had been illegally taking muskrats near the Carp River, the 27-year old trapper knocked the game warden to his knees and killed him with two shots near the heart. Kivela then dragged 45-year-old Schmeltz's body to a nearby swamp, covered it with brush, and, later that evening, attempted to destroy it with dynamite.

But, by that time, Schmeltz had been reported missing, and the tremendous explosion led searchers directly to not only pieces of the officer's body, but also evidence that resulted in Kivela's arrest and conviction for murder.

4. GERALD WELLING (Hermansville) — September 10, 1972

Shortly after midnight, the 54-year-old conservation officer and his partner spotted two men in a pickup truck illegally "shining" and shooting at bears on a dump. The two officers left their patrol car and signaled the truck to stop. But the driver roared into them, and a hydraulic snow-plow assembly mounted on the front of the vehicle struck and killed Welling.

The 24-year-old driver, who twice before had been arrested by Welling for poaching, served a nine-and-a-half-month prison sentence for the death of the fourth and last Michigan conservation officer killed while on duty.

5 FAMILY MURDERS

The five worst recent instances of entire Michigan families being murdered.

1. FERNDALE (January 25, 1965)

Thirty-three-year old Mary Belcher and her six children, ranging in age from two to nine, perished in a house fire. Belcher's husband, who prosecuting attorneys said set the fire because his wife had refused to grant him a divorce, was sentenced to life imprisonment.

2. GOODHART (July 1968)

Richard Robison (Lathrup Village), his wife Shirley, and their three sons and one daughter were found shot to death in an isolated vacation cabin 25 miles north of Petoskey. The case has never been solved.

3. FARWELL (February 16, 1982)

As George Post entered the basement recreation room of his rural house to set up a card table and chairs for a small family reunion, a 20-gauge shotgun roared from six feet away, killing him instantly. At the sound of the blast, Helen Gaffney, Post's daughter by a previous marriage, grabbed her four children and ran for a pickup truck parked in the driveway. But the truck wouldn't start, and with a shotgun and a .38-caliber pistol, the murderer shot and killed Gaffney and three of the children, then returned to the house.

Several minutes later, when Vaudrey Post and her daughter, Garnetta Haggart, returned from a shopping trip and entered the kitchen, the shotgun roared twice more, and mother and daughter died together.

Two days after the worst mass family-murder in Michigan history, police arrested Robert Lee Haggart, the estranged husband of Garnetta, and charged him with the seven murders. Haggart was tried, found guilty on six counts of first-degree murder and one of second-degree murder, and sentenced to seven life terms without parole.

4. ALLENDALE (March 13, 1982)

Maris Karklins, a self-described "hit man for God," shot Robert Paulson, his wife Mary Jane, and their three daughters, then set the house containing their bodies on fire. Four months later, 41-year-old Karklins donned a Nazi uniform and shot his mother in the head, killing her.

Karklins, who had confessed in vivid detail to the killing of the Paulsons, was found guilty on five counts of first-degree murder and one count of second-degree murder and sentenced to mandatory life imprisonment without parole.

5. YALE (April 7, 1982)

Fifty-year-old Bette Giuliani and her four children, ages nine to 19, were all shot in the head by a killer, who then reloaded a .22-caliber rifle and shot them again. Sixteen-year-old James Porter IV, who, according to court testimony, had had several disagreements with the Giuliani family, was tried as an adult in the killings, convicted on five counts of first-degree murder and sentenced to five life terms with no chance for parole.

3 LYNCHINGS

1. MENOMINEE (September 27, 1881)

At about 10 p.m., 20 men, who had spent the afternoon drinking and discussing the murder of a popular lumberjack, stormed the town's jail, broke down the door with a telephone pole, put ropes around the necks of the two brothers accused of the killing, and jerked them into the street.

There, the drunken mob tied the ropes to the back of a horse and wagon and dragged the brothers through the streets lined with hundreds of people, who kicked the screaming men and spit on them as they bounced and tumbled by. When the lynchers reached the railroad tracks outside of town, they tied the two battered, bloody, and lifeless bodies to the crossing sign then threw rocks and garbage at them.

2. MASON (1886)

A mob broke into the jail where a young black man was being held for allegedly trying to kill an employer who had refused to give him his pay, dragged the man to a nearby tree, and hanged him.

3. CORUNNA (May 23, 1893)

A mob rushed into the county jail, looped a rope around the neck of a man accused of the axe murder of a Durand farmer, jerked him into the street, and hung him from a nearby tree. Several members of the mob, including young children, then dragged the body through the muddy streets as others cut the rope into pieces and passed them out as souvenirs.

3 UNUSUAL MURDER TRIALS

1. In 1976, Jerry Wayne Evans (Detroit) clinically died during surgery for knife wounds but was revived. Six years later, Evans, a 42-year-old white man, picked a fight with a black man in a bar and, according to testimony, shot him to death. At a subsequent murder trial, Evans' attorneys argued that their client couldn't help the shooting because he had suffered brain damage during his 1976 "death."

But Evans was found guilty of second-degree murder, and the man — once dead — was sentenced to life.

2. In May 1984, shortly after John Aslin (Mt. Morris Township, Genesee County) had broken into the home of a 76-year-old woman and robbed her, the woman suffered a heart attack and died. Two months later, 21-year-old Aslin went on trial as the first person in Michigan ever to be charged with frightening someone to death during the commission of another crime. In December, Aslin was convicted of first-degree murder and sentenced to life imprisonment.

3. In January 1985, King Boots (Birmingham), a prize-winning sheepdog, went on "trial" for his life. During five days of testimony that took on all the trappings of a murder trial, city prosecutors charged that the 100-pound dog had

mauled his owner's 87-year-old mother to death and should, therefore, be put to death also. The dog's owners, on the other hand, claimed that the elderly woman had died of a heart attack and was only bitten after she had collapsed on top of the sleeping dog.

On January 22, 1985, the presiding judge ordered King Boots defanged, neutered, and confined to his home.

2 WORLD WAR II
DEATH SENTENCES

1. On January 31, 1945, Private Eddie Slovik (Detroit) died before a firing squad in the snowy forests of France and became the only U.S. soldier shot for desertion since the Civil War.

2. In 1942, Max Stephan, a Detroit restaurant owner, was convicted of being a Nazi spy, sentenced to death for treason, and scheduled to be hanged at the federal penitentiary at Milan. President Roosevelt, however, commuted the sentence to life imprisonment, and Stephan was transferred to an Atlanta, Georgia prison.

4 MICHIGAN SOLDIERS KILLED
DURING "CUSTER'S LAST STAND"

Of the 263 men who died during "Custer's last stand" at the Little Bighorn River, Montana, in late June 1876, four were from Michigan. They were:

1. GEN. GEORGE ARMSTRONG CUSTER (Monroe)
2. PVT. RICHARD DORN (Bronson)
3. PVT. FRANCIS MILTON (Hillsdale)
4. PVT. GEORGE POST (Adrian)

2 PROMINENT WAR CASUALTIES

1. PRIVATE JOSEPH W. GUYTON (May 24, 1918)

The Evart man was the first American World War I soldier to be killed on German soil.

2. LT. COL. WILLIAM NOLDE (January 28, 1973)

The 22-year career Army officer died when a communist artillery shell exploded in his bunker at An Loc. Eleven hours later, a cease-fire ended the role of American soldiers in Vietnam and made the Mount Pleasant man the last American soldier to die in the official conflict.

2 MOST WIDOWED COUNTIES

Two counties with the highest percentage of population composed of women whose husbands have died. State average = 4.5.

1.	GOGEBIC	8.1
2.	IRON	8.0

4 WIDOWERED COUNTIES

Four counties with the highest percentage of population composed of men whose wives have died. State average = 0.9.

1.	KEWEENAW	1.8
2.	GOGEBIC	1.7
3.	LAKE	1.7
4.	IRON	1.7

5 LIVING COUNTIES

Five counties with the lowest death rate in 1982, expressed in deaths per 10,000 population. State average = 8.2.

1.	WASHTENAW	5.4
2.	CLINTON	5.7
3.	LIVINGSTON	5.7
4.	INGHAM	5.9
5.	MECOSTA	5.9

4 DYING COUNTIES

Four counties with the highest death rate in 1982, expressed in deaths per 10,000 population. State average = 8.2.

1.	KEWEENAW	24.2
2.	GOGEBIC	14.4
3.	LAKE	14.4
4.	MONTMORENCY	14.2

3
FACTS OF LIFE

4 COUNTIES
WHERE MEN MOST OUTNUMBER WOMEN

Four counties with the greatest number of males per 100 females in 1980. State average = 95.

1.	HOUGHTON	116
2.	IONIA	109
3.	KEWEENAW	108
4.	MARQUETTE	105

5 COUNTIES
WHERE WOMEN MOST OUTNUMBER MEN

Five counties with the greatest number of females per 100 males in 1980. State average = 105.

1.	SCHOOLCRAFT	109
2.	WAYNE	108
3.	IRON	108
4.	ISABELLA	108
5.	KENT	108

2 ELIGIBILITY EXTREMES

1. According to the December 1984 issue of *Money* magazine, for every 100 single women between the ages of 20 and 59 who live in Detroit, there are only 58 eligible men.

2. Ann Arbor, as of 1979, had Michigan's highest and the nation's seventh-highest percentage of single males 14 and over — 50.5%.

3 UNIQUE FIRST WEDDINGS

1. AERIAL ELOPEMENT (October 28, 1912)

Art Smith and Aimee Cour left Fort Wayne, Indiana, in a biplane, flew 75 miles with only one stop for gas, then crash-landed on the campus of Hillsdale College. Despite their injuries, the couple made their way to a Presbyterian church where the pastor completed the nation's first aerial elopment.

2. RADIO WEDDING (June 15, 1920)

From the First Presbyterian Church (Detroit), Mabelle E. Ebert pronounced her wedding vows into a telephone connected to the local telegraph office. The telegrapher then wired the ceremony to personnel at the Great Lakes Naval Training Station near Chicago who, in turn, sent it by wireless radio to the U.S.S. *Birmingham* in the Pacific Ocean. There, Seaman John R. Wichman said, "I do," and completed the world's first radio wedding.

3. RECORDED MARRIAGE (May 5, 1710)

Jean Baptiste Turpin and Margaret Fafard, both French, were married at St. Anne's Church (Detroit) in the first known Michigan wedding involving two white people.

8 CREATIVE "I DO'S"

1. In 1965, 20-year-old EARNEST DIXON (Inkster) entered into his first marriage. In 1971, according to Michigan state police, Dixon wedded a second woman but waited another year before divorcing his first wife. Nine years later, while still married to his second wife, he got married for a third time then in April 1983 married a fourth woman while still married to wives numbers two and three. In September 1983, after Dixon's third wife had learned of the situation and had obtained an annulment, he tied the knot with a fifth woman.

Finally, wife number four, who had discovered that she was one in a group of three wives and two ex-wives, turned the matter over to police. In December 1983 the man who loved too well, too often, pleaded guilty to polygamy.

2. In July 1973, 67-year-old EDDIE BROWN (Sault Ste. Marie) married his deceased wife's twin sister.

3. HAZEL GORHAM and WILLIAM LARUE were married August 30, 1968, on the *Straits of Mackinac*, the last of the state highway department's Mackinac Straits auto-ferry fleet. The 40-year-old craft, which, with the opening of the Mackinac Bridge in 1957, had been converted to a passenger ferry, was retired from service at the end of the 1968 season (see page 158), and the Milford couple was married on one of its final runs between Mackinaw City and Mackinac Island.

4. CYNTHIA OWENS and ALEXANDER WHITE had 56 people — 20 bridesmaids, 20 groomsmen, three flower girls, two ringbearers, two junior

bridesmaids, one junior groomsman, one princess, the maid of honor, the best man, the bride and groom, and four parents — in their October 10, 1981, Kalamazoo wedding.

5. During a 1981 Cincinnati-to-Dayton bus trip, YVONNE PRINCE (Winchester, Tennessee), a front-seat passenger, and RONALD JOHNSON (Royal Oak), the driver, met and fell in love. A year later at Royal Oak, the couple pronounced their wedding vows — on a Greyhound bus.

6. MICHAEL "RENEGADE" HAMMOND (Nashville, Michigan) and SUE "WILD HONEY" PINE (Lansing), who, as drivers for different trucking firms, had carried on an eight-year courtship over the CB airwaves, got married February 17, 1982, atop a flatbed truck at a Dimondale truck stop in a ceremony performed in CB lingo.

7. JEFF ALDERDYCE (Davison), who wore baseball cleats, and JUDY ARMSTRONG (Davison), who carried a bat wrapped with daisies, were married on the pitcher's mound of a softball diamond shortly after the groom's team had lost a May 13, 1983 game.

8. Each year, the Builders Association of Southeastern Michigan advertises for, then marries, a couple at its Builders Home, Flower, and Furniture Show held at Detroit's Cobo Hall.

4 MOST WEDDED COUNTIES

Four counties with the highest marriage rates per 1,000 people in 1980. State Average = 9.4.

1. OGEMAW		12.9
2. GRAND TRAVERSE		12.4
3. WEXFORD		12.3
4. KALKASKA		12.0

3 MOST SLOW-TO-MARRY COUNTIES

Three counties with the lowest marriage rates per 1,000 people in 1980. State average = 9.4.

1. HOUGHTON		7.0
2. LAKE		7.0
3. ONTONAGON		7.5

3 REMARRIAGES

Of the 160,064 people who were married in Michigan in 1982, 107,880 (67.4%) tied the knot for the first time. The rest were taking the plunge again, including:

1. SECOND MARRIAGES	40,808 (25.5%)
2. THIRD MARRIAGES	9,190 (5.7%)
3. FOURTH OR MORE MARRIAGES	2,064 (1.3%)

2 MOST DIVORCED COUNTIES

Two counties with the highest divorce rate per 1,000 population in 1980. State average = 4.9.

1. CRAWFORD	7.5
2. SCHOOLCRAFT	7.0

4 MOST HAPPILY MARRIED COUNTIES

Four counties with the lowest divorce rate per 1,000 population in 1980. State average = 4.9.

1. MACKINAC	0.5
2. ONTONAGON	2.0
3. LAKE	2.1
4. GOGEBIC	2.2

5 MOST PREGNANT COUNTIES

Five counties with the highest birth rate per 1,000 population from April 1980 to July 1983. The average birth rate for the entire state during the same period was 49 per 1,000 residents.

1. MISSAUKEE	66
2. KALKASKA	66
3. IOSCO	65
4. KENT	62
5. CRAWFORD	62

4 MOST FERTILE COUNTIES

Four counties with the highest ratio of married couples with children to married couples without children in 1980. State average = 1.18.

1. LAPEER	1.83
2. LIVINGSTON	1.62
3. MONROE	1.54
4. CLINTON	1.52

5 LEAST PREGNANT COUNTIES

Five counties with the lowest birth rate per 1,000 population from April, 1980 to July, 1983. The average birth rate for the entire state during the same period was 49 per 1,000.

1. ALCONA   35
2. KEWEENAW   38
3. ONTONAGON   38
4. GOGEBIC   39
5. MECOSTA   39

3 MOST BARREN COUNTIES

Three counties with the highest ratio of married couples without children to married couples with children in 1980. State average = 0.85.

1. KEWEENAW   2.08
2. ROSCOMMON   1.72
3. LAKE   1.59

6 UNUSUAL BIRTHS

1. On February 13, 1982, shortly after she had checked into a hospital with mysterious stomach pains, Deborah Baker (Rochester) gave birth to a five-pound, 14-ounce boy without knowing or suspecting, until that moment, that she was pregnant. Baker had dismissed early aches and pains as heartburn and, though she had gained a little weight, wore the same size clothes throughout her unknown pregnancy.

2. While traveling by ambulance to a Petoskey hospital on May 11, 1983, Kim Shuman (Kinross, Chippewa County) began giving birth, prematurely, as the vehicle crossed the Mackinac Bridge. The ambulance stopped, and the woman completed the birth, the first-ever on the span, of a boy.

3. On Christmas Day 1944, a 37-year-old Battle Creek victim of infantile paralysis, who had spent the previous 15 weeks inside an iron lung, gave birth to a two-and-a-half-pound daughter. During the hour-long delivery at Community Hospital, the woman alternated five-minute periods inside the lung with two-minute periods outside, during which the attending doctor and four nurses administered artificial respiration.

4. Two-and-a-half years after Antoine de la Mothe Cadillac founded Detroit, his wife in February 1704 gave birth to a daughter, the first recorded white child born in Michigan. Though other French children may have been born earlier, the records of those births were destroyed in a fire that burned St. Anne's church.

5. On August 29, 1983, Fraser police stopped a Mt. Clemens woman and, though she told them her "water had broken" and she was on her way to the hospital to have a baby, arrested her because a check of her record showed an unpaid traffic ticket. The police then held her at the Fraser station for nearly 40 minutes until her parents arrived and posted $25 bail. Six hours later, at a hospital, she delivered a healthy boy. Officials later discovered that the ticket had been properly paid.

6. Nancy Scaggs (Monroe) gave natural birth on February 6, 1984, to a 13-pound, six-and-a-half-ounce baby boy. The mother said the baby, only two days overdue, was the easiest of her four children to deliver.
  —*Item contributed by Louise Bauerschmidt, Monroe*—

3 TEST-TUBE-BABY FIRSTS

1. FIRST BABY (March 23, 1984)

Cheryl Shveida (Hazel Park) gave birth to Michigan's first "test-tube" baby, a seven-pound, 13-ounce boy, at Detroit's Hutzel Hospital. Almost exactly nine months before, doctors had removed four eggs from the woman, fertilized them in a small glass saucer with her husband Greg's sperm, then transferred one fertile egg back into the mother's uterus, where the baby developed normally.

2. FIRST TWINS (June 10, 1984)

Glenda Higgison (Bay City), who had undergone *in vitro* ("test-tube") fertilization at Blodgett Hospital (Grand Rapids), gave birth, six weeks prematurely, to twin girls at Saginaw General Hosptial.

3. FIRST TRIPLETS (November 4, 1984)

George and Sharon Burns (Manistique) became parents of Michigan's first and the nation's fifth set of test-tube triplets, two boys and a girl, delivered eight weeks prematurely at Blodgett Memorial Hospital (Grand Rapids).

4 ALL-IN-THE-FAMILY BIRTHS

1. In 1944, Ed Howard (Traverse City) told his pregnant wife that he thought it would be nice if she had their baby on her birthday, August 27. She obliged, with a son. Ten years later, Howard repeated his request, only this time asked to have a baby on his birthday. Again, Mrs. Howard complied, this time with a daughter on her husband's birthday, June 28.
  — *Item contributed by Edmund Howard, Traverse City* —

2. According to the 1935 edition of Ripley's *Believe It or Not*, Keith Philo Galpin (Ann Arbor) was the oldest son — of an oldest son — of an oldest son — of an oldest son — of an oldest son — of an oldest son — of an oldest son.
  — *Item contributed by Dale Leslie, Ann Arbor* —

3. On April 3, 1983, Mary Allen, 22, (Flint) gave birth to a daughter. Fourteen hours later, Mary's mother, Sharon Buchanan, 41, became her daughter's hospital roommate after giving birth to a boy.

4. Jackson's Mary Anne Woodard (1976), her mother, Rosann (1953), and her grandmother, Mary Anne Vandusen (1918), were all born on April 20.

— Item contributed by Rosann Woodard, Jackson —

3 REMARKABLE MULTIPLE BIRTHS

1. Jolie Westers (Rives Junction, Jackson County) shocked the medical world on December 29, 1981, when she gave birth to twins — at age 51. Childbearing by women over age 50 happens so rarely that the American College of Obstetricians and Gynecologists doesn't even keep records of such births.

2. On May 19, 1930, Sarah and Carl Morlok (Lansing) became parents of four girls whom in 1957 the National Institute of Mental Health discovered were, at that time, the only all-identical quadruplets in the world.

3. Connie Schermerhorn (Marcellus), 25, became one of the very few kidney-transplant patients in the United States to have twins when on April 10, 1983, she gave birth to two healthy boys.

3 YOUNGEST COUNTIES

Three counties with the lowest percentage of residents age 65 or older in 1980. State average = 9.85.

1.	LIVINGSTON	7.02
2.	ISABELLA	7.07
3.	LAPEER	7.14

5 OLDEST COUNTIES

Five counties with the highest percentage of population aged 65 or over in 1980. State average = 9.85.

1.	KEWEENAW	27.66
2.	IRON	21.90
3.	LAKE	21.09
4.	GOGEBIC	20.72
5.	ALCONA	20.56

4 MICHIGAN RETIREMENT HAVENS

Four Michigan areas among 107 listed in the 1983 book, *Places Ranked Retirement Guide*, in which authors Richard Boyer and David Savageau rated

otential U.S. retirement areas on climate, leisure activities, crime rate, cost of
iving, and quality of health-care centers.

1. OSCODA-HURON SHORELINE
2. TRAVERSE CITY — GRAND TRAVERSE BAY
3. PETOSKEY AREA
4. HOUGHTON LAKE

5 FASTEST-GROWING COUNTIES

Five counties, according to a Dun & Bradstreet study, with the largest
percentage in population gains from 1980 to 1983.

1. LAKE   10.9%
2. ROSCOMMON   10.3%
3. OSCODA   9.1%
4. OGEMAW   8.8%
5. OSCEOLA   8.2%

3 MOST RAPIDLY SHRINKING COUNTIES

Three counties, according to a Dun & Bradstreet study, with the largest
percentage in population losses from 1980 to 1984.

1. WAYNE   -7.3%
2. BERRIEN   -6.8%
3. JACKSON   -4.6%

6 FASTEST-SHRINKING
METROPOLITAN AREAS

Six of the nation's 12 fastest-shrinking metropolitan areas from 1980 to
1983 were in Michigan, according to a 1984 report prepared by the Dun &
Bradstreet Corporation (New York). Those Michigan metro areas and percent
population loss from 1980 are:

1. BENTON HARBOR   -4.4%
2. ANN ARBOR   -3.4%
3. DETROIT   -3.3%
4. JACKSON   -2.8%
5. BATTLE CREEK   -2.6%
6. FLINT   -2.5%

53

5 SHRINKING PAINS

According to a U.S. Census Bureau report, from 1980 to 1983, a period during which the U.S. economy suffered its worst slump since the Great Depression and Michigan's auto-industry-dependent economy experienced even greater pains:

1. Michigan led the nation in net population loss — 193,000.

2. As a result of the population loss, Michigan had to give up one of its 19 seats in the 435-member U.S. House of Representatives.

3. Including adjustments for births and deaths, 403,000 more people left Michigan than entered.

4. Fourteen thousand more Michigan men and women enlisted in the armed forces than left the services, the highest net figure in the nation.

5. A *Detroit News* poll, released only weeks before the Census Bureau's report, revealed that, though 91% of Michigan residents said that they were proud to be from Michigan, 54% of the same respondents said they would rather live someplace else, preferably warmer.

2 UNUSUAL MOVES

1. In 1921 mammoth trailer trucks moved the entire town of Jennings — 100 homes and a sawmill — to Cadillac, 11 miles to the south. The tiny village had decided to relocate closer to the mill's potential customers, and the specially built trucks accomplished the task at the rate of two houses every three days.

2. On March 5, 1959, 22-year-old Carol Sik, her husband, Marino, and 35 other Detroit residents set out in a caravan of cars, pickup trucks, and house trailers for Alaska, where, as the last of America's homesteaders, they built log cabins and cleared land in exchange for free 160-acre parcels of wilderness. By winter, however, only 13 families remained, and by 1984, though the town they had founded 100 miles north of Anchorage had grown to 1500 residents, the Siks were the only original "Fifty-Niners" left in the area.

6 MOST RENTED COUNTIES

Six counties with the highest percentage of year-round housing units that were renter occupied in 1980. State average = 25.3.

1. WASHTENAW	44.4
2. INGHAM	39.7
3. MARQUETTE	32.7
4. KALAMAZOO	32.6
5. WAYNE	31.6
6. ISABELLA	30.5

6 LEAST RENTED COUNTIES

Six counties with the lowest percentage of year-round housing units that were renter occupied in 1980. State average = 25.3.

1.	LAKE	6.1
2.	ALCONA	7.0
3.	OSCODA	7.1
4.	MONTMORENCY	7.3
5.	ROSCOMMON	7.3
6.	OGEMAW	7.4

2 SMALLEST CITIES

1. LAKE ANGELUS — population 397

The affluent community near Pontiac officially incorporated as a city on January 1, 1984.

2. OMER — population 406

Just before Lake Angelus incorporated in 1984, Omer officials persuaded state lawmakers to pass a special resolution permanently preserving the title of "Michigan's Smallest City" which their town had claimed since 1903.

4 MOST STABLE COUNTIES

Four counties with the highest percentage of residents who lived in the same house in 1980 as they did in 1975.

1.	ONTONAGON	66.6
2.	GOGEBIC	66.2
3.	IRON	63.9
4.	KEWEENAW	63.8

6 LEADING HOUSE-OWNING CITIES

Six Michigan cities, population greater than 50,000, with the highest percentage of owner-occupied housing, according to the U.S. Census Bureau. As a state, Michigan ranks second nationally, with 72.7 percent of all householders buying their homes rather than renting.

CITY	%	NATIONAL RANK
1. REDFORD TOWNSHIP	91.4	1

Of 463 U.S. cities with populations of more than 50,000, Reford Township led the nation in home ownership.

2. LIVONIA	90.24	2
3. DEARBORN HEIGHTS	85.76	5
4. ST. CLAIR SHORES	84.06	7
5. WARREN	80.23	13
6. STERLING HEIGHTS	80.18	15

2 SPECIAL HOUSE CONSTRUCTIONS

1. The first brick house in Michigan was constructed at Detroit in 1807 for Territorial Governor William Hull.

2. On July 13, 1984, 180 Traverse City workers erected a $60,000 three-bedroom house in a world-record six hours, 48 minutes. Though the basement and foundation had been previously built, the volunteers completed the remainder of the construction — including furnace installation and laying of sod — in the record time then raffled off the dwelling to raise money for a scholarship fund.

5 COUNTIES WITH THE NEWEST HOUSES

Five counties with the highest percentage of year-round housing units built between 1970 and 1980. State average = 22.1.

1. CRAWFORD	46.4
2. KALKASKA	45.4
3. LIVINGSTON	45.3
4. OTSEGO	42.5
5. GRAND TRAVERSE	42.1

5 COUNTIES WITH THE OLDEST HOUSES

Five counties with the highest percentage of year-round housing units built in 1939 or earlier. State average = 27.6.

1. KEWEENAW	73.3
2. HOUGHTON	70.0
3. GOGEBIC	64.4
4. DICKINSON	58.8
5. IRON	57.6

11 FIRST CHURCHES

Dates and locations of the founding of the first Michigan churches of eleven selected denominations.

1. BAPTIST (Pontiac) — 1819

The first Baptist church in Michigan was organized by a group of New York immigrants who paid the pastor of the church $100 a year, one-third in cash and the remainder in produce.

2. CATHOLIC (Detroit) — July 26, 1701

Two days after the founding of Detroit by Antoine de la Mothe Cadillac, the foundation for St. Anne's church, Michigan's oldest and the nation's second-oldest continuous Catholic parish, was laid. The original structure burned to the ground two years later, and, because of other fires or expansion programs, the church moved or was rebuilt six more times over the next 180 years.

3. CONGREGATIONAL (Romeo) — 1828

4. EPISCOPAL (Detroit) — November 22, 1824

Michigan's first Episcopal group held services at the Detroit Council House and Fort for three years, then purchased a lot on Woodward Avenue and began construction of St. Paul's.

5. LUTHERAN (Ann Arbor) — 1833

6. METHODIST (River Rouge) — March 31, 1818

The Society of Methodists erected the first formal permanent Protestant church building in the Michigan Territory.

7. MOSQUE (Highland Park) — 1919

The first Moslem Mosque in the country was built to serve Highland Park's large Arabic-speaking population.

8. NAZARENE (Grand Rapids) — 1909

9. QUAKER (Farmington) — 1831

10. SEVENTH DAY ADVENTIST (Battle Creek) — 1855

The denomination's first world headquarters, publishing house, sanitarium, school, and college were also established in Battle Creek.

11. SYNAGOGUE (Detroit) — September 22, 1850

Twenty-five German Jewish families, who had arrived at Detroit from the New York area, formally organized the Beth El Society and became Michigan's first Jewish congregation. The members met initially in a private house, then a room over a downtown store before purchasing an old French Methodist church in downtown Detroit.

9 FIRST CLERGY

1. BAPTIST MINISTER

Elon Galusha, the first Baptist minister to establish a pastorate among whites in Michigan, came to Pontiac in 1819.

2. BLACK METHODIST BISHOP

In July 1976, Edsel A. Ammons, a seminary professor from Sioux Falls, South Dakota, was named as the head of his demonination's West Michigan Conference and Detroit Conference and became Michigan's first black methodist bishop.

3. CATHOLIC BISHOP

Frederick Rese on October 6, 1833, was consecrated as the first bishop of the Diocese of Detroit, Michigan's first Roman Catholic diocese.

4. CATHOLIC MISSIONARIES

Fathers Isaac Jogues and Charles Raymbault, French missionaries from the Christian Island Mission on Georgian Bay, made contact with Chippewa Indians on October 4, 1641, at the rapids that connect Lake Superior to Lake Huron. After conducting the first Christian religious services ever held in Michigan, the missionaries named the spot Sault de Sainte Marie (St. Mary's Rapids) then returned to Canada.

5. FEMALE EPISCOPAL PRIEST

The Rev. Meredith Hunt on June 18, 1977, became the first woman ordained to the Episcopal priesthood in a Michigan ceremony. Three months earlier, Rev. Georgia Helen Shoberg had become the first Michigan Episcopal woman to be ordained, but in an Alexandria, Virginia ceremony.

6. FEMALE BAPTIST MINISTER

Muriel Andrew (Detroit) became Michigan's first licensed female Baptist minister in September 1978.

7. METHODIST MINISTER

Nathan Bangs, the first Methodist preacher in Michigan, arrived in 1803.

8. MICHIGAN-BORN PRIEST

Charles Ange, who was ordained in 1744, was the first native of Michigan to enter the priesthood.

9. PROTESTANT MISSIONARY

David Bacon, who was sent by the Congregational Missionary Society of Connecticut, arrived at Detroit on September 11, 1800, conducted religious services, but found that all but a few residents were confirmed Catholics so returned to the East.

5 RELIGIOUS LEADERS

1. Grand Rapids has more churches per capita than any other city in America.

2. The Grand Rapids area, with seven "Christian" broadcasting outlets, has more religious radio stations per capita than any other city in the nation.

3. Of the nation's 100 largest cities, Grand Rapids and Flint have the two highest concentrations in the country of adherents to Reformed Churches — Grand Rapids, 213 per 100,000, and Flint, 18 per 100,000 residents.

4. Flint, with a 13.61% increase, led the nation's 100 largest cities between 1970 and 1980 in Church of God membership growth.

5. Between 1970 and 1980, Detroit Catholics left their city's churches at a rate three times faster than city residents as a group and faster than Catholics in any other of the nation's 100 largest cities.

2 MICHIGAN MONASTERIES

1. ST. GREGORY'S PRIORY (Three Rivers)

   The first Episcopal Benedictine monastery in the Western Hemisphere.

2. ST. AUGUSTINE'S HOUSE (Oxford)

   Lutheran

3 NOTABLE RELIGIOUS EDUCATIONS

1. Michigan's first Protestant Sunday School, founded by members of various Protestant denominations, began October 4, 1818, at Detroit.

2. The first doctor of ministry program to be accredited to any college in Michigan was inaugurated by the Seventh-Day Adventist Theological Seminary at Andrews University (Berrien Springs) in June 1972.

3. The Louhelen Baha'i School (Davison) is one of only four Baha'i learning institutes in North America. The Baha'i faith, founded in Persia in 1893, currently has approximately six million adherents world-wide.

3 SPECIAL SCHOOL SUPERINTENDENTS

1. JOHN PIERCE (Marshall) was appointed in 1836 as Michigan's first state superintendent of public instruction.

2. ANNA MINVERVA CHANDLER (Marquette) in 1888 became the first female superintendent of a Michigan public school system.

3. DR. JOHN W. PORTER on October 14, 1969, became Michigan's and the nation's first black state superintendent of public instruction.

6 MOST EDUCATED COUNTIES

Six counties with the highest percentage of their population, 25 years and over, with a high-school education. State average = 67.9%.

1.	WASHTENAW	80.9
2.	EATON	78.0
3.	INGHAM	77.9
4.	OAKLAND	77.8
5.	LIVINGSTON	77.2
6.	GRAND TRAVERSE	77.1

3 LEAST EDUCATED COUNTIES

Three counties with the lowest percentage of their population, 25 years and over, with a high-school education. State average = 67.9%.

1.	LAKE	49.0
2.	KEWEENAW	49.7
3.	ARENAC	53.3

2 SMALLEST SCHOOL DISTRICTS

Both offer only grades one through eight and in 1983 both had a total enrollment of eight.

1. BOIS BLANC PINES SCHOOL DISTRICT (Bois Blanc Island)
2. GRANT TOWNSHIP PUBLIC SCHOOLS (Keweenaw County)

15 ONE-ROOM SCHOOLHOUSES

Fifteen Michigan schools where in 1984 one teacher instructed multiple grades in one classroom.

1. ADAMS ELEMENTARY SCHOOL (Sigel Township, Huron County)
   Fourteen students, kindergarten through eighth grades.

2. BECKING SCHOOL (Sheridan Township, Huron County)
   Nine students, kindergarten through eighth grades.

3. BIG BURNING SCHOOL (Colfax Township, Huron County)
   Twelve students, kindergarten through seventh grades.

4. CHASSELL NEW ELEMENTARY SCHOOL (Chassell Township, Houghton County)

Twenty-eight students.

5. CHURCH SCHOOL (Huron County)

Nineteen students, kindergarten through eighth grades.

6. ECCLES SIGEL NO. 4 SCHOOL (Sigel Township, Huron County)

Eighteen students, kindergartern through eighth grades.

7. ELLIS CORNERS SCHOOL (Ellis Corners, Calhoun County)

Twenty-six students, kindergarten through sixth grades.

8. HAYNOR SCHOOL (Easton Township, Ionia County)

Twenty-five students, kindergarten through sixth grades.

9. LOUCKS ELEMENTARY SCHOOL (Roxand Township, Eaton County)

Eighteen students, kindergarten through eighth grades.

10. PINES SCHOOL (Bois Blanc Island, Mackinac County)

Five students, kindergarten through eighth grades.

11. RAPSON ELEMLENTARY SCHOOL (Bloomfield Township, Huron County)

Twenty-six students, kindergarten through eighth grades.

12. RED SCHOOL (Filion, Huron County)

Nineteen students, kindergarten through eighth grades.

13. STRANGE SCHOOL (Oneida Township, Eaton County)

Fifteen students, kindergarten through eighth grades.

14. SHILOH SCHOOL (Orleans Township, Ionia County)

Thirty-seven students, kindergarten through sixth grades.

15. WOOD SCHOOL (Bangor, Van Buren County)

Fifteen students, kindergarten through eighth grades.

2 OLDEST SCHOOLHOUSES

1. "WOODEN" OLD STONE SCHOOL (Cambridge Township, Lenawee County)

The structure, built in 1850, is believed to be the oldest remaining original school building in Michigan.

2. GLENN SCHOOL (Glenn, Allegan County)

The school, which has held classes every year since 1854, claims to be the oldest continuously used public school in Michigan.

— *List contributed by Ronald C. Ryan, Adrian* —

4 SPECIAL STUDENT ACCOMMODATIONS

1. The Michigan State University resident-hall system, with a 1983-84 population of 16,500, is the nation's largest.

2. Central Michigan University's yearly board-and-room cost — $2,350 for the 1985-86 school year — is the cheapest of any of the state's four-year colleges.

3. When veterans flocked to Michigan campuses following World War II, dormitory space became so scarce that, at one time, Michigan State University housed students in their gym and had to move beds on and off the floor according to the basketball schedule.

4. When John Wesley College operated at Owosso, their student union was a converted underground stone-and-brick-lined cavern once used by a brewery to store beer.

10 TOP-RANKED COLLEGES

From the *1983-84 Gourman Report: A Rating of Undergraduate Programs in American & International Universities*, which rated schools on a 2.01-to-4.99 scale. Michigan's 10 top-ranked colleges and universities, according to the report, were:

1. UNIVERSITY OF MICHIGAN (Ann Arbor)	4.93
2. MICHIGAN STATE UNIVERSITY	4.51
3. WAYNE STATE UNIVERSITY	4.38
4. UNIVERSITY OF MICHIGAN (Dearborn)	3.94
5. UNIVERSITY OF MICHIGAN (Flint)	3.92
6. OAKLAND UNIVERSITY	3.90
7. MICHIGAN TECHNOLOGICAL UNIVERSITY	3.88
8. UNIVERSITY OF DETROIT	3.87
9. WESTERN MICHIGAN UNIVERSITY	3.85
10. GENERAL MOTORS INSTITUTE	3.40

9 BOTTOM-RANKED COLLEGES

From the *1983-84 Gourman Report: A Rating of Undergraduate Programs in American & International Universities*. The college guidebook, which rated schools on a 2.01-to-4.99 scale, was criticized because the author did not clearly explain the criteria and sources of information used in determining his ratings and for appearing to be biased against private colleges. According to the controversial report, Michigan's nine worst colleges are:

1. SHAW COLLEGE AT DETROIT   2.64
2. SAINT MARY'S COLLEGE   2.66
3. MARYGROVE COLLEGE   2.67
4. MADONNA COLLEGE   2.68
5. HOPE COLLEGE   2.70
6. CONCORDIA COLLEGE   2.71
7. AQUINAS COLLEGE   2.72
8. CALVIN COLLEGE   2.73
9. HILLSDALE COLLEGE   2.74

4 COLLEGES WITH THE GREATEST ENROLLMENT DECLINES

At four-year public institutions from 1980 to 1984.

1. NORTHERN MICHIGAN UNIVERSITY   14.1%
2. MICHIGAN STATE UNIVERSITY   11.7%
3. WAYNE STATE UNIVERSITY   11.2%
4. WESTERN MICHIGAN UNIVERSITY   10.3%

4 COLLEGES WITH THE GREATEST ENROLLMENT INCREASES

At four-year public institutions from 1980 to 1984.

1. UNIVERSITY OF MICHIGAN (FLINT)   30.0%
2. SAGINAW VALLEY STATE COLLEGE   7.6%
3. UNIVERSITY OF MICHIGAN (DEARBORN)   1.7%
4. LAKE SUPERIOR STATE COLLEGE   1.3%

5 SPECIAL COMMENCEMENTS

1. August 6, 1845

At Ann Arbor's Presbyterian Church, 11 graduates received bachelor-of-arts degrees in the first-known University of Michigan commencement.

2. March 27, 1871

Amanda Sanford received a Doctor of Medicine degree and Sara Killgore, a Bachelor of Laws degree, and became the first women to graduate from the University of Michigan. One year earlier, when the college first allowed women to enroll, both ladies had transferred from other schools to complete their education.

3. January 20, 1975

Jackson Community College presented 20 Associate degrees to inmates of Southern Michigan Prison (Jackson) in the nation's first college-commencement exercises ever held within the walls of a prison.

4. April 1984

Lynne Gordon (Farmington Hills) became the sixth and last member of her family to graduate from the University of Michigan, a school record for members of one immediate family.

5. May 31 1984

The Hannahville Indian School (Wilson, Menominee County), Michigan's first and only Indian-run school, graduated its first class, composed of four students from the nearby Potawatomi reservation.

FIRST 2 NURSING SCHOOLS

1. HARPER HOSPITAL NURSING SCHOOL (Detroit) — 1883

2. THE MARION L. WHITHEY SCHOOL FOR NURSES (Union Benevolent Association Hospital, Grand Rapids) — 1886.

FIRST 2 MEDICAL SCHOOLS

1. THE UNIVERSITY OF MICHIGAN (1850)

2. THE DETROIT MEDICAL COLLEGE (February 1869)

The school became the Wayne State University College of Medicine, currently the nation's largest medical school.

2 MEDICAL FIRST LADIES

1. DR. FRANCES A. RUTHERFORD was named by the Grand Rapids common Council in 1870 as the City Physician, and she became the first woman in the United States to hold that type of office.

2. MARY STONE (Shih Mai-yu) graduated from the University of Michigan on June 22, 1896, and became the first Chinese woman in the nation to receive a Doctor of Medicine degree.

2 MOST DOCTORED COUNTIES

Two counties with the most doctors per 100,000 people in 1983. State average = 150.8.

1. WASHTENAW   632.7
2. EMMET   347.9

4 LEAST DOCTORED COUNTIES

Four counties with the fewest doctors per 100,000 people in 1983. State average = 150.8.

1. KEWEENAW   0
2. CLARE   8.4
3. MISSAUKEE   20.0
4. ARENAC   20.4

4 COUNTIES WITH THE MOST DENTISTS

Four counties with the most dentists per 100,000 people in 1982. State average = 51.9.

1. WASHTENAW   120.5
2. GRAND TRAVERSE   91.1
3. EMMET   73.9
4. IRON   73.3

5 COUNTIES WITH THE FEWEST DENTISTS

Five counties with the fewest dentists per 100,000 people in 1982. State average = 51.9.

1. KEWEENAW   0
2. MONTMORENCY   13.3
3. OSCODA   14.6
4. CASS   16.2
5. KALKASKA   18.3

4 SPECIAL DENTISTS

1. HENRI BELISLE

The French doctor, who in 1704 was a resident of the newly established settlement at Detroit, was the first practitioner of dentistry in Michigan but only worked on teeth as a sideline to his medical practice.

2. GEORGE F. GREEN (Kalamazoo) patented the nation's first electric dental drill on January 26, 1875. His version of the tool never caught on, however, because it was too heavy and the batteries were too expensive for general use.

3. The first dental clinic in Michigan to be staffed entirely by volunteer dentists and dental assistants opened at Corunna on April 3, 1970, to provide free dental care to low-income families.

4. A Detroiter, who described himself as "God's dentist," traveled the country during 1982 fighting moral decay by making miracles appear in the teeth of true believers. The man claimed that, simply by speaking, he had made a whole set of teeth appear where there were none; restored a chipped tooth to normal; and caused silver and gold fillings to appear in teeth, sometimes in the shape of a cross.

3 OPTICAL MILESTONES

1. 1850

L. Black opened Michigan's first exclusive optical (eyeglasses) store at Detroit. Initially, Black only fitted glasses but later also ground lenses and manufactured frames.

2. September 10, 1896

The Michigan Optical Society organized at Grand Rapids. In 1904 the professional society changed its name to the Michigan Society of Optometrists.

3. May 1, 1910

All persons beginning the practice of optometry in Michigan were required, for the first time, to pass an examination and be licensed.

FIRST 4 MENTAL INSTITUTIONS

1. THE MICHIGAN ASYLUM FOR THE INSANE (Kalamazoo) admitted its first patient on April 23, 1859. For many years, however, most families, rather than suffer the social disgrace of committing a relative, continued to confine mentally ill family members in attics, sheds, or even backyard iron cages.

2. THE EASTERN MICHIGAN ASYLUM (Pontiac) opened August 1, 1878, to serve 20 southeast Michigan counties.

3. THE TRAVERSE CITY STATE HOSPITAL opened on November 30, 1885.

4. The UPPER PENINSULA HOSPITAL FOR THE INSANE (Newberry) opened in 1895.

12 UNIQUE MEDICAL FACILITIES

Dates inside parentheses are opening dates of the facilities.

1. The ACNE HEALTH CARE CENTER (Lathrup Village — January 1983) is the only known facility in Michigan that treats acne exclusively.

66

2. The AMERICAN LEGION HOSPITAL (Camp Custer, Battle Creek) was, at the time of its December 15, 1921 opening, the only tuberculosis hospital in the country operated by the American Legion for the treatment of servicemen.

3. The INGHAM MEDICAL CENTER (Lansing — May 1980) is the nation's, and perhaps the world's, first arthroscopic surgery center. There, surgeons insert miniscule instruments through tiny punctures then, by watching the tools on a small television screen, repair the human body's most hidden bones without making incisions.

4. The MCLAREN HOSPITAL "WELLNESS CENTER" (Flint — January 1983) is Michigan's first hospital-sponsored facility to encourage and teach people to adopt a healthier lifestyle and stay well instead of getting sick.

5. The MICHIGAN HEADACHE AND NEUROLOGICAL INSTITUTE (Ann Arbor — 1983) is the nation's first in-patient facility devoted exclusively to headache treatment and research.

6. In 1966, PINE REST CHRISTIAN HOSPITAL (Grand Rapids), supported and controlled by the Christian Reformed Church and the Reformed Church in America, became the largest church-supported mental hospital in the United States.

7. In April 1979, ST. JOSEPH HOSPITAL (Mount Clemens) opened the nation's first hospital shopping-mall branch in a suburban Clinton Township shopping center.

8. Michigan's first hospital, ST. VINCENTS, opened in a log building at Detroit on June 9, 1845. The facility, run by the Sisters of Charity, later changed its name to St. Mary's.

9. The SUNSHINE HOSPITAL (Grand Rapids — 1907) was the first municipally owned tuberculosis hospital in the country.

10. The TURNER CONTINENCE CLINIC (University of Michigan, Ann Arbor — October 1981) is the nation's first clinic designed to diagnose and cure people who suffer from urinary incontinence, that is, inability to control bladder functions.

11. The UNIVERSITY OF MICHIGAN HEREDITY CLINIC (Ann Arbor — November 12, 1941) was the nation's first facility designed to research and counsel families on the effects of inherited characteristics.

12. The UNIVERSITY OF MICHIGAN HOSPITAL (Ann Arbor — May 1983) inaugurated the state's first hospital-based-and-staffed helicopter ambulance service.

4 UNIQUE TRANSPLANTS

1. FIRST TRIPLE TRANSPLANT (Ann Arbor) — April 1970

A 26-year-old Kalamazoo man and a 21-year-old Croswell woman each received a kidney, and a 54-year-old Portage man received the heart of a 42-year-old Jackson architect who had died of a brain hemorrhage.

2. SMALLEST KIDNEY RECIPIENT (Ann Arbor) — September 4, 1982

Doctors at the University of Michigan's Holden Perinatal Hospital placed a new kidney into a 17-day-old, four-pound, 14-ounce Ypsilanti baby girl and, a month later, discharged her as the smallest infant in the nation to successfully undergo a kidney transplant.

3. YOUNGEST LIVER TRANSPLANT (Minneapolis, Minnesota) — June 1983

At the University of Minnesota, a one-year-old Warren child received the liver of a traffic-accident victim, but the boy, Michigan's youngest liver transplant patient, died a week later from cardiac arrest.

4. MOST DONATED ORGANS — July 1984

A 17-year-old Mount Clemens boy, who was killed in a car accident, had his organs donated to five people — three in Michigan and two out-of-state — the most patients ever helped by a single Michigan donor.

4 UNIQUE HEART SURGERIES

1. FIRST HEART PUMP (Detroit) — August 11, 1971

Doctors at Sinai Hospital implanted the nation's first permanent, mechanical heart pump in Haskell Shanks, a 63-year-old Warren plant guard who had suffered congestive heart failure. Shanks survived with the implanted silicone-and-dacron chamber longer than any other recipient of such a device before dying three months later from infection.

2. FIRST BLOODLESS OPERATION (Detroit) — July 31, 1978

Doctors at Harper Hospital successfully bypassed two partly clogged arteries in a retired toolmaker's heart without using a transfusion during the operation. The doctors were forced to perform Michigan's first bloodless open-heart surgery because the 72-year-old Jehovah's Witness would not allow transfusions because of his religious beliefs.

3. YOUNGEST HEART TRANSPLANT (Ann Arbor) — June 20, 1984

A two-year-old Detroit girl became the youngest person in the nation to undergo a heart-transplant operation when doctors at C.S. Mott Children's Hospital (University of Michigan) replaced her diseased heart with that of a three-year-old Romulus boy who had died of meningitis.

4. YOUNGEST SURVIVOR (Benton Harbor)

On Christmas day 1977, a Benton Harbor boy was born with a heart that had a defective valve and no pulmonary artery. At Detroit Children's Hospital during the next year and a half, the infant underwent two separate operations to repair his damaged heart and recovered to become the nation's youngest known survivor of two open-heart surgeries.

3 SPECIAL PACEMAKER IMPLANTATIONS

1. During surgery performed at a Newark, New Jersey medical facility on April 9, 1973, 12-year-old Roxanne Hutchinson (Grand Rapids) became Michigan's first recipient of a nuclear-powered pacemaker.

2. On August 7, 1973, in the first such operation performed in Michigan, doctors at William Beaumont Hospital (Royal Oak) implanted a nuclear-powered heart pacemaker — which lasts five times longer than battery-operated models — in a 59-year-old Hazel Park auto worker.

3. Nalani Grover, a nine-day-old baby girl who received a $1^{1}/_{2}$-ounce pacemaker during a two-hour operation at Butterworth Hospital (Grand Rapids) on October 25, 1984, is the youngest Michigan survivor of such surgery.

6 UNUSUAL MEDICAL PROBLEMS

1. Boyne City became so desperate for a physician that in 1968, the Boyne Valley Lions Club put four billboards along the main roads leading to the city advertising for a doctor. R.W. Mansfield D.O., who was attracted by the ads while skiing in the area, decided to relocate to the resort community and in July 1969 opened an office where he still practices today.

Photo courtesy of Curt Frook — P.P.C. (Traverse City)

2. Doctors who had examined a man who had broken every window in a Spring Lake office building in March 1907 declared the man insane and attributed his mental illness to "excessive use of cigarettes."

3. On January 14, 1982, a 55-year-old Benton Harbor man underwent surgery to reattach his left ear, which his girlfriend's son had bitten off during a fight.

4. In November 1982, seven children in the Grand Rapids area became the first "cluster group" in Michigan to be struck by Kawaski disease, a mysterious illness characterized by persistent high fever, redness and cracking around the lips, a red tongue, "pink eye," and a sunburn-like rash around the hands and feet. Since all but one of the affected children had walked or crawled on freshly shampooed rugs shortly before exhibiting symptoms, researchers speculated that the disease may be carried by mites that reside in rugs and become airborne during cleaning.

5. Because Geraldine Preston (Grand Blanc) had Rh-negative blood and her unborn triplets had Rh-positive blood, the woman's body began to produce antibodies that threatened to cross the placenta and destroy the fetuses. But, in an experimental treatment, Mrs. Preston swallowed capsules of Rh-positive blood-cell membranes to "trick" her body into diverting the destructive antibodies away from the fetuses, and on December 2, 1980, gave birth to healthy triplet girls.

6. During the late 1970s, Hemlock-area (Saginaw County) residents experienced abnormally high incidences of cancer, hair and weight loss, kidney ailments, skin rashes, enlarged spleens, and dizziness. In 1979 state health officials concluded a lengthy investigation which failed to turn up any clues as to what had caused the community's mysterious health problems.

4 CASES OF INDIGESTION

1. On December 10, 1909, the Michigan Supreme Court ruled that, though Michigan law did not allow sausage to be adulterated, the Armour & Company (Chicago) could sell sausage containing cereals and water in Michigan as long as they listed the contents clearly on their labels.

2. A Federal Appeals Court ruled in October 1972 that a lenient federal law preempted Michigan's strict standards governing the contents of hot dogs and luncheon meats. The U.S. Supreme Court rejected Michigan's appeal of the ruling, and, for the first time, hot dogs and lunch meat sold in Michigan could contain animal ears, lips, eyes, lungs, udders, snouts, spleens, and bladders.

3. On November 29, 1983, a group of state employees at Lansing dined on a specially prepared meal — Great Lakes fish seasoned with a touch of pesticide. The volunteer diners then had their blood carefully analyzed for the next week by health department toxicologists, who had prepared the experimental meal in an attempt to discover the short-term effects on humans who eat contaminated fish.

4. At an Ossineke farm on March 5, 1973, Mario Fabrini, a frozen-food manufacturer, buried 44,000 pizzas that contained contaminated mushrooms.

3 UNUSUAL ALLERGIES

1. Linda Weiss (Franklin) is allergic to just about everything. Gas heat, draperies, automobiles, carpeting, prepared food, and many other simple conveniences or pleasures that the rest of the world take for granted can, because of the chemicals they contain, cause her to have asthma, hives, headaches, rheumatism, arthritis, digestive problems, depression, or a host of other nagging symptoms.

To help the growing number of individuals who suffer from the same immune-system breakdown, Mrs. Weiss and her husband, Milton, wrote in 1983, *How To Live With the New 20th-Century Illness — A Resource Guide for Living Chemically-Free*, which lists companies who sell chemical-free products.

2. In November 1982, underwear, accidentally contaminated by a toxic fumigant before being sold at a discount outlet, caused at least five Grand Rapids area boys — all between the ages of three and 10 — to suffer painful blistering and swelling of their buttocks and genitals.

3. Coldwater, Michigan, has the highest ragweed pollen index of any city in the nation.

5 ENVIRONMENTAL-ACTION FIRSTS

1. SEWER

Michigan's first underground sewer, a stone-and-brick-lined underground drain, was built in 1836 to replace an unsightly and unsanitary series of open ditches that ran through the city of Detroit.

2. POLLUTION-CONTROL PROGRAM

In 1928 the Michigan Conservation Department and Department of Health, in a joint effort to eliminate human and industrial waste in Michigan lakes and streams, launched the state's first concerted pollution-control program. The two departments combined because, under existing laws, the conservation department had more power to protect fish from contamination than the health department had to protect people.

3. FISH-CONTAMINATION RESPONSE

A 1971 regulation mandating public notice of mercury levels in fish was Michigan's first response to toxic-chemical contamination of fish. The regulation was swept away by the Legislature's Joint Committee on Administrative rules in 1984.

4. RECYCLED TEXTBOOK

In February 1972, Michigan State University published the first textbook in the nation to be printed on 100% recycled paper. The book, *Environmental Quality: Now or Never*, advised readers to recycle waste materials.

5. LEAD-BASED PAINT BAN

In October 1972, Pontiac became the first Michigan city to ban the use or sale of lead-based paint, which can cause brain damage if ingested by children.

2 RECENT POLLUTION-CONTROL LAWS

1. A law that banned smoking in grocery stores and required restaurants seating 50 or more people to have designated nonsmoking areas took effect in Michigan April 2, 1977.

2. Unswayed by a million-dollar advertising bitz by beverage and bottling industries, Michigan voters on November 2, 1976, overwhelmingly approved a ban on the sale of nonreturnable bottles and flip-top cans.

4 WORST POLLUTION SITES

As listed in December 1984 by the Michigan Department of Natural Resources, which annually ranks problem sites according to the toxicity of pollutants, their volume, and the threat of their release into the environment.

1. MONITOR AND WILLIAMS TOWNSHIPS SITE (Auburn)

Groundwater contaminated with traces of heavy metals from abandoned coal mines.

2. PINE GROVE SUBDIVISION (Grand Traverse County)

Organic chemicals in the groundwater.

3. G & H LANDFILL (Macomb County)

Industrial paints and oils.

4. STEVENS' LANDFILL (Monroe County)

The abandoned landfill in the middle of a subdivision of $100,000 homes holds volatile organic chemicals.

5 UNUSUAL POLLUTION PROBLEMS

1. The Michigan Air Pollution Control Commission in January 1984 ordered the University of Michigan Medical School (Ann Arbor) to install pollution-control devices on its crematorium after an analysis showed that the black smoke that was released into the air from the burning of medical students'

dissected cadavers violated state clean-air standards.

2. During the 1940s, the surface of Detroit's Rouge River, which became infamous as the receptacle for any and all industrial waste, was so polluted with oil that, once, it actually caught on fire.

3. In 1970, Pontiac barbers complained to the city council that the city's air pollutants, which settled in their customers' hair, caused their tools to wear out twice as fast as those in pollution-free suburbs.

4. Workmen who were painting the Mackinac Bridge in July 1976 were ordered to stop because overspray from the oil-based paint that settled on the water below violated pollution standards. The problem was solved by changing the size of the nozzles being used in the spray painting.

5. When Mount St. Helens (Washington) erupted on May 18, 1980, personnel at the A.C. Corporation (Flint) were called upon to quickly solve an unusual pollution problem. Extremely fine, abrasive volcanic ash, that traveled as far as 500 miles downwind, was being sucked through conventional air filters into automobile engines and was ruining them. AC quickly developed and shipped 10,000 breathable strips of polyurethane plastic that, when wrapped around conventional air filters, trapped the volcanic dust.

4

NATURE'S WAY

4 UNUSUAL ANIMAL DEATHS

1. Six sea lions and seals and two rheas (ostrich-like birds) died from lead poisoning at the Detroit Zoo in 1971, after licking, chewing, or eating self-developing-film debris that litterbugs had tossed near the animals.

2. Cleveland Amory, in an article in the March 1984 issue of *Town & Country* magazine, placed Copper Harbor at the top of a list of "America's (8) Cruelest Towns." Copper Harbor earned the spot, according to the founder and president of the anti-hunting Fund for Animals organization, because, "All year long, bears are encouraged to feed at the town dump without being molested. Then, at the start of the hunting season, the bears that have developed a trust of humans are shot like fish in a barrel by alleged 'sportsmen' who go home proud of their trophies."

3. A visitor at the Detroit Zoo in June 1971 threw a tennis ball into the mouth of a two-ton hippo named Barney. The ball lodged in an opening between the hippo's stomach and small intestine, causing gangrene to set in and kill him.

4. At about 8:30 p.m. on April 13, 1980, a raccoon stepped onto some transformer lines at a power sub-station at Michigan State University, electrocuted himself, and caused a six-hour blackout on the campus.

2 WILDLIFE CATASTROPHES

1. In the years immediately following the Civil War, much of Michigan's wildlife was wantonly slaughtered by market hunters and commercial fishermen. Professional hunters, for example, annually shipped the meat of more than 100,000 Michigan deer to national markets. Bird hunters, many using a small cannon on a pole that fired a half pound of ball shot at a time, killed so many quail, grouse, and prairie chickens that those birds completely disappeared in many southern Michigan areas. Commercial fishermen, often using dynamite, ravaged inland lakes and streams. One fishing party, for example, caught so many grayling along the Au Sable River in 1871 that they left more than 2,000 on the shore to rot.

But perhaps the most devastating slaughter of wildlife in Michigan history was that of the passenger pigeon, which once flew in Michigan skies in flocks so large they blocked out the sun for hours.

The beautiful birds arrived in Michigan in March and remained until early autumn. During that time, professional hunters systematically attacked the pigeon's nesting places, killed millions of the birds with poles, guns, and axes, salted them and sold them for $2 apiece to Chicago and New York restaurant buyers.

The systematic massacres continued until the last wild passenger pigeon, it is believed, was shot in Pike County, Ohio, on March 24, 1900. Martha, the last bird of the passenger-pigeon species, died at the Cincinnati Zoo on September 1, 1914.

2. With the opening of the St. Lawrence Seaway in 1959, alewives, small, oily "trash" fish, made their way through the waterway and invaded the Great Lakes. Without natural predators, the alewife population exploded, at times filling the lakes to depths of 500 feet.

But, lacking an adequate food supply, the fish died just as rapidly, and, during the summer of 1967, the rotting carcasses of billions of alewives, which littered 400 miles of Lake Michigan shoreline from Benton Harbor to Petoskey, cost tourist-related businesses in those areas an estimated $50 to $100 million.

The problem was finally solved by planting coho and chinook salmon, which gorged on the nuisance fish and grew to tremendous size, and by commercial netting of the alewives for use in cat food.

2 NOTABLE ANIMALS THAT DIED OF OLD AGE

1. G.I. JOE

In October 1943 a carrier pigeon named "G.I. Joe" saved the lives of more than 1,000 Allied soldiers by successfully delivering a critical message 20 miles. As a result, the bird received a medal of gallantry from London's mayor and recognition from the U.S. Congress before retiring to the Detroit Zoo, where he died of old age on June 6, 1961.

2. SAHARA

Shortly after the the Guinness *Book of World Records* had declared her the world's longest-living gerbil, eight-year-old Sahara died at the home of her Lathrup Village owners on October 3, 1981.

4 UNUSUAL ELEPHANT DEATHS

1. A 3,000-pound elephant broke loose from a parking-lot act at a Lansing shopping center on September 26, 1963, and, while being chased by a large crowd, bulled through the front window of a department store, crashed up and down the aisles, then cut a two-mile swath of destruction and confusion through nearby residential neighborhoods. After two futile hours of trying to capture the

animal, police finally killed "Little Rajjee" with rifles.

2. Two employees of the International Animal Exchange of Ferndale were sent to company-owned land in rural Rochester in July 1969 to bury a 600-pound baby Indian elephant that had died. But the men either got lost or couldn't find the burial ground and, instead, interred the dead pachyderm in a shallow sand pit on private property after a 15-year-old boy had given them permission to do so.

    The boy's father, however, knew nothing about his son's good turn and, after awakening the next morning to the ill wind of the rotting, partially buried carcass, called the company who removed and reburied it on their land.

3. During a June 1982 stop at Calvin College (Grand Rapids), a circus worker drove a three-foot stake into the ground then tethered a 12-year-old Asian elephant to it. But, unbeknownst to the worker, the metal stake hit a 440-volt underground line, which powered a water pump, and when the pump activated, the stake energized and electrocuted the 3,000-pound animal.

4. On June 7, 1979, Michigan State University veterinarians carefully made a 10-inch incision in the throat of Bingo the Elephant then removed a baseball-sized rock the animal had swallowed. At first, the 4,000-pound star attraction at Lansing's Potter Park Zoo appeared to be recovering normally but on August 13, 1979, suddenly developed pneumonia and died.

2 ANIMAL DENTISTRIES

1. In August 1972, a Grand Rapids dentist performed a $4^1/_2$-hour root canal on Ramu, a 400-pound lion who had snapped off a tooth while chewing on a steel bar in his cage at John Ball Park.

2. In December 1973, a Detroit dentist capped the molar of a one-year-old Doberman pinscher who had broken his tooth in a dog fight.

2 DOG PACEMAKERS

1. A nine-year-old Flint Township female schnauzer in April 1970, became the first Michigan dog, and only the second in the country, to have a heart pacemaker placed in its chest. Veterinarians at Michigan State University performed the operation after one of the dog's heart valves began to fail.

2. Surgeons at a Coldwater clinic became the first private-practice veterinarians in Michigan to implant a heart pacemaker in a dog when in January 1983 they performed the complicated operation on "Honey," a 15-pound pug.

3 UNIQUE DOG BIRTHS

1. Frosty, a snow-white samoyed (sled dog) belonging to a Burton Township

minister, tied a 19-year-old national American Kennel Club record for her breed when in October 1970 she gave birth to 11 pups.

2. A husky at Tun-Dra Kennels (Nunica) gave birth on January 12, 1983, to identical twin pups, an event, according to a Michigan State University canine expert, that occurs only once in every 400,000 to a million births.
— *Item contributed by Cheryl Cheadle, Nunica* —

3. During a 15-hour delivery in April 1967, a Fenton Township couple's St. Bernard had a 16-puppy litter. Since the mother Bernard did not have enough teats to feed all her pups, the dog's owners had to feed half the litter by bottle.

3 DISTINCTIVE DOGS

1. Trapper, a year-old English springer spaniel owned by a 10-year-old Kentwood girl, won $25,000, a year's supply of dog food, and a ride on a float in Macy's Thanksgiving Day parade as the Purina Dog Chow company's 1983 "Great American Dog."

2. & 3. On November 2, 1966, national wire services carried a a photograph of Karla Foutch (Flint) holding her seven-week-old, 1 1/2-inch-high, four-inch-long toy poodle in a teacup. Sixteen years later, a Yorkshire terrier owned by Foutch gave birth to a pup that also, at seven weeks old, was only 1 1/2 inches high and four inches long. (See photo, page 78)

2 CONSPICUOUS ANIMAL OWNERS

1. In 1983, Doug Kneller (Moran), Michigan's only skunk rancher, was forced by clean-air requirements to move his business from near Monroe to the Upper Peninsula. Kneller, who breeds, raises and sells approximately 500 vaccinated, dewormed, and descented baby skunks each year, decided to change locations when chemical pollution at his Monroe-area site began damaging his animals' eyes, skin, and fur.

2. In response to a call by police, the Humane Society arrived at the former home of Herman Mangum (Detroit) in April 1983 to find three full-grown cockatoos, three monkeys, three dogs, eight puppies, one chinchilla, six doves, four rabbits, one guinea pig, and a large number of rats in cages.
Fifty-three-year-old Mangum explained that he actively traded and sold animals and that his former home seemed like a good place to keep his fluctuating animal collection.

2 FUGITIVE SNAKES

1. When "Big Sid," a 140-pound, 20-foot-long python that was accustomed to a diet of small animals, escaped from a circus near Walker in June 1978, worried residents kept small children and pets inside during the five weeks it took to find

Tina the Terrier is the second 1 1/2-inch-high dog owned by a Flint-area woman. (See story, page 77)

Flint Journal photo

and capture the snake.

2. On May 11, 1984, as a Thomas Township (Saginaw County) woman transplanted a new weeping-fig tree she had just purchased, a snake that had nested in the roots coiled around her hand and bit her on the index finger. The 40-year-old woman shook the snake loose, and, as it tried to escape under a railroad tie, her husband killed it with a shovel. The snake was later identified as a non-poisonous corn snake from Florida.

10 UNIQUE ANIMAL ADDITIONS

1. 1706

The first livestock in Michigan, 10 cattle and three horses, arrived at Fort Ponchartrain (Detroit).

2. 1840s and 1850s

During the early days of mining in the Upper Peninsula, before any docks were built along the Lake Superior shoreline, oxen, cattle, horses, and other animals brought by boat to the area were dumped overboard and made to swim for shore.

3. 1918

A herd of Rocky Mountain elk — ancestors of what is claimed today to be the largest elk herd east of the Mississippi River — were released at Pigeon River.

4. 1919

A pair of large, graceful mute swans were released near Charlevoix. By 1982 their progeny, having thrived on Michigan's lakes and streams, numbered nearly 1500, which prompted some naturalists to suggest that the swan population should be limited so that the environment they live in isn't destroyed.

5. 1920s

In an attempt to establish a new animal in Michigan for hunting, a small herd of imported reindeer was released in the vicinity of Newberry. But, because the area did not contain proper food, minerals or nutrients, the entire herd died out.

6. Mid-1950s

The first successful reintroduction of wild turkeys (see page 85) in Michigan took place when the Department of Conservation released 50 Pennsylvania birds in the Allegan State Game Area. Additional releases were made in northern lower Michigan, and, by 1964, some 2,000 turkeys ranged freely.

7. June 11, 1966

For the first time in history, a herd of cattle set hooves on Mackinac Island. The 21 head, brought by boat for a "world-championship livestock-market auctioneer contest," were penned in the Grand Hotel's tennis courts, and the auction was conducted on the hotel's spacious lawn.

8. Spring-summer 1984

Two large, potentially dangerous jungle cats, suspected to be abandoned by someone who owned them illegally, were reported prowling the Manchester and Wixom areas. Reliable sources, including a U.S. Fish & Wildlife Service worker, police officers from two departments, and a sheriff's deputy, reported 14 sightings of a black leopard or panther near Manchester and 10 sightings near Wixom.

9. January 1985

In an effort to re-establish moose in the Upper Peninsula, the first of 29 of the half-ton animals were transported by helicopter from Canada and released north of Marquette.

10. February 1985

The province of Sichuan, Michigan's Chinese sister state, sent 23 adult blackneck pheasants to help revitalize the state's dwindling pheasant population. One thousand eggs from Chinese pheasants, which are not affected by modern farming practices which have depleted Michigan's ring-necked-pheasant population, followed in May.

7 KIRTLAND'S-WARBLER COUNTIES

The numbers of singing males of the endangered bird species — which breeds only in a limited range of Michigan's north-central Lower Peninsula — as counted by the Department of Natural Resources in 1982.

1.	OSCODA	72
2.	CRAWFORD	67
3.	OGEMAW	44
4.	KALKASKA	17
5.	ROSCOMMON	5
6.	IOSCO	1
7.	MARQUETTE	1

The discovery in Marquette County, near Gwinn, was the first of a male Kirtland's Warbler in the Upper Peninsula.

2 EAGLE FIRSTS

1. In the first successful prosecution of an eagle killer in Michigan history, a 34-year-old Burton auto worker, who had killed one of the protected birds while deer hunting near Lake City in 1975, was fined $1,500 and placed on two months probation.

2. Near Munising in 1977, American bald eagles, for the first time in Michigan's and perhaps the nation's wildlife history, hatched and raised eaglets on man-made platform nests. A total of five eaglets were produced at two nests originally built for osprey hawks.

5 UNIQUE ANIMAL LEGISLATIONS

1. After upper-peninsula lawmakers had objected to mitten-shaped dogtags that were proposed in May 1983 for statewide use, a compromise was reached: tags shaped like mittens were ordered for lower-peninsula dogs, and tags resembling the Upper Peninsula — vaguely rabbit-shaped — were designed for dogs residing above the Mackinac Straits.

2. In October 1972, the Michigan Department of Natural Resources issued an order making it illegal to import wolves as pets because, in part, the animals ". . . cause anxiety for . . . neighbors."

3. Seventy-five noisy fifth-graders jammed into Governor William G. Milliken's office on February 21, 1978, to watch him sign into law their bill protecting house cats from hunters. The St. Clair elementary-school students had initiated the legislation by bombarding their state senator with letters protesting a 1929 law that made it legal to shoot cats.

4. Although in 1879, Detroit was the nation's 17th-largest city, many residents still treated parks as pastureland and streets as herding areas, so the Detroit City Council on May 29, 1879, passed an ordinance forbidding the "running at large of cattle in public places."

5. State legislators on July 28, 1976, turned down a proposal to replace the robin, Michigan's official state bird since 1935, with the Kirtland's Warbler. A compromise, however, named the Kirtland's Warbler as the official Michigan bicentennial bird.

7 HUNTING "DON'TS"

It is unlawful in Michigan to:

1. Use tracer or explosive ammunition.

2. Use a silencer on your gun.

3. Use drugs, poison, chemicals, gas, or explosives to take wild birds or animals.

4. Set fires to drive out game.

5. Carry a slingshot, except on your own private property, without a license.

6. Hunt from a motorized vehicle of any kind, including boat, snowmobile, or airplane.

7. Use a semi-automatic shotgun.

7 PROTECTED ANIMALS

The following seven animals are protected from hunting at all times in Michigan.

1. BADGERS
2. EAGLES
3. HAWKS
4. LYNX
5. MOOSE
6. OWLS
7. WOLVES

9 DEER-HUNTING MILESTONES

1. 1859

Michigan's first deer-hunting law was enacted. The law limited hunting to the last five months of the year, but no license was required, no limit was set, and no means of enforcement was provided.

2. 1895

A limit of five deer of either sex was imposed, and a license fee of 50 cents for residents and $25 for non-residents was charged.

3. 1901

The limit was reduced to three deer.

4. 1905

The limit was reduced to two deer and the license fee raised to $1.50.

5. 1915

The limit was reduced to one deer.

6. 1921

A one-buck law was enacted and the license fee raised to $2.50.

7. 1937

A special bowhunting season was established. One hundred eighty-six hunters took a total of only four deer during that first season.

8. 1952

Hunters were allowed to take any deer they saw during the last three days of the fall season and, as a result, killed 162,000 bucks, does, and fawns — nearly three times the normal kill at that time. Following the special season, an avalanche of angry letters poured into the Conservation Department protesting the perceived virtual wipeout of the state's herd, so the practice of "antlerless" hunting, though not eliminated, was limited.

9. 1975

Michigan's first muzzle-loading deer season opened. More than 1,000 hunters, using black powder and a round ball in a single-shot gun or rifle like American's forefathers used, stalked bucks only during the 10-day season.

3 BEST DEER-HUNTING SEASONS

Three years with the most deer killed during the firearms season.

1. 1981	173,000
2. 1952	162,000
3. 1982	153,000

4 UNIQUE DEER KILLS

1. On the opening day of firearm deer season, November 15, 1984, an eight-point buck smashed through the window of a downtown Ionia bar, barged into a plumbing-and-heating establishment next door, then finally crashed through the plate-glass window of an antique market where it broke furniture, china, and glassware until killed by city police.

2. In November 1984, as Paul Stilson drove back to his deer-hunting camp near Iron Mountain after phoning his wife at their Burton home, he rammed and killed a deer on the highway. The next day, his wife, while driving to Chicago, hit and killed a deer near Lansing.

3. Two deer wandered into the University of Michigan stadium on November 8, 1963. One, a doe with a broken leg, was shot and killed by police, and the other, a large buck, escaped.

4. Steven Cloud, a freshman at Lake Superior State College, went out at daybreak on November 15, 1979, the first day of hunting season, sighted a deer about 35 miles from campus, downed it, dressed it, and was back at school in time for his first class.

4 RECORD BUCKS

Four bucks with the largest antlers ever measured in Michigan, as certified by Commmemorative Bucks of Michigan. The bucks were scored using the Boone and Crockett antler-measurement method for firearm-killed deer or the Pope & Young Club standards for deer taken with bow and arrow. Both categories have classifications for typical (symmetrical) antlers and non-typical (irregular) antlers.

1. 232⁵/₈ points

Paul Mickey (Kawkalin) shot the buck, which tops the non-typical firearm category, in 1976 in Bay County.

2. 187⁶/₈ points

The state-record, non-typical bow-killed buck, was taken by Bob Morey in Saginaw County in 1975.

3. 186 points

The leading firearm-taken typical deer was shot by Mark Ritchie (Dexter) in Washtenaw County in 1984.

4. 164⁵/₈ points

The 12-point buck, taken by Gary Hull (Williamston) in Ingham county in 1980, is the state record for typical bucks taken with bow and arrow.

TOP 6 TROPHY-BUCK COUNTIES

Six counties where the most trophy bucks, that is bucks with antlers larger than a specified minimum size, were killed through the 1982 season, as compiled by Commemorative Bucks of Michigan.

1.	LIVINGSTON	26
2.	WASHTENAW	23
3.	MACKINAC	22
4.	HILLSDALE	21
5.	DELTA	20
6.	MARQUETTE	19

3 LARGE BEAR

1. The largest Michigan bear ever officially weighed and recorded was a 613-pound (dressed weight) black bear shot by archer Hawley Rheu in Emmet County in 1974.

— *Item contributed by Tom Huggler, Otisville* —

2. On November 24, 1966, near Hoar Lake (Keweenaw County), Robert Haatja (Ahmeek) shot a 570-pound (dressed weight) bear which, at the time, was a state record.

3. In the early 1940s, Carl T. Johnson (Grand Rapids) shot a 625-pound bear, live weight, in the Dead Stream Swamp of Missaukee County. But Johnson, Michigan's Conservation Commissioner at the time, didn't weigh the animal dressed so it never made the record books.

4 RECORD GAME ANIMALS

Though no official records are kept of many of the biggest game animals ever taken in Michigan, Department of Natural Resources personnel have assembled a manila folder full of unofficial record-weights, including those for:

1. BEAVER

In December 1980, Jered Emerick (Lovells) caught an 80-pound female from the North Branch of the Au Sable River.

2. BOBCAT

Duncan Parrish shot a 47-pound bobcat on Drummond Island in December 1955. Twenty-three years later, Wilho Hautamaki (Greenland) shot a cat of identical weight in Ontonagon County.

3. DEER

The biggest whitetail ever reported weighed 354 pounds dressed and an estimated 425 pounds on the hoof. Albert Tippett (Flint) shot the huge buck at Trout Creek in 1919.

4. RACCOON

Milo Perkins (Escanaba) shot a record 45-pound raccoon near Rock in 1978.

— List contributed by Tom Huggler, Otisville —

4 UNIQUE TURKEY HUNTS

1. January 1897

The last recorded Michigan native wild turkey was taken in Arlington Township (Van Buren County). But, over the next 50 years, by releasing hand-reared wild turkeys from other areas of the United States, conservationists successfully re-established the bird.

2. November 6, 1965

The first modern-day Michigan wild-turkey hunt began, with some 400 hunters stalking about 600 of the birds scattered throughout Allegan County. Eighty-two turkeys were killed during the nine-day season.

3. 1979

Al Palmer shot the state's biggest turkey, a 24-pound, six-ounce tom, in Alcona County.

— Item contributed by Tom Huggler, Otisville —

4. May 8, 1983

Thomas W. Passow (Saginaw) killed a 29-pound turkey while hunting in Butman Township (Gladwin County), but, since Department of Natural Resources field offices were closed (Sunday), did not officially register the bird. Passow later learned that his bird outweighed the official Michigan record by more than four pounds (see preceding item).

3 MODERN-DAY ELK HUNTS

1. & 2. December 1964 and December 1965

In December 1964, during Michigan's first elk-hunting season since the pioneer era, 300 hunters pursued 3,500 elk in four counties. An eight-day season was held again the next year to control elk overpopulation then discontinued for 19 years.

3. December 1984

Fifty hunters, chosen by lottery, killed 49 of the estimated 1,000 elk living in and around the Pigeon River Country State Forest east of Vanderbilt.

7 FISH TALES

1. PLAINWELL (July 1982)

When William Hart (Kalamazoo) caught a black-and-green, 12 3/4-inch fish that didn't look like any he had seen before, he took the creature to the Department of Natural Resources for identificiation. Two weeks later, DNR officials informed Hart that his catch was a piranha, which, since it cannot survive in cold water, they speculated must have just been dumped from someone's aquarium.

2. DOWAGIAC (1880)

While fishing for bass, James Heddon tossed a small piece of whittled wood into the pond only to have a bass that had been eluding his hook leap for the carving. Heddon experimented with and perfected his discovery, and, by the turn of the century, his casting plugs appeared on fishing poles everywhere.

3. SAGINAW (March 29, 1910)

After a lengthy investigation at a residence that had suddenly lost its water supply, plumbers finally removed a service pipe from the street to the house and found that the line was completely clogged with seven-inch fish.

4. LUDINGTON (Sepember 1, 1983)

Todd Miller, a 12-year-old Ann Arbor boy who used earnings from his newspaper route to enter the American Salmon Derby, landed a 32-pound chinook and won the event's top prize — $15,550.

5. ROUGE RIVER (September 1, 1983)

Roy Wright (River Rouge), who was fishing for walleyes, hooked a mean-looking, 22-inch-long, inch-and-a-half-in-diameter eel. The eel, one of the very few caught in Michigan waters each year, had hatched in the mid-Atlantic Ocean and entered the Great Lakes via the St. Lawrence Seaway.

6. KLINGER LAKE (St. Joseph County) — June 1971

When Department of Natural Resources fish biologists examined the scales of a 43-inch, 61-pound state-record carp that had been speared, they discovered that, at nearly 25 years of age, it was the oldest fish of its species ever taken from the wild in the country.

7. ST. CLAIR (January 4, 1929)

A 1 1/2-foot bullhead, which had entered the intake pipe at the city's water plant, deprived residents of water for more than an hour while pumps were stopped so that the fish could be removed.

4 SPECIAL FISH ADDITIONS

1. April 11, 1884

J.F. Ellis, a member of the Northville fish hatchery, lugged a can containing 5,000 brown-trout fry to the banks of the Pere Marquette River near Baldwin and upended it. With a gurgle and a splash, Ellis unceremoniously dumped the first German brown trout ever released in American waters.

2. 1912

The first smelt were brought to Michigan from Maine as food for Crystal Lake's salmon population. The salmon resisted the food and eventually died, but the smelt, though originally a saltwater inhabitant, lived on and, according to conservation experts, are the source of all Great Lakes smelt except those found in Lake Ontario.

3. 1955

Ontario fish biologists, who had hatched pink-salmon eggs at a Thunder Bay hatchery for release into a Hudson Bay tributary, dumped about 200 leftover fingerlings into Lake Superior. Over the next 25 years, the descendants of those fingerlings expanded their range and are now found in more than 50 Michigan Great Lakes tributaries.

— Item contributed by Tom Huggler, Otisville —

4. April 2, 1966

Conservation Commissioner Carl T. Johnson upended a bucket and spilled the first of 850,000 six-inch Coho salmon into the Platte River. Though Coho had never been successfully planted anywhere outside of their native Pacific Coast, massive and continued releases successfully established the salmon as the backbone of Michigan open-water sport fishing.

3 SPECIAL FISH PONDS

1. Michigan's first fish hatchery was opened at Detroit in 1873.

2. The state's first portable fish ladder, four 10-foot aluminum sections developed to help fish over dams at remote sites, was used at Traverse City in 1968.

3. The Platte River anadromous fish hatchery, with rearing ponds for chinook and coho salmon and rainbow, brown, and steelhead trout, is the largest of its type in the world.

3 UNSUAL WATER BODIES

1. LAKE DUBONNET (also called Big Mud Lake), near Interlochen, has a one-acre floating island, complete with 40-foot trees and brush, that is blown across the surface by the wind.

2. The LITTLE OCQUEOC RIVER (Presque Isle County) dives underground near Ocqueoc Falls, disappears as it takes a 500-foot shortcut through limestone slabs, then reappears on the other side of a hill.

3. RAINY LAKE (Millersburg)

When water action periodically disturbs sediment and debris on the lake's bottom, it empties through holes into a series of underground limestone chambers as though someone pulled a bathtub plug. Then, when mud and silt plugs the cracks and holes, the 200-acre lake, which drained itself competely dry in 1894, 1925, and 1950, fills up again.

7 INTERESTING GREAT LAKES FACTS

1. Michigan is sinking into the Great Lakes, as it has been for the past 500 million years, at the rate of one millimeter per year.

2. No matter where you stand in Michigan, you are never more than 85 miles from a Great Lake.

3. Appproximatley 38,459 square miles of Great Lakes water is included within Michigan's boundaries.

4. Michigan is the only state that borders on four of the five Great Lakes.
   — Item contributed by M.A. Smith, Arvada, Colorado —

5. The Great Lakes contain 99 percent of America's fresh surface water.

6. The Great Lakes account for one-fifth of the world's fresh water.

7. Lake Superior is the second-largest lake in the world; only the Caspian Sea is larger.

5 "ALL WET" FACTS

1. No matter where you stand in Michigan, you are never more than five miles from a lake or stream.

2. Michigan has 15,800 lakes two acres or larger in size.

3. Michigan has 1,573 square miles of inland lakes.

4. Michigan has 36,350 miles of rivers.

5. The St. Clair Flats is the largest freshwater delta in the world.

5 WETTEST COUNTIES

Five counties with the most inland water area in square miles.

1.	CHIPPEWA	184.77
2.	CHEBOYGAN	77.30
3.	MACKINAC	66.60
4.	ROSCOMMON	52.00
5.	MARQUETTE	51.88

5 DRIEST COUNTIES

Five counties with the least inland water area in square miles.

1.	SANILAC	0.00
2.	SHIAWASSEE	0.30
3.	MACOMB	0.30
4.	SAGINAW	0.40
5.	EATON	0.90

7 STATES WE ARE CONNECTED TO BY INLAND WATER ROUTES

1. ILLINOIS
2. INDIANA

3. MINNESOTA
4. NEW YORK
5. OHIO
6. PENNSYLVANIA
7. WISCONSIN

5 STATES WE SHARE
WATER BOUNDARIES WITH

1. ILLINOIS
2. INDIANA
3. MINNESOTA
4. OHIO
5. WISCONSIN

3 STATES WE SHARE
LAND BOUNDARIES WITH

1. INDIANA
2. OHIO
3. WISCONSIN

3 SURPRISING GEOGRAPHICAL FACTS

1. Port Huron is further east than Atlanta, Georgia.

2. Hancock is further north than Montreal.

3. Ironwood is as far west as St. Louis, Missouri.

8 SURPRISING DISTANCES

Eight out-of-state cities that are closer to Detroit that Ironwood, Michigan, is to Detroit, based on highway mileage as listed in the Rand McNally *Road Atlas*. The distance from Detroit to Ironwood, as listed on the official Michigan Highway Department road map, is 593 miles.

1. DES MOINES, IOWA	587
2. NASHVILLE, TENNESSEE	534
3. ST. LOUIS, MISSOURI	534
4. WASHINGTON, D.C.	516
5. BALTIMORE, MARYLAND	514
6. CHARLESTON, WEST VIRGINIA	399
7. LOUISVILLE, KENTUCKY	382
8. BUFFALO, NEW YORK	361

— *List idea contributed by Dennis Guerriero, Harrison* —

4 GREATEST WIDTHS AND LENGTHS

1. The greatest width (east to west) of the Upper Peninsula is 334 miles.

2. The greatest width of the Lower Peninsula (east to west) is 200 miles.

3. The greatest length of the Lower Peninsula (north to south) is 286 miles.

4. The greatest length of the Upper Peninsula (north to south) is 215 miles.

5 UNIQUE WEATHER CONDITIONS

1. February 5, 1663

   An earthquake shook the area of North America known as New France, which, at the time, included Michigan. The reports of the quake, as recorded by Catholic missionaries in *Jesuit Relations*, are the earliest written account of a Michigan earthquake.

2. April 17, 1893

   A six-foot-high seiche, or tidal wave, surged from Lake Michigan and swept 700 feet beyond the high-water mark at St. Joseph.

3. 1912

   For the first time in recorded history, Lake Superior completely froze, and, as a result, moose and wolves crossed from the mainland to Isle Royale, where they had not been previously known.

4. November 9, 1913

   The most devastating storm in Great Lakes history began with winds blowing at hurricane force for 16 straight hours. When the storm finally rolled eastward after three long days, it had sunk 40 ships and killed 235 seamen.

5. May 2, 1983

   The worst property-damage storm in Michigan history struck southeastern Michigan when hail caused approximately $165.2 million in damage to homes and automobiles.

3 MOST AIR-CONDITIONED COUNTIES

Three counties with the highest percentage of year-round housing units with air conditioning. State average = 34.2.

1. OAKLAND	53.0
2. MACOMB	49.9
3. WASHTENAW	48.0

8 CITIES COMPARED TO A DEGREE

Average January and July 1982 temperatures in degrees Farenheit for eight selected cities.

CITY	JANUARY	JULY
1. ALPENA	11.2	67.9
2. CADILLAC	11.7	67.1
3. DEARBORN	17.6	72.9
4. GRAND RAPIDS	17.2	73.1
5. IRONWOOD	-0.2	65.9
6. JACKSON	15.8	73.0
7. MIDLAND	15.8	72.0
8. SAULT STE. MARIE	4.7	62.7

3 UNIQUE SNOW-JOBS

1. In 1983 a movie company hauled 600 yards of snow from Michigan and dumped it in Public Square, downtown Cleveland, Ohio, so that they could film a realistic Christmas-parade scene.

2. Midland-based Snow Machines Inc., which has placed its equipment in more than 100 American ski resorts and another 200 resorts elsewhere in the world, is the largest manufacturer and supplier of snowmaking equipment in America.

3. Mt. Brighton ski area (Brighton), with a 125-machine snowmaking system, bills itself as the "snowmaking capital of the midwest." The average ski resort in Michigan has between 30 and 40 such machines.

6 MOST WOOD-HEATED COUNTIES

Six counties with the highest percentage of owner-occupied housing units that were heated predominately with wood in 1980. State average = 2.1%.

1. OSCODA		30.7
2. MONTMORENCY		24.5
3. LAKE		21.6
4. MACKINAC		19.4
5. BARAGA		17.0
6. ANTRIM		16.6

5 NOTABLE FORESTS

1. In 1903 the legislature established Michigan's first state forest on cut-over, burned-over lands in Roscommon and Crawford counties.

2. Michigan's first national forest was established in 1909 in Iosco County along the Au Sable River and in the Upper Peninsula west of Sault Ste. Marie.

3. Michigan's state forest system, with 3.8 million acres, is the largest dedicated system in the lower 48 states.
   — Item contributed by Henry H. Webster, State Forester, Lansing —

4. The Upper Peninsula is 84 percent forested.
   — Item contributed by Henry H. Webster, State Forester, Lansing —

5. In 1876, a farmhand, in a personal observance of the 100th anniversary of the signing of the Declaration of Independence, planted a row of sugar maple tree seedlings on his employer's farm near Niles.

One hundred years later, more than 1,000 seeds were gathered from the resulting stand of hardy trees and distributed to groups around the state, who planted them in commemoration of the nation's 200th birthday.

3 SPECIAL TREES

1. In late 1984, the Washtenaw County Road Commission announced plans for what they expected to be the routine removal of an oak tree which they felt was too close to a two-lane county road near Manchester. But, when more than 100 area residents, including former governor John Swainson, protested the move, the commission spared the 300-year-old burr oak, considered to be Michigan's second-oldest tree.

2. & 3. Two Michigan-grown blue spruce were selected as official 1984 White House Christmas trees. An eight-footer from the Harvey Koop farm (Allegan) was used in the Reagan family quarters, and a 20-footer from the front yard of 87-year-old Russell Hammond (Lake City) was placed in the "Blue Room" (see also page 263).

2 HISTORIC OAKS

1. Fifteen hundred Michigan Whigs, Democrats, and Abolitionists gathered at Jackson on July 6, 1854, to protest slavery and other prevailing policies of their day. When the large group could not fit into the town hall, they moved to a stately grove of oaks on the outskirts of the village, where they organized the nation's first Republican party.

2. During the summer of 1834, Isaac Craary and Reverend John Pierce held several informal discussions under a white oak in Marshall, during which they mapped out a plan for a public school system for Michigan. Their educational system was enacted into law in 1836, and Pierce was named as Michigan's first Superintendent of Public Instruction.

4 MONSTER TREES

Michigan has more than 90 recognized national-champion trees, each representing the biggest known tree of a particular species found in the United

States. The four Michigan champion trees with the biggest girths (circumferences) are:

1. WHITE WILLOW — 343 inches
   Located west of Jackson.

2. BLACK WILLOW — 337 inches
   Located on the grounds of the State Hospital at the edge of Traverse City.

3. COTTONWOOD POPLAR — 315 inches
   In Wayne.

4. BRITTLE WILLOW — 305 inches
   Northwest of Utica.

5

MONEY MATTERS

9 FINDERS — A FEW KEEPERS

1. THAO CHANG (Saginaw) — February 1984

The 10-year-old member of an impoverished refugee family picked up a bottlecap he had been kicking along the sidewalk and discovered it was a $1,000 winner in a soft-drink-company contest.

2. THOM MILBOURNE (Lansing) — January 1985

When a courier unknowingly dropped a money bag in the parking lot of a chain discount store, Milbourne, a 20-year-old bagger at the outlet, picked it up and turned the contents — $150,000 in cash and checks — over to his manager. For his honesty, Milbourne received $5 cash and a $10 gift certificate.

3. NATIONAL BANK & TRUST (Ann Arbor)

On July 1, 1970, an employee of the J.C. Penney Company's Arborland store dropped $1,900 cash and $1,000 in checks into the bank's night deposit box. The bank, however, said it never received the money, and, after a thorough investigation, which included a lie-detector test that cleared the store's employee, the fate of the deposit bag remained a mystery.

Twelve years later, the Michigan National Corporation, which had purchased the National Bank & Trust, closed the Arborland branch and distributed the bank's fixtures to its other branches around the state. While workmen installed one of the used night-deposit boxes in a southern-Detroit-suburb branch, they found a worn bag — deposited July 1, 1970, and containing $3,000 — wedged in the neck of the box.

4. DAN ODEN (Mount Clemens) — January 20, 1983

At 9:00 a.m., an armed bank robber fled on foot carrying $140,000 in stolen cash in a plastic garbage bag, and, as he ran past an apartment-complex entrance, several bundles of money spilled out of the bag and littered the pavement.

Minutes later, as Oden left the complex in his van, he saw the cash, quickly scooped several bundles — worth $9,000 — into a blanket, then spent the rest of the day trying to figure out where it came from and what to do.

That evening, when Oden, a 34-year-old unemployed school teacher, heard about the bank robbery, he turned the money over to the police. Whoever picked up the rest of the cash, however, did not.

5. VERNARD OLSEN (Newberry) — October 1982

While bulldozing an old house in the Tahquamenon Area State Park, the 50-year-old Department of Natural Resources equipment operator found $90,000 in small bills that had been stuffed into glass jars and placed under the building's foundation.

Olsen reported the find to his superiors, whereupon relatives of Edmund Leduc, a deceased lumber baron who had previously owned the property, claimed the entire find.

6. SUE and KEVIN WAGNER (Caledonia) — April 1984

The couple's goat, which they had purchased a month earlier for $15, coughed then belched out a 14-karat-gold, diamond-studded ring worth $2,000.

7. DUANE WILLSMORE (Livingston County) — 1974

While hunting squirrels near the farm of a reputed international drug dealer, Willsmore came across a hole covered with cross-hatched sticks, reached in, and pulled out a sturdy aluminum suitcase with a combination lock. Willsmore, a 21-year-old unemployed Howell truck driver, then called police, who opened the metal valise and found, inside, $384,000 in small bills neatly wrapped in bank wrappers.

When a lengthy police stakeout and investigation did not turn up the money's owner, Willsmore filed claim to the buried treasure — but so did the owner of the land, the Michigan Attorney General, and Osceloa Township. After five years of legal haggling, the state appeals court in 1981 awarded 55% of the money, which through investments had grown to $650,000, to Willsmore and the rest to Osceola Township.

8. In November 1984 a man in a burgundy Chrysler picked up a dufflebag that had tumbled from an open rear door of an armored car onto Detroit's Lodge Freeway, quickly jammed it into his vehicle's undercarriage, and sped off. The bag was jarred loose, however, and retrieved by the occupants of a second vehicle, who took it to their home.

There, family members, including an 80-year-old grandmother and young children, gathered in the attic, opened the bag and, upon discovering $407,000 in cash, threw money into the air and grabbed at the fluttering bills. The group then, according to police, who charged them with larceny, spent all but $5,000 on two pickup trucks, a Cadillac, a Lincoln, a Chevrolet, and cocaine.

9. When two Holland men who had just stolen $2,000 at knifepoint from a convenience store appproached a police roadblock on I-96 near Grandville on November 1, 1984, they threw the cash out of the car window. While fortunate passers-by leaped from their vehicles and stuffed the fluttering bills into their socks, pants, and coats, the robbers eased through the blockade.

One suspicious motorist, however, reported the strange incident to police, who then caught the robbers but only recovered $587 of the money.

6 SPECIAL GAMBLERS

1. VALERIE KACZOR (Rochester Hills) — March 1985

The 32-year-old housewife, who was charged with more than two dozen counts of criminal fraud for writing, altering, and passing more than $120,000 worth of phony checks and money orders, claimed she did so to support her addictive $1,000-a-day Michigan lottery habit.

2. VIVIAN LOHR (Royal Oak)

In 1978 the housewife won $1,000 in the Michigan state lottery. Four years later, she won $20,000 for correctly guessing the number of nails — 75,360 — in a builders-show contest.

3. TOM MCEVOY (Grand Rapids) — May 16, 1983

The 38-year-old former accountant, who had been fired from or quit eight jobs, entered the World Series of Poker tournament at Las Vegas with only $3,000 to his name. Four days later, McEvoy left the tables with two championship titles and $657,000. The following September, the father of three won another $43,875 by capturing the Dublin (Ireland) International poker-playing championship.

4. TERRY NAZURIJCHUK (Flint)

By playing as many as 130 bingo cards at the same time and — incredibly — not using markers to cover the numbers as they are called, the 25-year-old clothing-store manager has earned the title of Michigan's "Bingo King." Nazurijchuk, who needs two tables to set up his cards, has won as much as $800 in a single night, and his memory and concentration skills have also won him appearances on television's *PM Magazine, The Tonight Show*, and *Good Morning America*.

5. VICTOR WILKERSON (Northville) in September 1982 hit a $14,245 jackpot while playing the 25-cent slot machines at the MGM Grand Hotel in Reno.

6. REBECCA WRIGHT (Detroit) — March 1984

The 27-year-old unemployed cosmetologist and single parent became the American Family Publishers' $2-million, grand-prize sweepstakes winner.

2 MEMORABLE LOTTO WINNERS

1. THOMAS G. LAPENNA (Marquette) — September 1, 1984

The 45-year-old banking executive, by picking numbers from his wife's birth date, his daughter's grade in school, and the year of his birth, won $2.9 million in the first jackpot paid by the six-digit weekly Lotto game.

2. PATRICIA PARKER (Kalamazoo) — November 17, 1984

The accounting clerk won $10.4 million, the largest prize in Michigan lottery history (as of July 1, 1985), when she matched the weekly Lotto numbers 5, 6, 8, 12, 19, and 39.

3 MOST POPULAR LOTTERY NUMBERS

1. 1 2 3

The most often-played number in the three-digit daily game had, as of 1983, hit four times.

2. 1 2 3 4

The most popularly played number in the four-digit daily game had, as of 1983, never hit.

3. 1 2 3 4 5 6

The most heavily bet weekly Lotto combination is played an average of 5,000 times per week.

2 UNPOPULAR LOTTERY NUMBERS

The least-played numbers in the three-and four-digit daily games as of 1983.

1. 9 9 4

The least-played number in the three-digit game has hit twice.

2. 9 9 9 2

The least-played number in the four-digit game has never hit.

4 SUCCESSFUL CONSECUTIVE NUMBERS

Three-digit game as of 1983.

1. 3 4 5

Selected six times.

2. 7 8 9

Selected four times.

3. 1 2 3

Selected four times.

4. 5 6 7

Selected four times.

2 UNSUCCESSFUL CONSECUTIVE NUMBERS

Two three-digit numbers that, as of 1983, had never been drawn as winners.

1. 2 3 4

2. 6 7 8

2 MILLION-DOLLAR WINNERS WHO LOST

1. KEN PROXMIRE (Hazel Park)

In 1977 the Michigan lottery winner moved to California with his $50,000-a-year income. Four years later, he and his wife declared personal bankruptcy, and in 1982 he and his business partners also filed for bankruptcy.

2. CHARLES RIDDLE (Trenton) — October 1984

Nine years after becoming the lottery's 19th million-dollar winner, Riddle, who had already suffered through a highly publicized divorce case, was indicted by a federal grand jury on one count of distributing about a half-pound of cocaine and on a cocaine-conspiracy charge.

6 SPECIAL MONEY MAKERS

1. Governor JOHN S. BARRY bolstered the state treasury in the 1840s by having the grass on the capital lawn cut and sold for hay.

2. RICHARD GILSBACH (Sterling Heights) — May 1977

A pet-food manufacturer paid Gilsbach, an automobile draftsman, $500 for his cat, who, after a nationwide "look-alike" search, was chosen to replace television's retired cat-food-advertising star, "Morris the Cat."

3. JOSEPH HARRISON (Grand Rapids) — January 1985

The 79-year-old man, who pleaded guilty to a misdemeanor after police had arrested him for operating a house of prostitution, said that he had rented one of his upstairs bedrooms to a prostitute and a vice officer to supplement his Social Security income.

4. PORTAGE NORTHERN HIGH SCHOOL (November 20, 1982)

According to the *World Almanac and Book of Facts, 1984*, the school's students raised $6,212, the largest amount by any high school in the U.S., for the March of Dimes Breadlift charity program.

5. STATE HIGHWAY DEPARTMENT (1978)

When repainting center lines on Michigan's 9,450 miles of highways, the department saved $100,000 by shortening the white stripes from 20 to 12.5 feet and lengthening gaps between the marks from 30 to 37.5 feet.

6. WHITTIER HOTEL (Detroit) — September 1964

When the Beatles, who had stayed at the Whittier during their first American tour, left Detroit, the hotel's management sold the group's sheets — unlaundered — for $1,150 to two enterprising Chicago men. The two businessemen then cut the linen into one-inch squares and, along with sworn affidavits by the hotel's managers that testified to the articles' authenticity, marketed them.

2 UNIQUE BUDGET SURPLUSES

1. On November 1, 1937, the city of Kalamazoo paid a final bond installment and became the only city in the nation, 50,000-or-more population, at that time, to be free of debt.

2. In April 1983, at a time when its membership had dropped by nearly a half million, 300,000 of its members were laid off, and concessions were preferred to walkouts, the United Auto Workers Union (UAW) had accumulated the largest strike fund in the world, $510 million.

3 UNIQUE BUDGET DEFICITS

1. Michigan Bell Telephone Co. in April 1982 cut off service to 250 Highland Park city-government offices because the financially troubled city of 28,000 hadn't paid a $52,000 phone bill. The city, which, at the time, had a $5.6-million deficit, also owed about $50,000 to Detroit Edison and $20,000 to Michigan Consolidated gas.

2. On May 5, 1959, the state government of Michigan, which had run up a deficit of nearly $95 million, temporarily did not have enough money in the treasury to pay its employees. Newspapers and national television news programs across the country bannered the story of the "payless payday" under the headlines, "Michigan — the state that has gone broke."

3. In April 1981, officials of the state Medical Practice Board wanted to mail warnings to Michigan physicians about mounting abuse of prescription drugs (see page 7) but couldn't because they had run out of money for stamps.

3 TOWNS FOR SALE

1. DAMON (15 miles west of West Branch)

In 1981, Nancy Howard listed for sale, at $52,000, all that was left of the former lumbering boom town of Damon — six acres of land, a house, two cabins, two barns, and a general store.

2. JONES (Intersection of M-60 and M-40, Cass County)

Ed Lowe (Cassopolis), who had made a fortune selling kitty litter, bought

Jones in 1973 then spent $1.5 million over the next four years turning the dilapidated former farm village into a 50-acre, turn-of-the-century tourist attraction. But when the tourists failed to come, Lowe gave up his dream, and in June 1977 Jones was again sold — this time piece by piece by an auctioneer.

3. TAFT (M-55 between East Tawas and West Branch)

In November 1982, 74-year-old John Sibley, Taft's sole remaining resident, put his town up for sale. Sibley, who was born in the town and whose father owned the general store, said he'd part with the three acres and nine buildings for $50,000.

8 EARLY REAL-ESTATE DEALS

1. 1707

At Detroit, Antoine de la Mothe Cadillac conducted the first legal real-estate transaction in Michigan when he granted a long, narrow "ribbon farm," extending from the Detroit River, to Francois Fafard Delorme.

2. August 3, 1795

The first Michigan Indian land — a strip six miles wide along the Detroit River, all of Mackinac Island, a strip of the mainland along the Straits of Mackinac and another strip north of Mackinac Island — was ceded the to the United States in the Treaty of Greenville.

3. March 26, 1804

The federal government established at Detroit the first United States land office in what is now the state of Michigan and began settling disputes over deeds issued during French and English rule.

4. August 29, 1805

The first act requiring the registering of deeds in the Michigan territory was passed.

5. November 7, 1807

The first major block of Indian lands in Michigan — the southeastern quarter of the Lower Peninsula — was ceded to the United States for $10,000 and an annual payment of $2,400.

6. July 6, 1818

The first public auction sale of Michigan land took place with parcels being sold for an average of $4 per acre.

7. January 20, 1837

The Saginaw Bay Chippewas signed a treaty and turned over to the United States the last Indian-owned land in the Lower Peninsula.

8. July 10, 1838

Ludwik Wesolowski purchased a lot in the village of Marcellus (Macomb County) and became, according to *Enduring Poles*, the first recorded property owner of Polish lineage in the new state of Michigan.

4 COUNTIES WITH THE MOST-EXPENSIVE HOMES

Based on the median value of owner-occupied housing units in 1980. State average = $39,000.

1.	LIVINGSTON	$61,000
2.	WASHTENAW	$60,800
3.	OAKLAND	$56,300
4.	MACOMB	$50,600

3 COUNTIES WITH THE LEAST-EXPENSIVE HOMES

Based on the median value of owner-occupied housing units in 1980. State average = $39,000.

1.	KEWEENAW	$14,400
2.	GOGEBIC	$17,400
3.	LAKE	$19,800

3 COUNTIES WITH THE MOST EXPENSIVE RENT

Based on median monthly contract rent of renter-occupied housing in 1980. State average = $196.

1.	OAKLAND	$286
2.	WASHTENAW	$271
3.	MACOMB	$259

3 COUNTIES WITH THE CHEAPEST RENT

Based on median monthly contract rent of renter-occupied housing in 1980. State average = $196.

1.	LAKE	$109
2.	IRON	$112
3.	GOGEBIC	$113

2 RICHEST COUNTIES

Based on 1982 per-capita income. State average = $10,942.

1. OAKLAND	$14,186
2. MACOMB	$12,268

3 POOREST COUNTIES

Based on 1982 per-capita income. State average = $10,942.

1. OSCODA	$5,587
2. MECOSTA	$6,030
3. LAKE	$6,187

4 MOST MEDICAIDED COUNTIES

Four counties with the highest percentage of population collecting medicaid benefits in 1983. State average = 5.1%.

1. LAKE	10.5
2. LUCE	9.2
3. OGEMAW	8.7
4. WAYNE	8.1

3 LEAST MEDICAIDED COUNTIES

Three counties with the lowest percentage of population collecting medicaid benefits in 1983. State average = 5.1%.

1. OTTAWA	1.9
2. LEELANAU	2.0
3. CLINTON	2.2

3 MOST NEEDY COUNTIES

Three counties with the highest percentage of population collecting welfare benefits in 1983. State average = 12.9%.

1. LAKE	29.2
2. CRAWFORD	23.2
3. KALKASKA	21.4

3 MOST SELF-RELIANT COUNTIES

Three counties with the lowest percentage of population collecting welfare benefits in 1983. State average = 12.9%.

1. OTTAWA	4.0
2. LEELANAU	5.2
3. CLINTON	5.4

3 POOREST CONGRESSIONAL DISTRICTS

Three poorest Michigan U.S. congressional districts, based on U.S. Census Bureau information on typical home values and rent costs as indexed by the *Detroit Free Press*. National average = 100.

1. DISTRICT 13 — 40

The 13th district, composed largely of part of Detroit plus the cities of Grosse Pointe and Grosse Pointe Park, is, according to the Census Bureau, the poorest congressional district in the country.

2. DISTRICT 1 — 51

Part of Detroit and Highland Park

3. DISTRICT 11 — 70

Entire Upper Peninsula; all of Emmet, Cheboygan, Presque Isle, Alpena, Montmorency, Otsego, Charlevoix, and Alcona counties; and the northern third of Oscoda and Crawford counties.

3 RICHEST CONGRESSIONAL DISTRICTS

Three richest Michigan U.S. congressional districts, based on U.S. Census Bureau information on typical home values and rent costs as indexed by the *Detroit Free Press*. National average = 100.

1. DISTRICT 18 — 179

Most of the southeast half of Oakland County plus small areas of Macomb and Livingston counties.

2. DISTRICT 2 — 113

All of Hillsdale County; western half of Lenawee County; northwest two-thirds of Washtenaw County; and the southern 80% of Jackson County.

3. DISTRICT 12 — 108

Most of St. Clair County and the eastern two-thirds of Macomb County.

5 HIGHEST GOVERNMENTAL SALARIES

In 1983 more than 500 taxpayer-supported employees in Michigan state government earned more than the $70,000 a year taken home by Governor Blanchard. In fact, of the 59,000 workers receiving their paychecks from the state, the governor's salary ranks 275th. The five highest-paid state-government officials, all of whom made $95,422 in 1983, are:

1. DR. MAURICE REIZEN — Department of Public Health medical consultant

2. DR. THOMAS SULLIVAN — Director of Lafayette Clinic

3. DR. KENNETH WILCOX — State laboratory and epidemiology administrator

4. DR. HAROLD WRIGHT — Director of Northville Regional Psychiatric Hospital

5. DR. HERMAN ZIEL — State health facilities services administrator

4 ELECTED STATE OFFICIALS' SALARIES

In December 1984 the Michigan Officers Compensation Commission approved pay increases for elected state officials, which kept them among the highest paid in the nation. Salaries for elected Michigan officials are:

Official	*1985 Salary*	*1986 Salary*
1. GOVERNOR	$81,900	$85,800
2. LT. GOVERNOR	$56,175	$58,850
3. SUPREME COURT JUSTICES	$77,700	$81,400
4. LEGISLATORS	$34,860	$36,520

6 TOP-PAID PRIVATE-INDUSTRY EXECUTIVES

Total compensation for 1983 as reported by the *Detroit Free Press*.

1. ROGER SMITH (General Motors Corporation) — $1,490,490

2. PHILIP CALDWELL (Ford Motor Corporation) — $1,420,534

3. JAMES GROSFELD (Pulte Home Corporation) — $910,000

4. W. MICHAEL BLUMENTHAL (Burroughs Corporation) — $900,000

5. WILLIAM LAMOTHE (Kellogg Company) — $685,000

6. PAUL OREFFICE (Dow Chemical Company) — $644,970

4 RECORD PROFITS

1. General Motors made $4.5 billion in 1984, the largest yearly profit in its corporate history.

2. Ford Motor Company in 1984 earned a record $2.9-billion profit.

3. Chrysler Corporation recorded a $2.4-billion profit in 1984, the largest in the company's 60-year history.

4. While winning the 1984 world championship, the Detroit Tigers earned an estimated $8-9 million profit, the largest in their history.

5 COUNTIES WITH THE HIGHEST
WEEKLY EARNINGS

Based on 1983 average weekly earnings of employees covered under the state unemployment insurance program. State average = $374.60.

1. GENESEE	$460.47
2. MIDLAND	$452.55
3. MONROE	$436.94
4. WAYNE	$420.27
5. INGHAM	$401.45

6 COUNTIES WITH THE LOWEST
WEEKLY EARNINGS

Based on 1983 average weekly earnings of employees covered under the state unemployment insurance program. State average = $374.60.

1. OSCODA	$151.14
2. KEWEENAW	$157.35
3. LEELANAU	$162.22
4. LAKE	$165.12
5. GOGEBIC	$168.00
6. ROSCOMMON	$168.82

4 BELOW-AVERAGE WAGE-EARNING YEARS

The only four years since 1929 that Michigan residents' per-capita income has been less than that of their fellow Americans. Numbers represent Michigan percent of average American per-capita income.

1. 1933	93.0
2. 1932	98.5
3. 1982	98.6
4. 1983	99.1

4 OUTSTANDING WAGE-EARNING YEARS

Four years since 1929 that Michigan residents' per-capita income has outpaced that of their fellow Americans by the greatest margin. Numbers represent Michigan percent of average American per-capita income.

1. 1943	122.3
2. 1953	119.4
3. 1937	119.1
4. 1944	116.3

106

4 COUNTIES WITH THE MOST WORKING WOMEN

Four counties with the highest percentage of the total labor force composed of women in 1980. State average = 41.4.

1.	ISABELLA	45.6
2.	INGHAM	45.2
3.	EMMET	44.4
4.	IOSCO	44.2

3 COUNTIES WITH THE FEWEST WORKING WOMEN

Three counties with the lowest percentage of the total labor force composed of women in 1980. State average = 41.4.

1.	PRESQUE ISLE	35.0
2.	KALKASKA	36.9
3.	MISSAUKEE	36.9

3 MOST SOCIALLY SECURE COUNTIES

Three counties with the highest percentage of total personal income composed of social security benefits in 1982. State average = 6.5%.

1.	ROSCOMMON	21.3
2.	KEWEENAW	21.0
3.	MONTMORENCY	20.6

3 LEAST SOCIALLY SECURE COUNTIES

Three counties with the lowest percentage of total personal income composed of social security benefits in 1982. State average = 6.5%.

1.	WASHTENAW	3.9
2.	CLINTON	4.4
3.	LIVINGSTON	4.6

4 VETERANS BENEFITS

1. December 26, 1944

Floyd M. Edwards (Kalamazoo), a World War II navy veteran, purchased a home with the help of a loan guaranteed by the Veterans Administration and became the first Michigan veteran to take advantage of the "G.I. bill of rights."

2. November 5, 1946

Sixty-one percent of Michigan's voters approved a $270,000 bonus for Michigan's 600,000 World War II veterans.

3. November 2, 1954

Michigan voters, by more than two-to-one, approved an $80-million bonus to Korean War veterans.

4. 1974

By only a 1.8% margin, Michigan voters approved a $190 million-bonus to Vietnam veterans.

4 UNIQUE BEQUESTS

1. In her will, Patricia Roney (Grosse Pointe), who died January 4, 1982, at the age of 62, left $10,000 to anyone who would adopt and care for her German shepherd, Adolph. When news of the unusual bequest was broadcast nationally, the attorney who administered the will was contacted by more than 200 people from all over the country offering to take the orphaned dog.

But, since Roney had left the remainder of her estate to Notre Dame University and had also stipulated that if Adolph died before the money was spent the balance of his inheritance would also go to Notre Dame, the attorney gave Adolph to a secretary at the school.

2. Homer E. Nowlin, an 86-year-old Lapeer County farmer who had attended school only through the eighth grade, left an estate worth at least $1 million to Michigan State University upon his death in October 1979.

3. Russ Bengel, a former Jackson mayor and businessman, and his wife Ruth gave $1 million to the Michigan Wildlife Habitat Foundation, a private group that finances and directs habitat improvement and reclamation projects. The Bengel's February 1984 donation was the largest ever to a Michigan conservation organization.

4. In 1892, Helen Look Daly was born in Lowell (Kent County), lived in the small town for the next 66 years, then moved to Arizona, where in November 1981 she died at the age of 89. Though she had not returned to her native Lowell for 23 years, Daly willed the city an estimated $300,00 in stocks and bonds and named her former physician to chair a committee to decide how to spend the gift, which equalled about one-sixth of the city's annual budget.

MICHIGAN'S 3 LARGEST PRIVATE FOUNDATIONS

Based on 1983 assets.

1. KELLOGG FOUNDATION (Battle Creek) — $1 billion
The nation's fourth-largest private foundation.

2. KRESGE FOUNDATION (Troy) — $792 million
Ranks eighth nationally.

3. CHARLES STEWART MOTT FOUNDATION (Flint) — $471 million
Ranks 15th nationally.

8 LARGEST SAVINGS & LOANS

Based on assets as of June 30, 1982.

1.	FIRST FEDERAL OF MICHIGAN (Detroit)	$4.4 billion
2.	STANDARD (Troy)	$3.6 billion
3.	DETROIT & NORTHERN (Hancock)	$1.2 billion
4.	GREAT LAKES (Ann Arbor)	$938 million
5.	AMERICAN (Southfield)	$841 million
6.	FIRST OF OAKLAND (Pontiac)	$755 million
7.	CAPITOL (Lansing)	$473 million
8.	MUTUAL (Bay City)	$445 million

9 BANK CLOSINGS

1. February 14, 1933

After nearly 200 Michigan banks had failed, Governor William Comstock, in order to prevent further panic withdrawals, ordered a bank "holiday" which closed the state's few remaining banks for nine days.

2. November 27, 1935

An assistant cashier at the Lennon State Bank embezzled $14,000, which so depleted the bank's assets that it was forced to close for good.

3. October 11, 1966

In a secret, late-night court session, a Detroit judge declared the Detroit Public Bank insolvent, and Michigan experienced the largest bank failure since the days of the Great Depression. Within a few hours, however, the Federal Deposit Insurance Corporation (FDIC) sold all assets and liabilities to the larger Bank of the Commonwealth, which opened the bank the next day without officially losing a day of business or a customer's dollar.

4. April 16, 1970

FDIC examiners closed the Peoples State Savings Bank (Auburn) and charged the bank's board of directors and officers with "complete collapse" and "mismanagement and poor judgment" for their involvement in a fantastic financing scheme that involved hundreds of people.

The bank's problems started with a normal $5,000 loan to a Sanford man who wanted to build a small mobile home park. But the developer's plans kept expanding and ultimately included a golf course, shopping center, subdivisions, marina, and condominuim complex. Peoples expanded with him and, by misusing "letters of credit," which they issued like certificates of deposit, unethically secured $1.5 million for the developer from banks in Bay City, New Jersey, and

New York, a Richmond, Virginia union trust fund, and individual east-coast investors.

5. February 11, 1971

The Michigan financial institutions commissioner seized and declared insolvent the Bloomfield Bank (Pontiac). Over the next four days, all banking holidays, the FDIC, in the largest assistance transaction in its 37-year history, made $100 million available to a Detroit business family, who then incorporated, bought the insolvent bank, and reopened as The Fidelity Bank of Michigan.

The changeover was the first in Michigan banking history to involve the organization of a new bank to assume the liabilities of a closed bank without losing any banking days.

6. 1974

Michigan National Corporation took over the insolvent Tri-City Bank (Warren) and reopened it as Michigan National Bank of Macomb.

7. May 15, 1982

The Community Bank of Washtenaw (Ypsilanti) was declared insolvent, the FDIC appointed as receiver, and takeover bids accepted. Two days later, the bank reopened as a branch of Michigan National Bank.

8. February 1983

Metropolitan Savings Association of Farmington Hills, Michigan's 10th-largest savings and loan, was declared insolvent by federal regulators and merged into Empire of America, one of the nation's largest savings and loan associations.

9. March 9, 1984

National Bank and Trust of Traverse City was declared insolvent after losing nearly $10 million over two years. The bank opened four days later as NBD Northwest Bank, an affiliate of the corporation which owns National Bank of Detroit.

3 NOTABLE BLACK MONEY-HANDLERS

1. RICHARD AUSTIN in 1941 became the first black certified accountant in Michigan. Thirty years later, Austin took office in Michigan as the nation's first elected black Secretary of State.

2. FIRST INDEPENDENCE NATIONAL BANK opened its doors in Detroit on May 14, 1970, as the first bank in Michigan to be owned and operated by blacks.

3. CASSANDRA SMITH GRAY (Detroit) in July 1976 became the first black-female tax assessor in the country.

3 UNIQUE LOANS TO MICHIGAN

1. On March 20, 1836, the State of Michigan borrowed its first funds, $36,000, from Robert Hollingsworth (New York), who charged six-per-cent-per-year interest payable over 20 years.

2. When, on December 18, 1908, the state treasury was out of money and could not meet its employees' next payroll, several railroad companies volunteered to pay $750,000 in advance on their taxes to help out.

3. On August 27, 1982, a consortium of Japanese banks agreed to help Michigan's borrowing problems by providing the state with a $500-million line of credit. At the time, Michigan had the lowest credit rating of any state in the nation, which made it both difficult and expensive to borrow money in America. Many Michigan residents and officials, however, viewed the Japanese aid with irony since the state's economic problems, high unemployment, and sagging auto industry had been blamed on domestic inroads made by Japanese automakers.

MICHIGAN STATE GOVERNMENT'S
10 LARGEST STOCK HOLDINGS

The Michigan Treasury Department, which handles the investment of about $8.2 billion from five state pension funds, had, as of October 1983, 30 percent of those funds invested in stocks, the 10 largest holdings being:

1.	IBM (863,129 shares)	$109.3 million
2.	MOBIL OIL (3,373,500 shares)	$101.2 million
3.	BRISTOL-MYERS (1,929,100 shares)	$84.8 million
4.	SCHLUMBERGER LTD. (1,481,700 shares)	$77.4 million
5.	GENERAL MOTORS (842,800 shares)	$65.3 million
6.	SMITHKLINE BECKMAN (956,100 shares)	$64.7 million
7.	DIGITAL EQUIPMENT (990,600 shares)	$64.7 million
8.	STANDARD OIL OF CALIFORNIA (1,828,700 shares)	$64.4 million
9.	STANDARD OIL OF INDIANA (1,304,200 shares)	$64.0 million
10.	GTE CORPORATION (1,357,200 shares)	$61.9 million

9 TAXING MILESTONES

1. March 2, 1799

Detroit became an official port of entry with the first collector earning a $250 annual salary plus three percent of any customs fees he took in.

2. September 10, 1805

A Michigan territorial law directed that ". . . every male inhabitant in the territory over the age of 16 years should pay annually the sum of one dollar as a capitation tax." The total number of taxpayers in the territory at the time was 525, and all paid.

3. May 8, 1820

The territorial legislature levied, for the first time in Michigan, taxes on personal property and land and authorized sheriffs to imprison delinquents.

4. April 21, 1825

A Michigan territorial law directed that, instead of jailing property owners for nonpayment of property taxes, the territory would confiscate and sell the tax-delinquents' lands.

5. March 15, 1867

The state legislature, by approving a levy of 1/20th of a mill on each dollar of taxable property in the state, made the University of Michigan the nation's first university to be supported by a direct property tax.

6. June 1, 1933

The legislature eliminated a state tax on real estate and, in its place, enacted an unpopular three-percent sales tax to get the state out of debt. Most Michigan residents blamed Governor William Comstock for the measure, and sales personnel often told their customers, "That will cost you $1.00 plus three cents for Comstock." Rumors spread that Comstock might even be personally profiting from the tax and didn't stop until he finally offered a cash reward to anyone who could prove them.

7. 1960

The sales tax was increased to four percent.

8. October 1, 1967

Michigan's first state income tax, 2.6 percent on individual incomes, 5.67 percent on corporate profits, and seven percent on banks and other financial institutions, went into effect.

9. November 5, 1974

Voters repealed the state sales tax on food and drugs.

6 GAS-TAX INCREASES

1. In 1926, Michigan levied its first gasoline tax at 2 cents per gallon. In the ensuing years, that tax increased as follows:

2. 3 cents per gallon — 1927

3. 4$^1/_2$ cents per gallon — 1951

4. 7 cents per gallon — 1967

5. 9 cents per gallon — 1972

6. 11 cents per gallon — 1978

11 AUTOMOBILE REGISTRATION FEES

What it has cost to purchase automobile license plates in Michigan since they were first required in 1905.

1. $2.00 one-time fee — 1905

2. $1.00 for initial registration and 50 cents annually for renewal — 1907

3. $3 annually — 1909

4. 25 cents per horsepower plus 25 cents per 100 pounds of weight — 1916

5. 25 cents per horsepower plus 35 cents per 100 pounds of weight — 1919

6. 55 cents per 100 pounds of weight — 1925

7. 35 cents per 100 pounds of weight — 1934

8. 55 cents per 100 pounds of weight — 1967

9. Fees ranging from $20 for 0-3,000 pounds weight up to $74 for 10,000 pounds weight — 1978

10. Fees ranging from $23 for 0-3,000 pounds weight up to $85 for 10,000 pounds weight — 1982

11. Effective October 1, 1983, each passenger vehicle of the 1984 or subsequent model year is taxed on the basis of list price.

3 MOST TAXED COUNTIES

Three counties that paid the most state income tax per capita in 1981.

1.	OAKLAND	$283
2.	MIDLAND	$261
3.	INGHAM	$226

4 LEAST TAXED COUNTIES

Four counties that paid the least state income tax per capita in 1981.

1. HURON $0

Overall, people in Huron County received more money back in refunds than they paid in taxes.

2. KEWEENAW	$23
3. LAKE	$28
4. GRATIOT	$34

4 COUNTIES THAT RECEIVE
THE LEAST STATE MONEY

Four counties that received the least money per from any and all forms of state aid in 1981.

1. EATON	$352.47
2. LEELANAU	$361.21
3. OAKLAND	$402.65
4. BRANCH	$407.41

5 COUNTIES THAT RECEIVE
THE MOST STATE MONEY

Five counties that received the most money per capita from any and all forms of state aid in 1981.

1. LUCE	$2,310.79
2. ISABELLA	$1,302.48
3. INGHAM	$1,249.75
4. IONIA	$1,185.44
5. HOUGHTON	$1,136.17

3 TAX MALDISTRIBUTIONS

1. In 1983, Michigan received back from the federal government less money — only 69 cents of every $1 state residents and businesses paid to the U.S. treasury — than any other state.

2. According to a 1984 study by the Advisory Commission on Intergovernmental Relations, middle-income Detroiters paid more in total taxes than their counterparts in 50 other large U.S. cities. A typical family of four in Detroit earning $25,000 a year, according to the non-partisan government-research group, paid $6,542.50 or 26.17 percent of its income in taxes, compared to a national average of 22 percent.

3. In nearly doubling its cigarette tax from 11 cents per pack to 21 cents per pack on May 1, 1982, Michigan tied three other states for the highest cigarette tax in the nation.

3 CONSPICUOUS TAX PROTESTS

1. In a highly publicized, organized tax protest in 1981, as many as 5,000 Flint and Pontiac autoworkers claimed excessive numbers of exemptions on the W-4 witholding forms they filed with their employers. Others, claiming that the tax system was unconstitutional, refused to file their 1040 forms.

The protest movement all but died, however, when on April 14, one day before the annual filing deadline, three leaders of the movement were indicted on charges of filing fraudulent W-4 forms and its founder later sentenced to two years in prison.

2. Like Lady Godiva — the devoutly religious 11th-Century English noblewoman who rode naked through the marketplace to convince her husband to eliminate an oppressive tax — an unidentified Kalamazoo woman, clad only in a nude body suit, rode a horse in a Libertarian Party's April 16, 1983 "Tax-Protest-Day" parade.

3. In March 1982 a Sterling Heights man, who had had his taxes lowered by the Michigan Tax Tribunal in 1981 only to see them raised again by the city tax assessor the following year, trimmed $50 from his property tax bill by shattering his $1,800 patio with a sledgehammer.

3 BEST-FUNDED SCHOOL DISTRICTS

Based on amount spent per pupil in 1981-82.

1. DEARBORN		$4,126
2. BIRMINGHAM		$4,030
3. SOUTHFIELD		$3,955

4 LOWEST-FUNDED SCHOOL DISTRICTS

Based on amount spent per pupil in 1981-82.

1. VASSAR (Tuscola County)	$1,558
2. MORLEY STANWOOD (Mecosta County)	$1,601
3. MARCELLUS (Cass County)	$1,601
4. KINGSLEY (Grand Traverse County)	$1,605

4 MOST EXPENSIVE COLLEGES

Based on 1983-84 tuition and fees for freshhmen at four-year public and private colleges and universities.

1. ALMA COLLEGE	$6,072
2. KALAMAZOO COLLEGE	$6,882
3. ALBION COLLEGE	$5,850
4. HILLSDALE COLLEGE	$5,720

4 MOST ECONOMICAL COLLEGES

Based on 1983-84 tuition and fees for freshhmen at four-year public and private colleges and universities. (Does not include community colleges.)

1.	OAKLAND UNIVERSITY	$1,271
2.	UNIVERSITY OF MICHIGAN (Flint)	$1,356
3.	EASTERN MICHIGAN UNIVERSITY	$1,365
4.	WESTERN MICHIGAN UNIVERSITY	$1,397

3 TOP-SPENDING LIBRARIES

Three libraries with the highest per-capita 1982 budgets.

1.	OAKLAND	$47.00
2.	BLOOMFIELD TOWNSHIP	$23.30
3.	DEARBORN	$23.10

5 LOW-BUDGET LIBRARIES

Five libraries with the lowest per-capita 1982 budgets.

1.	DOWLING	$0.90
2.	DEWITT	$1.00
3.	LYONS VILLAGE	$1.00
4.	ATHENS	$1.20
5.	DEXTER	$1.20

6 FINEST LIBRARIES

Six libraries that collected the most fines in 1982.

1.	DETROIT	$688,405
2.	MONROE	$447,876
3.	WAYNE	$358,756
4.	KENT COUNTY	$252,567
5.	LAPEER	$229,895
6.	GRAND RAPIDS	$229,524

5 LIBRARIES THAT COLLECTED THE FEWEST FINES

In 1982.

1.	WALKERVILLE	$94
2.	FIFE LAKE	$387
3.	MCMILLAN	$611
4.	AMASA	$669
5.	OSCEOLA	$954

6

GETTING DOWN TO BUSINESS

8 MICHIGAN INVENTORS

1. MELVILLE R. BISSELL (Grand Rapids)

The dusty packing straw Bissell used in his china shop aggravated his allergic headaches, so in 1876 he invented and patented the nation's first carpet sweeper to scoop up the dust rather than scatter it.

2. LLOYD G. COPEMAN (Flint and Hadley) died in 1956 holding patents on more than 650 inventions, including the automatic electric toaster, the electric refrigerator, the rubber ice-cube tray, and an automatic electric stove, the rights to which he sold to George W. Westinghouse.

3. JOSEPH GIBBONS (Adrian) on August 25, 1840, patented the nation's first practical seeding machine, a grain drill with cavities to deliver seed at a regulated volume.

4. DALE W. GRAY (Mundy Township, Genesee County) and Ted Lawson (Oregon, Illinois) in 1970 invented a tracker for bow hunters. The men marketed their device — a string which, when attached to the arrow, winds off a spool like a fishing reel and leads the hunter to the animal — in 1980.

5. BOB KAISER (Milford) invented a better mousetrap — a small, narrow box that holds bait and a killing spring mechanism — that makes it possible to capture, bloodlessly kill, and dispose of mice without ever touching or seeing them. Kaiser's trap was chosen as the 1982 Product of the Year by the National Hardware Retailing Association after being selected in 1980 by the *Smithsonian* magazine as the most encouraging patent of the year.

6. C.B. KING (Detroit) patented the nation's first pneumatic jackhammer in 1894.

7. LEO PETERS of Butterball Farms (Grand Rapids) holds more than 60 patents, including one for the Butterball turkey and another on the process of making "designer" butter pats, used exclusively throughout the nation by McDonald's, Walt Disney World, and Hyatt Regency hotels.

8. LEONIDAS G. WOOLLEY (Mendon) on May 3, 1881, patented the nation's first electric locomotive headlight. Woolley suspended his polygonal lamp frame in position with opposing strings which neutralized jarring.

3 EARLY BLACK INVENTORS

By 1915 the United States Patent Office had registered 76 patents to 17 black inventors in Michigan. Leading the list of those early Michigan black inventors were:

1. JOSEPH H. DICKINSON (Detroit)

The designer of chapel and parlor organs had registered, by 1912, more than a dozen patents for musical instruments.

2. ELIJAH MCCOY (Ypsilanti and Detroit), who in 1923 received his last patent at the age of 81, created 78 inventions over his lifetime, 48 of them for lubricating devices used on ships and locomotives around the world.

3. ROBERT A. PELLHAM (Detroit) in 1905 invented a fast, economical, and precise statistical tabulating machine, which was leased by the U.S. government.

10 UNIQUE MANUFACTURERS

1. ABBOTT'S MAGIC MANUFACTURING COMPANY (Colon) is the world's largest manufacturer of magical supplies.

2. THE FRANKENMUTH WOOLEN MILL (Frankenmuth), which uses machinery that dates back to its 1894 establishment to process fleece shorn from Michigan sheep, is Michigan's only woolen mill. The mill, which knitted 66,000 pairs of socks for World War I doughboys, currently manufactures 5,000 comforters each year.

3. GEODESIC DOMES, INC. (Davison) in the 1950s paid $2,000 to become one of the nation's three original licensed manufacturers of Richard Buckminster Fuller geodesic domes. The company now sells an average $750,000 worth of the uniquely shaped structures annually.

4. HOEGH INDUSTRIES (Gladstone) is the world's largest manufacturer of pet caskets, annually shipping 15,000 animal coffins to more than half of America's 60 pet cemeteries. (See photo, page 119)

5. ICT, INC. (Shelby) is the world's largest manufacturer of man-made gemstones — synthetic diamonds, rubies, and sapphires made from chemicals under extreme heat and pressure.

6. MICHIGAN BRICK INCORPORATED (Corunna) is Michigan's only brick manufacturer.

7. PREEMIE FASHIONS (Lansing) makes and sells clothing for premature babies.

8. RANIR COPORATION (Grand Rapids) is Michigan's leading manufacturer of private-label dental floss, servicing over 100 stores and wholesalers.

9. The THETFORD COPORATION (Ann Arbor) is the nation's largest manufacturer of portable-toilet systems.

10. WHITEHALL METAL STUDIOS (Montague), the world's largest manufacturer of weather vanes, built 60,000 in 1983, including one for the California ranch of President Ronald Reagan.

2 UNIQUE COBBLERS

1. WOLVERINE WORLD WIDE (Rockford), the country's largest pigskin tanner and eighth-largest footwear manufacturer, is best known for its line of Hush Puppy shoes.

2. The WOODEN SHOE FACTORY (Holland), which has produced poplar and aspen footwear by hand and machine since 1926, is the only original wooden-shoe factory on the North American continent.

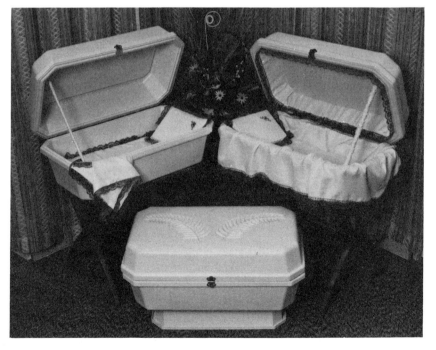

Three of the 20 styles of regular or deluxe styrene caskets manufactured by Hoegh Industries, Inc. (Gladstone) for dogs, cats, birds, turtles, snakes, squirrels, mice, rabbits, ducks, chickens, skunks, monkeys, gorillas, and other pets. (See story, page 118)

2 OVERSTUFFINGS

1. STUFFED SAFARI (Farmington), with 1,000 square feet holding more than 3,400 plush toys from aardvarks to zebras, advertises itself as the world's largest stuffed-animal specialty store.

2. TEDDY & ME (Grand Ledge) claims to have the Midwest's largest selection of Teddy bears and Teddy-bear-related gift items.

4 PROMINENT PRINTERS

1. ROSPATCH CORPORATION (Grand Rapids) is the nation's leading producer of sewn-in labels for clothing manufacturers.

2. SCIENTIFIC GAMES (Madison Heights and Sparta) prints 200 million tickets annually for Michigan's instant-lottery game as well as 300 million tickets for lotteries in four other states and Australia.

3. GEORGE F. VALASSIS & CO. (Livonia) is the nation's largest printer of the cents-off coupon booklets that flutter out of newspapers.

4. The ZONDERVAN CORPORATION (Grand Rapids) is the country's largest publicly held evangelical publishing house.

4 UNIQUE SERVICES

1. DEAD LETTERS

Afterworld Communications (Southfield) will, for $40, place a message with a terminally ill "courier" who, upon reaching the afterworld, will then deliver the memorized passage to the spirits of the customer's deceased friends or relatives. For $100, Afterworld will place communications with three messengers, usually cancer patients, to increase chances of "early delivery."

2. HUMAN HAZARDS TESTING

International Research and Development (Mattawan) is one of the world's half-dozen largest independent laboratories that studies the possible hazards to humans of new food additives, drugs and cosmetics. International has, for example, conducted the largest study of the effect of saccharin on humans and has determined the saftey limits of birth-control pills and asbestos.

3. TEMPORARY SERVICES

Kelly Services (Troy) is the nation's largest and the world's second-largest temporary services company. Five hundred Kelly offices in five countries provide 450,000 temporary employees — clerical workers, personal computer operators, registered nurses, draftsmen, product demonstrators, design engineers, and others — to 170,000 customers annually.

4. WEATHER WATCHER

Esther Lahti retired in 1984 after spending 21 years measuring precipitation and daily high-, low-, and 5 p.m.-temperatures as a National Weather Service volunteer weather observer at Herman (near Marquette), the state's highest weather-reporting station.

2 CLOCKWATCHERS

1. LOIS ANDERSON (Northville), after passing a day-long essay and practical examination in 1974, became the first woman in Michigan to be licensed as a clock repairer.
   — *Item contributed by Thomas Anderson, Northville* —

2. SEAN (PAT) MONK (Birmingham), a master watchmaker and founder of the Michigan Watchmakers Guild, holds Michigan horological license No. 00001.

6 SUCCESSFUL DRUG DEALERS

1. SIDNEY BARTHWELL founded Barthwell Drug Stores, Inc. (Detroit), which, during the 1940s, was the nation's largest chain of black-owned drug stores.

2. DR. SAMUEL DUFFIELD opened a drugstore in Detroit in 1862 that eventually grew into the pharmaceutical giant, the Parke, Davis & Co., with annual sales of over $3 billion.

3. The L. PERRIGO COMPANY (Allegan), begun in 1887 as a patent-medicine distributor, is currently the world's largest producer of pharmaceuticals, vitamins, and health and beauty products for "private labels" such as A & P, Cunningham, and Revco.

4. PERRY DRUGS, begun in 1957 in a rented store in Pontiac, is the largest drug store chain in Michigan.

5. W.E. UPJOHN (Kalamazoo), during the 1880s, revolutionized the pharmaceutical industry when he enclosed pills in a hard, yet easily dissolvable, coating.

6. JAMES VERNOR (Detroit), manufacturer of Vernor's soft drink (see also pages 128 and 190) was Michigan's first registered pharmacist.

2 FIRST BUSINESSES

1. Michigan's first papermill was established in 1834 on the Raisin River near Monroe.

2. The first window-glass factory in Michigan opened on January 10, 1836,

near Monroe. Before the shop's opening, glass in Michigan buildings had been a luxury and a broken window a disaster.

6 OLDEST BUSINESSES

As of 1983, more than 400 businesses in Michigan had been in existence for more than 100 continuous years. Six of the oldest of their particular type of business and the years of their founding are:

1. ARNOLD TRANSIT CO. (Mackinac Island) — 1878

   The state's oldest passenger ferry-service.

2. J.D. CHANDLER ROOFING CO. (Detroit) — 1879

   Believed to be the oldest roofing company in Michigan.

3. M. HALE CO. (South Haven) — 1855

   The oldest general-merchandise store in Michigan.

4. GEORGE JEROME and CO. survey engineers (Detroit) — 1828

   The oldest continuous-operating business in Michigan.

5. THE *MINING JOURNAL* (Marquette) — 1846

   The Upper Peninsula's oldest and largest newspaper.

6. ZEMPER STUDIO (Holland) — 1858

   Claims to be the oldest photographic studio in America.

TOP 10 MICHIGAN PERFORMERS

Based on net 1983 income as compiled by John Yeager, CPA of Arthur Young & Co. and Don Durocher of the public relations firm, Durocher & Co., and printed in the *Detroit Free Press*. The list does not include any private companies or large subsidiaries of companies headquartered outside of Michigan.

1. **GM**
   $3.7 billion

2. *Ford*
   $1.9 billion

3. Chrysler Corp.
   $701 million

4. **Kmart**
   $492 million

5. Detroit Edison

$365 million

6. Consumers Power Company

$348 million

7. DOW

$334 million

8. Kellogg's

$243 million

9. Burroughs Corp.

$197 million

10. ANR
American Natural Resources

$171 million

TOP 5 DEFENSE CONTRACTORS

The top five Michigan contractors for the U.S. Department of Defense, based on dollar value of contracts awarded during fiscal year 1982.

1. GENERAL DYNAMICS CORPORATION (Warren)

$372,365 for armed-vehicle production and research and development.

2. TELEDYNE INDUSTRIES, INC (Muskegon)

$194,793 for armed-vehicle components.

3. WILLIAMS INTERNATIONAL CORP (Walled Lake)

$171,622 for missile components and research and development.

4. GENERAL MOTORS CORPORATION (Flint)

$143,166 for armed-vehicle and personnel-carrier components, trucks, and diesel engines.

5. LEAR SIEGLER, INC (Grand Rapids)

$62,579 for aircraft components and systems engineering.

TOP 10 BLACK FIRMS

Michigan's 10 largest black-owned firms, based on 1983 gross sales, as published in the June 1984 issue of *Black Enterprise* magazine.

1. PORTERFIELD WILSON PONTIAC-GMC TRUCK INC (Detroit)

$40 million

2. PORTERFIELD WILSON MAZDA INC (Detroit)

$33 million

3. WOODRUFF OLDSMOBILE INC (Detroit)

$17.7 million

4. AL BENNETT FORD INC (Flint)

$17.3 million

5. DICK HARRIS CADILLAC INC (Detroit)

$16.2 million

6. MEL FARR FORD INC (Oak Park)

$14.5 million

7. CONYERS FORD (Detroit)

$11.3 million

8. THE BARFIELD CO (Ypsilanti)

$10.4 million

9. KEYS GROUP CO (Detroit)

$9.6 million

10. JIM BRADLEY PONTIAC-CADILLAC-GMC INC (Ann Arbor)

$9.3 million

10 FASTEST-GROWING COMPANIES

Ten Michigan companies among the 500 fastest-growing privately owned U.S. businesses, based on compounded annual growth from 1979 to 1983 as published in *Inc.* magazine, December 1984.

1. COMPUTER ALLIANCE (Farmington Hills)		171%
2. RENAISSANCE PRINTING (Detroit)		119%
3. CARBIDE TECHNOLOGIES (Fraser)		101%
4. JWI (Holland)		101%
5. GREAT LAKES MICROGRAPHICS (Kalamazoo)		99%
6. ELLIOTT STORE FIXTURES (Lansing)		85%
7. R.J. MARSHALL CO. (Detroit)		79%
8. TELECHECK MICHIGAN (Oak Park)		78%
9. PISCOR (Brighton)		67%
10. DEUCALION RESOURCES GROUP (Ann Arbor)		66%

5 SHOPPING FIRSTS

1. HUDSONS

On April 2, 1881, Joseph Lowthian Hudson held a grand opening of a men's, boy's and furnishings store he had opened in leased space at the Detroit

Opera House. By the late 1920s, Hudson's had become the third-largest department store in America and carried more than a half-million items displayed over 49 acres of sales space in a mammmoth 25-story red-brick downtown-Detroit building. On January 17, 1983, Hudson's closed that downtown store and on May 1, 1984, moved its headquarters to Minneapolis, Minnesota.

2. K MART

The S.S. Kresge Company opened the nation's first K mart at Garden City on March 1, 1962. Over the next 20 years, the firm opened more than 2000 of the discount stores nationwide.

3. PEDESTRIAN MALL

The nation's first permanent pedestrian mall, a shopping area created by closing several city blocks to traffic, opened at downtown Kalamazoo August 19, 1959.

4. SHOPPING MALL

Northland, the nation's first regional shopping mall, opened at Southfield on March 22, 1954. The success of the 1¼-mile circle of stores, anchored by the then world's-largest branch department store, J.L. Hudsons, began a retail revolution that saw American shoppers flee the city to the suburbs.

5. WICKES LUMBER

The world's first supermarket cash-and-carry building-supply outlet — Wickes Lumber — opened at Bay City in 1952. Over the next two decades, Wickes became the world's largest retailer of lumber and building supplies but, during the past several years, has suffered many corporate problems, including reorganization under Chapter 11 bankruptcy.

6 UNIQUE PUBLIC-RELATIONS CAMPAIGNS

1. On Monday, September 20, 1982, 37 people began a contest at a Grand Rapids Oldsmobile/Honda dealer who promised that the two participants who could keep their hands on one of two 1974 Oldsmobiles the longest could keep the vehicles.

For many of the contestants who didn't drop out quickly, the contest turned sour. At the 53-hour mark, one contestant slumped to the ground and began convulsing. Four hours later, a 24-year-old man became incoherent and was taken home by relatives. Another contestant's legs shook violently from severe leg cramps as he collapsed into the arms of a friend. Another disoriented man, who couldn't understand why people wanted him to hold his hand on the car, started to cry.

By Thursday morning, four contestants — two each on a Cutlass and an Oldsmobile 88 — remained. Finally, a 25-year-old man dropped his hand from the Olds 88 and walked silently away. Another man, after clutching the Cutlass for 65 hours, stumbled back a half step and, while shouting that the winner had put something in his drink, walked to a nearby creek and fell asleep.

2. After comedian Eddie Murphy wore a faded "Mumford Phys. Ed. Dept." T-shirt in his role as a Detroit detective in the 1985 hit movie, *Beverly Hills Cop*, Detroit's Samuel C. Mumford High School was so deluged with orders for their burgundy-on-blue athletic wear that they had to turn to a national distributor to handle the demand.

3. A group called "Promote Michigan" hired an Ohio advertising firm to fight a "Voter's Choice" tax-cutting proposal on the November 1984 ballot.

4. On May 3, 1976, the American Federal Savings branch bank (Farmington) sold $10,000 worth of money at a discount — $100 for $80, $50 for $40, $20 for $16 and silver dollars for 50 cents — as an opening-day promotion.

5. In a publicity stunt designed to attract national attention, Henry Ford on January 12, 1904, drove one of his automobiles a world-record 91.37 m.p.h. on cinders strewn atop frozen Lake St. Clair.

6. The Low Power Technology Corp. (Burton) began marketing in 1983 a device called AMCAST that broadcasts a sales message that can be picked up by an AM radio within 600 feet of the transmitter. A sign attached to the bottom of a realtor's "For Sale" sign in front of a house, for example, would tell interested buyers to tune their car radios to a specific AM frequency for more information.

2 EARLY "SAY YES TO MICHIGAN" CAMPAIGNS

1. In 1749 the governor general of Canada, in an attempt to attract people to France's new settlement at Detroit, offered to every man who would settle there, a spade, an axe, a ploughshare, one large and one small wagon, a cow, a sow, seed, and family support for one year. Over the next two years, 103 persons accepted the offer and came to Michigan.

2. In 1845, John Almy (Grand Rapids), who was sent by Michigan Governor John S. Barry to New York City to encourage arriving European immigrants to come to Michigan, published a six-page pamphlet extolling the attractions of the state. Three years later, Edward H. Thompson (Flint), another Michigan agent in New York City, published a 47-page pamphlet entitled, *The Emmigrant's Guide to Michigan*.

2 CONSPICUOUS GROCERY STORE ADS

1. The Hamady Brothers grocery store chain (Flint area), to commemorate its 40th anniversary in 1951, ran a 49-page newspaper ad, the largest number of advertising pages ever placed by a single firm in a single edition of any newspaper in the country. In celebrating its 71st anniversary in 1982, the company broke their own record, this time by running 88 pages.

2. In the state's first scented-ink grocery ad, the pleasant aroma of vanilla wafted from the pages of a January 23, 1985 *Detroit Free Press* Farmer Jack

advertisement which featured a special on the flavoring.

2 DISTINCTIVE GROCERY STORES

1. ALLEN'S SUPERMARKET (Inkster), opened by Lafayette Allen in 1954, is, according to *Ebony* magazine, the first black-owned supermarket in the country.

2. The BENTON HARBOR OPEN-AIR MARKET, which opened in 1930, is the world's largest fruit-and-vegetable stand.

3 WELL-KNOWN MICHIGAN-DEVELOPED FOODS

1. CELERY

Michigan became the birthplace for a new vegetable industry when in 1856 a Scotsman named Taylor planted some stalks of celery near Kalamazoo. By 1872, Dutch farmers had turned the Kalamazoo mucklands into fields of celery, and by the end of the century, 4,000 acres of celery on 400 farms made Kalamazoo County the world's largest grower of the vegetable. Celery became so popular that ambitious manufacturers even included it in breakfast cereal, chewing gum, soap, pickles, and medicines.

2. HAVEN PEACHES

The Hale Haven peach, a favorite of commercial growers because of its tough skin for shipping and early season ripening, was developed at South Haven orchards in 1932 by the Michigan State Agricultural College (now Michigan State University) horticultural department. Eight years later, the South Haven experimental station developed the Red Haven, now the most widely planted peach variety in the world.

3. SUGAR BEETS

Robert Clark Kedzie, a chemistry professor at the Michigan Agricultural College, imported 1,760 pounds of sugar-beet seed from France and Germany in 1890 and distributed it to Michigan farmers with instructions on planting and cultivating. Eight years later, the state's first successful sugar beet factory opened at Bay City, and today the Saginaw Valley, Michigan's "sugar bowl," processes $60 million worth of sugar-beet crops a year.

7 NOTABLE FOOD PRODUCERS

1. DRAKES BATTER MIX CO (Grass Lake), founded in 1937, was the first U.S. producer of commercial batter mix.

2. GERBER PRODUCTS (Fremont)

In the summer of 1927, Dorothy Gerber complained about the difficulty of straining peas for her baby daughter's dinner and suggested to her husband, Dan, that he process them for her at his father's canning company. Her suggestion led to the development of Gerber Products, which, as the world's largest processor of baby foods, now ships 150 varieties to more than 80 countries.

3. KELLOGG COMPANY (Battle Creek)

From the first box of Toasted Corn Flakes sold by Will Kellogg in 1906, the company grew to become the world's largest maker of ready-to-eat cereals, now producing nearly six million packages of cereal daily.

4. LIFE SAVERS INC (Holland), as the world's sole production site of Life Saver roll candy, ships 33.6 million boxes of the sweet donut-shaped candies annually.

5. LUDWICKS FROZEN DONUTS (Grand Rapids) introduced the original Sour Cream Donut over 25 years ago.

6. C.W. POST (Battle Creek)

In 1891, Charles W. Post, a smalltime businessman, stayed at a Battle Creek health sanitarium run by Dr. John Harvey Kellogg. While there, Post sampled some new foods — including a cereal-based substitute for coffee and cold cereal — that Kellogg had developed.

Post recognized the commercial possibilities of the foods and in the 1890s became almost an overnight success by marketing his own versions — Postum coffee and Grape Nuts Cereal — of Kellogg's products.

Today, Post is a part of the food-processing giant, General Foods.

7. VLASIC (West Bloomfield)

What started out as a small pickle distributor for Hamtramck's polish community in the 1930s is now the nation's leading distributor of pickles, peppers, relishes, and sauerkraut.

3 DISTINCTIVE BEVERAGES

1. FAYGO (Detroit)

With the help of one friend and a horse and wagon, two Russian brothers, Perry and Ben Feigenson, started the Faygo Beverage Company in 1907. By 1980 the Faygo plant had the largest capacity in the nation, supplying 21 states with 20 million cases of 33 different flavors of pop.

2. In 1983 the SQUIRT & CO (Holland) became the first U.S. soft-drink company to market a diet drink sweetened only by aspartame, an expensive artificial sweetener used to replace saccharin, which had been linked to cancer.

3. VERNORS (Detroit), first made in 1866 (see also page 190), is the nation's oldest soft drink.

5 TOP WINERIES

Based on liters shipped in 1983, as reported by the Michigan Beer & Wine Wholesalers Association.

1.	WARNER (Paw Paw)	651,386
2.	ST JULIAN (Paw Paw)	576,710
3.	TABOR HILL (Bridgman)	170,319
4.	LAKESIDE (Harbert)	149,681
5.	FRONTENAC (Paw Paw)	137,445

5 TOP BREWS

The 1983 Michigan market share, in percent, of national beer brewers.

1.	MILLER	29.5
2.	ANHEUSER-BUSCH	26.9
3.	STROH	16.6
4.	HEILEMAN	13.3
5.	PABST	8.6

2 SPECIAL BREWERIES

1. The BOSCH BREWING COMPANY (Houghton) in September 1973 became the last of the Upper Peninsula's 22 breweries to close.

2. The REAL ALE COMPANY (Lansing), organized in 1982, is Michigan's smallest commercial brewery.

3 LEADING BARLEY-PRODUCING COUNTIES

Three Michigan counties that produced the most barley, a key beer-making ingredient, in 1982.

1.	HURON	367,400 bushels
2.	TUSCOLA	295,300 bushels
3.	SANILAC	180,600 bushels

6 TOP CROP-PRODUCING COUNTIES

Six counties that produced the most of six selected crops in 1982.

1.	EATON	Winter wheat
2.	HURON	Dry beans
3.	LENAWEE	Corn
4.	SAGINAW	Soybeans
5.	SANILAC	Oats
6.	TUSCOLA	Sugar beets

5 LARGEST CASH CROPS

Michigan's four largest cash crops, based on 1981 sales.

1. CORN — $481.5 million

2. MARIJUANA

The National Organization for the Reform of Marijuana Laws estimated the value of Michigan's 1983-84 marijuana harvest at $200 million, a claim that, if accurate, makes pot the state's second-largest cash crop.

3. DRY EDIBLE BEANS — $190.7 million

Michigan grows 75% of all navy beans and 12% of all varieties of dry edible beans in the nation — 721 million pounds in 1981 — to rank first nationally.

4. SOYBEANS — $165.3 million

5. WHEAT — $138.1 million

4 TOP FARMING COUNTIES

Based on 1982 cash receipts from crops marketings.

1.	SAGINAW	$101 million
2.	TUSCOLA	$92 million
3.	HURON	$85 million
4.	BERRIEN	$70 million

6 COUNTIES WITH
THE MOST CENTENNIAL FARMS

As of March 1984, there were 5,068 centennial farms in Michigan, that is, farms that have been in the same family for 100 years or more. The counties that have the most centennial farms are:

1.	LENAWEE	242
2.	KENT	195
3.	TUSCOLA	187
4.	SANILAC	181
5.	SAGINAW	167
6.	ALLEGAN	157

7 FARMING MILESTONES

1. 1834

Michigan's first large-scale farm began operations when Townsend E. Gidley sowed 300 acres of wheat and set out a great orchard and home nursery on his Jackson County land.

2. January 10, 1872

The Burnside Grange, Michigan's first, organized at Lapeer County. By 1875, 600 local Granges had formed throughout Michigan, and though first formed for educational and social purposes, they became a forceful lobbying group, leading the fight, for example, to lower railroad rates.

3. 1917

The Michigan 4-H program was launched.

4. 1919

The Michigan State Farm Bureau organized as a central cooperative to look after such matters as transportation, taxation, and legislation for farmers.

5. 1921

Several state agencies that had been previously created for the benefit of the farmer were combined into the State Department of Agriculture.

6. 1981

The number of farms in Michigan increased by 1,000 over 1980 to an estimated 67,000, the first such increase since 1933.

7. 1981

The Michigan legislature passed a "right-to-farm law," the first in the nation, that allows farmers to grow and harvest crops, raise animals, irrigate land, and spray for insects with little or no interference. The legislature wrote the law after dozens of Michigan farmers had faced complaints and lawsuits from transplanted city dwellers who objected to the smells of swine and manure, the dust of plowing, or the noise of a tractor being started at dawn.

5 LARGEST FRUIT CASH CROPS

Based on 1981 receipts from Michigan farm marketings.

1. APPLES	$79.4 million
2. CHERRIES	$52.6 million
3. BLUEBERRIES	$26.5 million

Michigan's 1981 52-million-pound crop was almost half the entire nation's harvest.

4. GRAPES	$14.3 million
5. STRAWBERRIES	$8.4 million

4 TREE FARMINGS

1. 2,262 firms are involved in various forest industries in Michigan.
   — *Item contributed by Henry H. Webster, State Forester, Lansing* —

2. Michigan is the nation's largest grower of plantation Christmas trees with 700 Michigan farmers shipping over four million Scotch pine, Douglas fir, and 50 other species in 1982.

3. The Mead Corporation (Escanaba), the largest corporate landowner in Michigan, owns or controls 677,000 acres of upper-peninsula forest land, and each year, the company's sprawling mill on the Escanaba River turns 700,000 cords of softwoods into paper.

4. Foreign interests own 181,000 acres, or one percent, of Michigan's forests.

3 UNIQUE DAIRY FARMS

1. As of 1984, GARY ABNER (Franklin Township, Lenawee County) operated the only licensed goat dairy in Michigan.

2. GREEN MEADOWS FARMS, which straddles the Shiawassee-Clinton county line, milks the world's largest holstein dairy herd — 1,500 cows a day. The 4,000-acre farm also produces its own electricity from barnyard manure by using special bacterial "cookers" to generate methane gas which is then stored and used to run two diesel-powered generators.

3. RON and BILL VAN ZEE (Eagle) own and operate one of only five computer-run dairy farms in the country. Every known or measurable characteristic of each of their approximately 165 heifers is entered into a computer system, which then calculates and feeds grain according to the genetic capability of each cow and also weighs and records milk production for each animal.

3 RARE RANCHERS

1. LEE DUNN (Dun-Haven Farms, Belleville) is the nation's pre-eminent breeder of Hackneys, small, trim, high-stepping show ponies.

2. GERALD OLESON (Traverse City), who has raised buffalo for 27 years, claims that his herd of 420 is the biggest east of the Mississippi River.

3. DR. SAM TAYLOR (Taylor Pony Farm, Hudson) is the nation's foremost producer of Shetlands, small ponies most often used as children's riding pets.

7 FIRST PRODUCTIONS

1. COAL

Coal mining first began in Michigan during the mid-1830s near Jackson, but by 1881 only two small mines were active, one in Jackson County and the other near Corunna in Shiawassee County. The first major Michigan coal mine was begun in Bay County in 1897.

2. COPPER

Indians systematically mined the rich copper deposits of the Ontonagon River basin as far back as 5,000 B.C., leaving shallow pits throughout the Keweenaw Peninsula that are evident today. The first serious modern copper mine began in 1772 when a British company sunk a 30-foot shaft in the Keweenaw Peninsula on the northeast shore of Lake Superior. The next year, the project was suspended, however, and profitable copper mining did not begin for another 70 years.

3. GAS AND OIL

Michigan's first commercial production of gas and oil began in 1886 when 22 wells were drilled at Port Huron.

4. GOLD

In 1883 near Ishpeming, Julius Ropes, a Marquette chemist and geologist, opened the first and only gold mine east of the Mississippi River. The Ropes mine produced $703,000 worth of gold and silver before labor disputes forced its closing in 1897.

5. GYPSUM

An underground mining operation was begun near Grand Rapids in the 1880s that has continued to the present.

6. IRON

In September 1844, while establishing township lines and making geological observations for the federal government near Negaunee, William A. Burt noticed peculiar fluctuations in his magnetic compass. Burt asked his men to find the cause and they soon returned with pieces of iron ore. Three years later, the Jackson Mining Company began Michigan's first iron mine at the spot.

7. SALT

Michigan's first commercial salt well was established in 1841 at Clare.

5 SLICKEST COUNTIES

Five counties with the most new oil wells drilled in 1982. A total of 966 new exploratory and developmental oil wells were drilled in Michigan in 1982.

1. GRAND TRAVERSE   125

2. MANISTEE	77
3. OTSEGO	68
4. MISSAUKEE	64
5. KALKASKA	62

4 UNUSUAL CONSTRUCTION MATERIALS

1. CHAMPAGNE BOTTLES

From 1914 to 1917, Henry Stephens Jr., the son of a wealthy lumberman, used nearly 15,000 champagne, wine, and whiskey bottles to construct a two-block-long fence on his property at Waters. (See photo, page 135)

2. GLASHPHALT

In 1971, Brooks Products, Inc. (Holland) resurfaced its 50,000-square-foot parking lot with "glassphalt," which made the area the nation's first to be paved with the new mixture of recycled, crushed glass and asphalt.

3. MACHINE GUNS

Thirty machine guns, formerly used by prison guards, were taken, along with other guns police had confiscated, to a Ford Motor plant in Detroit in 1977 and, under the watchful eyes of State Police representatives, melted down, recycled, and used in new autos.

4. OLD TIRES

In February 1979, 10,000 discarded tires, 38 tons of steel, and a freight car of lumber were carefully assembled and placed on the ice of Lake Charlevoix (Charlevoix). When the ice melted the following spring, the assemblage sank to create an artificial 150,000-square-foot harbor, the first such marine facility on the Great Lakes. (See photo, page 135)

3 UNIONS HEADQUARTERED IN MICHIGAN

1. BROTHERHOOD OF MAINTAINANCE OF WAY EMPLOYES (Detroit)

100,000 members, 961 locals.

2. UNITED PLANT GUARD WORKERS OF AMERICA, INTERNATIONAL UNION (Roseville)

29,243 members, 162 locals.

3. UNITED AUTOMOBILE, AEROSPACE AND AGRICULTURAL IMPLEMENT WORKERS OF AMERICA, INTERNATIONAL UNION (UAW) (Detroit)

1,151,086 members, 1,517 locals.

A shoulder-high whiskey-and wine-bottle fence was built near Waters by the heir to a lumber fortune. The man also covered an entire basement wall in his large home with caps from bottles of beer, all of which he claimed he had drunk himself. (See story, page 134)

An artificial harbor near Charlevoix, constructed largely of recycled automobile tires, holds boats up to 50 feet long. (See story, page 134)

3 MAJOR UAW RECOGNITIONS

1. February 11, 1937

After a 44-day sit-down strike that had involved 150,000 workers and closed more than 60 plants in 14 states, General Motors guaranteed, for the first time, that it would recognize the UAW as its employees' bargaining agent.

2. April 6, 1937

The UAW became the sole bargaining agent at Chrysler.

3. May 21, 1941

Seventy percent of Ford Motor Company workers voted to have the UAW-CIO represent them, and the automobile giant became the last of the Big Three automakers to recognize the UAW.

16 AUTO-INDUSTRY MILESTONES

1. May 21, 1892

The *Scientific American*, in the first national notice given to a mechanically driven vehicle made in Michigan, featured an article about a sophisticated steam-engine automobile developed by Ransom E. Olds.

2. August 1897

A group of Lansing investors joined with Ransom E. Olds to form Michigan's first operating automobile company, the Olds Motor Vehicle Company.

3. 1899

The Olds Motor Works erected at Detroit the first factory built in America for the manufacture of automobiles.

4. 1903

The Buick Motor Company organized at Flint.

5. June 16, 1903

The Ford Motor Company was incorporated.

6. September 16, 1908

William C. Durant, head of the Buick Motor Company (Flint), purchased more than 30 other existing automobile companies — including Oldsmobile, Pontiac (then called "Oakland"), and Cadillac — and chartered the General Motors Company.

7. November 3, 1911

After racing car driver Louis Chevrolet had developed a production-model six-cylinder car, William C. Durant, who had personally financed Chevrolet, organized the Chevrolet Motor Company

8. 1914

Henry Ford revolutionized the auto-manufacturing world by inaugurating his new "assembly-line" technique. By assembling a car while it was in continuous motion, Ford workers cut production time for one autombile from 12¹/₂ hours to 93 minutes.

9. 1914

In a 20-acre plant at Hamtramck, John and Horace Dodge started production of automobiles carrying their name.

10. February 4, 1922

The Ford Motor Company bought a bankrupt luxury-car manufacturer, the Lincoln Motor Company, at a receiver's sale for $8,000,000.

11. 1925

The Chrysler Corporation was founded.

12. May 30, 1928

The Chrysler Corporation purchased the Dodge Brothers and became the third largest auto manufacturer behind Ford and GM.

13. 1954

The Hudson Motor Car Company and Nash-Kelvinator Corporation merged to form the American Motors Corporation.

14. 1982

Checker Motors Corporation, builder of taxicabs at Kalamazoo since 1922, ended cab production.

15. November 30, 1984

The Mazda Motor Corp., the fourth major Japanese auto manufacturer to locate in the United States, announced that it would build its first American automotive assembly line in a vacant plant at Flat Rock, Michigan.

16. January 8, 1985

General Motors announced the formation of the Saturn division, GM's first new-car company since Chevrolet and the first domestic GM company started from scratch.

FIRST "BIG THREE" BLACK AUTO DEALERS

1. EDWARD DAVIS received a Detroit Chrysler-Plymouth franchise in November 1963 and became the first black in Michigan to become a "Big Three" new-car dealer.

2. JOHN and NATHAN CONYERS officially assumed ownership of Detroit's oldest Ford franchise on January 1, 1970, and became Michigan's first black Ford dealers and second black "Big Three" franchise holders.

3. CLARENCE S. CARTER, a veteran of 24 years in the automobile business, was awarded a Detroit Chevrolet dealership on April 29, 1970, and became General Motors' first black Michigan auto dealer.

5 NEW-CAR COUNTIES

Five counties with the highest percentage of 1983 registered vehicles being new, that is 1983 model-year, cars. State average = 9.5%.

1.	OAKLAND	13.9%
2.	WAYNE	11.4%
3.	INGHAM	11.3%
4.	MACOMB	11.3%
5.	GENESEE	11.1%

4 NOTABLE AUTO MECHANICS

1. CHARLES GAINES (Pontiac), 2. JUAN RAMANAUSKAS (Warren), and 3. JULIAN WILSON (Detroit) became Michigan's first state-certified, licensed automobile mechanics on November 22, 1976.

4. In 1977, JANIS SYROVY (Ann Arbor) became Michigan's first female certified master auto mechanic.

8 SPECIAL DELIVERIES

1. FIRST POST ROAD

The first Michigan mail route (post road), part of a line between Washington and Detroit, was established on March 3, 1801. By October 1, 1802, regular quarterly mail delivery was in operation, but letters, carried by men on horseback and on foot, typically took 40 days to arrive in Detroit from Washington D.C.

2. SECOND POST ROAD

The second post road for delivery of mail in the Michigan territory was established between Detroit and Mount Clemens via Pontiac on May 3, 1820. "Postboys" carried mail in leather saddlebags over this route and, from the time they entered a city until they reached the post office, blew horns to notify residents of the mail's arrival.

3. FIRST DAILY MAIL

In January 1831 the first daily mail from the east began arriving at Detroit, but it took 14 days and nights to receive a letter from New York City.

4. FIRST STAMPS

On August 15, 1847, postage stamps, issued in five-cent and 10-cent denominations, were used for the first time in Michigan prompting the *Detroit Free Press* to approvingly report that, "all that has to be done is to prefix one of the little appendages and the letter goes direct."

5. FIRST FREE CITY DELIVERY

The first free city-wide distribution of mail in Michigan began at Detroit in October 1864. At the same time, a large number of iron letter boxes, placed on lamp posts and in grocery and dry-goods stores, were first used.

6. FIRST FREE RURAL DELIVERY

On December 3, 1896, two carriers started out with horses and road carts from the Climax post office on the nation's first rural free-mail-delivery route.

7. FIRST AIR MAIL

A seaplane from Cleveland landed at Detroit on August 17, 1920, with the first batch of mail ever delivered to Michigan by air.

8. FIRST MARINE POST OFFICE

In 1894 the the world's only marine post office, located aboard a boat in the Detroit River, began delivering mail to Great Lakes seamen, who had no other communication with relatives during the week-to-10-day trip from Duluth, Minnesota, to Lake Erie ports.

3 FIRST TELEGRAPHIC CONNECTIONS

1. FIRST LINE

On November 29, 1847, Michigan's first telegraph line, built along the Michigan Central Railroad tracks between Detroit and Ypsilanti, was completed.

2. FIRST EASTERN CONNECTION

The O'Reilly Telegraph Company (Detroit) completed the first New York (Buffalo)-to-Detroit telegraph line on March 1, 1848, and transmitted a dispatch that day.

3. FIRST UNDERWATER CONNECTION

The world's first successful underwater telegraph cable was laid across the Detroit River from Detroit to Windsor on July 16, 1857.

14 PHONEY FIRSTS

1. After seeing Alexander Graham Bell's invention at the Philadelphia Exposition, an Ontonagon mine operator installed Michigan's first telephone system in 1876.

2. Michigan's first commercial telephone line was strung between Stearns' drugstore and laboratory in Detroit on September 21, 1877.

3. Michigan's first telephone booth was placed at Detroit **police** headquarters in November 1877.

4. Michigan's first telephone directory was issued at Detroit on September 15, 1878.

5. In January 1879, Detroit customers were assigned the nation's first phone numbers.

6. The world's first international telephone line opened between Detroit and Windsor on January 20, 1880.

7. Michigan's first public pay phones were installed in January 1881 at Detroit.

8. On October 25, 1889, a submarine telephone cable at the Straits of Mackinac joined the Upper and Lower peninsulas.

9. The Michigan State Telephone Company in 1905 bought the first vehicle — a one-cylinder Cadillac truck — used in Michigan to install and service phones.

10. The Michigan State Telephone Company introduced "weather report" service on March 10, 1906.

11. The first phone directory to feature classified business advertising on yellow pages was issued April 1, 1906, at Detroit.

12. On November 20, 1953, Birmingham became the first city in Michigan and only the second in the nation to have direct-distance dialing.

13. The first air-to-ground public telephone service in the country began September 15, 1957, in the Detroit-Chicago area when about 20 airplanes were equipped for the two-way service. Rates varied from $1.50 to $4.25 for a three-minute call, depending on the location of the airplane and the telephone on the ground.

14. Michigan Bell installed the nation's first trimline phone at Jackson on October 21, 1965.

3 SPECIAL PHONE COMPANIES

1. The TELEPHONE AND TELEGRAPH CONSTRUCTION COMPANY,

which incorporated October 31, 1877, provided Michigan's first organized telephone service.

2. The GRAND RAPIDS TELEPHONE EXCHANGE, established on June 1, 1879, later became the first in the state to regularly employ women as operators. The company hired the women when delivery boys, who were originally given the job, were discovered shooting marbles instead of tending switchboards.

3. THE MICHIGAN STATE TELEPHONE SYSTEM went into operation in January 1881, and about 200 Michigan cities and villages were connected for the first time by telephone. On January 1, 1924, the company changed its name to the Michigan Bell Telephone Company.

4 MICHIGAN AREA CODES

1. 313

    Eastern third of the Lower Peninsula

2. 517

    Center third of the Lower Peninsula

3. 616

    Western third of the Lower Peninsula

4. 906

    Entire Upper Peninsula

LAST 2 CITIES TO GET DIAL PHONES

In 1971 the last local telephone operators in Michigan were replaced with dial phones at:

1. MACKINAC ISLAND

2. ST. IGNACE

FIRST 2 ELECTRIC-LIGHT PLANTS

1. The first electric light plant of any kind in the country (aside from experimental) was an alternating-current dynamo and seven arc lamps used at the Calumet and Hecla mines (Calumet) in 1878.

2. The second electric light plant in Michigan was one used on the Detroit steamer *Garland* in 1880.

6 UNIQUE UTILTIES
AND POWER PLANTS

1. BIG ROCK POINT

On the Lake Michigan shoreline near Charlevoix, a button was pressed on September 27, 1962, that started a controlled chain reaction in the world's first high-power-density boiling-water nuclear reactor for generating electricity. A month later, the facility, Michigan's first nuclear power plant and only the fifth in the country, began producing commercial electricity for Consumers Power customers.

2. CONSUMERS POWER COMPANY built Michigan's first rural electrical power line from Mason to Dansville in 1926.

3. The EDISON ILLUMINATING COMPANY (Detroit) organized in 1886 as Michigan's first public utility.

4. GRAND RAPIDS ELECTRIC LIGHT AND POWER began operation on July 23, 1880, as Michigan's, and probably the world's, first commercial hydroelectric plant.

5. In 1919 the HOLLAND GAS WORKS became the first Michigan utility to have its rates set by a newly created state Public Utilities Commission.

6. MONROE POWER PLANT

The Detroit Edison facililty is the largest coal-fired power plant in the nation.

7

ON THE MOVE

7 MOST MOTORING COUNTIES

Seven counties with the most vehicle (passenger, commercial, trailer, and motorcycle) registrations per 100 people in 1983. All seven counties have more registered vehicles than people. State average = 77.9.

1. ROSCOMMON	108.4
2. KALKASKA	107.6
3. ALCONA	107.4
4. OSCODA	106.0
5. MONTMORENCY	104.8
6. OCEANA	103.9
7. GRAND TRAVERSE	100.1

5 LEAST MOTORING COUNTIES

Five counties with the fewest vehicle (passenger, commercial, trailer, and motorcycle) registrations per 100 people in 1983. State average = 77.9.

1. WAYNE	63.2
2. HOUGHTON	64.2
3. MECOSTA	65.5
4. ISABELLA	66.0
5. WASHTENAW	69.9

4 FIRST DRIVES

1. 1885

Thomas J. Clegg (Memphis, Michigan) made the first recorded trips in a self-propelled vehicle built in Michigan. Clegg drove his steam-powered vehicle, which could reach a top speed of 12 m.p.h., an estimated 500 miles on 30 trips through rural St. Clair and Macomb counties during the summer of 1885.

2. March 6, 1896

After two years of private testing on Belle Isle, Charles B. King, a 27-year-old college-trained engineer, became the first person in Michigan to publicly drive a gasoline-powered horseless carriage. But during his test drive on Detroit's main streets, King's handmade vehicle broke down causing spectators to jeer, "Get a horse."

3. June 4, 1896

Having built his first gasoline-powered "quadricycle" too wide for the door, Henry Ford broke out part of a brick wall of an old storage shed in what is now downtown Detroit, then drove the vehicle around the darkened streets in a successful trial run.

4. 1900

Marie Comstock (Detroit) became Michigan's first female driver.

4 UNUSUAL LONG-DISTANCE TRIPS

1. In 1912 a Nebraska man personally picked up a Buick in Flint, drove it 823 miles to his home, then reported to the company that he had used 44³/₄ gallons of gas, seven pints of oil, 10 pints of water, and five cents worth of hand grease on the trip. The man also added that he had traveled 22 m.p.h. on Iowa's good dirt roads but was lucky to do 16 m.p.h. "plowing through the sands of Michigan."

2. Dwight B. Huss (Detroit) set the nation's first transcontinental automobile time record when in 1905 he traveled in his Oldsmobile runabout from New York City to Portland, Oregon, in 44 days.

3. Otto Hyslop's (St. Ignace) 1978 Chevrolet short-bed pickup truck had, as of 1982, traveled farther — 260,000 miles — on its original six cylinders than any product in General Motors history. GM offered to buy the truck from Hyslop and use it in an advertisement, but the motor-route newspaper carrier turned down the offer.

4. A production model 1984 GMC suburban, built at the General Motors Flint Truck Plant, was driven by two 33-year-old Canadian men on a 28-day, 12,000-mile record-setting trip from the southern tip of Africa to the northern tip of Norway.

8 HIGHWAYS THAT WERE
ONCE INDIAN TRAILS

1. US-2

Sault Ste. Marie to St. Ignace and Green Bay

2. US-10

   Detroit to Saginaw (Ottawa)

3. US-12

   Detroit to St. Joseph (Potawatomi)

4. US-16

   Detroit to Lansing and Grand Rapids (Ottawa)

5. US-25

   Detroit to Port Huron

6. US-41

   L'Anse to Marquette

7. US-112

   Ypsilanti to Chicago ("The Great Sauk Trail")

8. Michigan Route 26, which divides the Keweenaw Peninsula, was used for thousands of years by Indians in their migration to the rich copper deposits of the area.

8 FIRST ROADS

1. INTERIOR ROAD

The Moravian Road, which Macomb County's first settlers constructed in 1785-86 from the western edge of present-day Mount Clemens to a mill at Detroit.

2. SURVEYED ROAD

The Pontiac Road, now known within Detroit as Woodward Avenue, which was laid out by commissioners at Detroit beginning December 13, 1819.

3. MILE OF CONCRETE HIGHWAY

A 17-foot, eight-inch-wide stretch on Woodward Avenue between Six and Seven Mile Roads, which opened July 4, 1909.

4. RURAL SUPERHIGHWAY

M-102 (Eight Mile Road), which was built as an eight-lane highway from Detroit's northern boundary to the city of Pontiac along Woodward Avenue in the mid 1920s.

5. CROSS-STATE CONCRETE TRUNKLINE

M-16, which linked Detroit with Grand Haven in the 1920s.

6. EXPRESSWAY

The Willow Run expressway, which was constructed from Detroit to the Ford Motor Company's Willow Run bomber plant and formally opened on September 12, 1942. The expressway was later obliterated by the construction of I-94.

7. URBAN FREEWAY

The Davison Freeway through Highland Park, which opened in 1942.

8. INTERSECTING DOWNTOWN FREEWAYS

An 11-mile stretch of I-196 officially, which opened on December 14, 1964, and made Grand Rapids the first city in the nation to have two freeways (I-196 and U.S. 131) intersect in its downtown district.

5 SPECIAL REST AREAS

1. The nation's first permanently staffed travel-information center operated by a state highway department opened in 1935 on old US-12 south of New Buffalo.

2. Michigan's first roadside park, built on US-16 near the Red Cedar River east of Lansing, opened in 1935. (See photo, page 147)

3. A log cabin built on US-41 near Menominee in 1937 is the oldest continuously active travel information center in the United States.

4. A rest area on eastbound I-94 near Battle Creek has $348,000 solar-powered restrooms.

5. A rest area on northbound I-69 near Coldwater beat out 51 entries from 27 states to win first place in a 1970 nationwide highway beauty contest conducted by the U.S. Department of Transportation.

Where the Highway Ends I
4 EXPRESSWAYS
THAT END IN MICHIGAN

Every interstate expressway that enters Michigan ends here.

1. I-69

Begins at Indianapolis, Indiana, and ends at Port Huron.

2. I-75

Begins near Ft. Myers, Florida, and ends at Sault Ste. Marie.

3. I-94

Begins at Billings, Montana, and ends at Port Huron.

The nation's oldest active travel information center. (See story, page 147)
Michigan Department of Transportation photo.

4. I-96

Begins at Muskegon and ends near the Ambassador Bridge in Detroit.

Where the Highway Ends II
7 U.S. HIGHWAYS THAT END IN MICHIGAN

1. US-10

Begins at Coeur D'Alene, Idaho, and ends at Detroit.

2. US-12

Begins at Aberdeen, Washington, and ends at Detroit.

3. US-23

Begins at Jacksonville, Florida and ends at Mackinaw City.

4. US-27

Begins at Miami, Florida, and ends four miles south of Grayling.

5. US-31

Begins at Mobile, Alabama, and ends at Mackinaw City.

6. US-41

Begins at Miami, Florida, and ends at Copper Harbor.

7. US-127

Begins at Chattanooga, Tennessee, and ends at Lansing.

7 UNIQUE HIGHWAYS

1. M-185

The 7.5-mile-long two-lane paved roadway, which encircles Mackinac Island, is the only state highway in the nation from which motor vehicles are banned.

2. M-39, between Plymouth Road and the Jeffries Freeway in Detroit, is Michigan's busiest road, carrying an average of 140,000 vehicles a day, year-round.

3. M-119, between Harbor Springs and Cross Village, is the least-traveled stretch of state highway in Michigan, carrying an average of 200 or fewer cars per day.

4. I-375, which connects the Lodge and Chrysler Freeways in downtown Detroit, is Michigan's shortest freeway at 1.1 miles.

5. M-209, a .4-mile access from M-109 to Glen Haven (Leelanau County), is Michigan's shortest highway.

6. I-69 (from Lapeer to Port Huron)

The 40-mile section, with its official opening December 14, 1969, became the longest stretch of highway to be opened at one time in Michigan in more than 20 years.

7. When a 22-mile segment of I-75 opened in the Upper Peninsula on November 1, 1963, drivers could travel from the Ohio border to Sault Ste. Marie on what was then the nation's longest toll-free four-lane expressway. Though I-75 itself was not completed for another 10 years, drivers could use a nonstop 380-mile route composed of I-75, US-23, US-10, and US-27.

9 DRIVERS LICENSE DEVELOPMENTS

1. 1916

Chauffeur's licenses were first required.

2. July 1, 1919

A Michigan law requiring all drivers of motor vehicles to carry licenses while driving went into effect, with license number one being issued to Governor Albert Sleeper. The 4^1/$_2$-by-5^1/$_2$-inch linen-backed paper licenses, which had no expiration date, were issued, without either a road or written test, to anyone 14 or older who requested them.

2. 1931

Drivers were required to renew their licenses every three years.

3. 1938

Tests to obtain a drivers license were finally required.

4. 1953

The expiration date of licenses was set up to correspond with the applicant's birthdate.

5. 1955

Permanent license numbers, derived from numbers assigned to letters in a person's full name and birthdate, were first issued.

6. January 1, 1957

No person under the age of 18 could be licensed unless he or she had passed an approved course in driver education.

7. 1964

Photographs on drivers licenses were required for the first time.

8. 1965

Color, instead of black-and-white, photographs were used on licenses.

9. 1971

All-plastic licenses, made of polycarbonate treated with photosensitive material so the driver's picture could be photographed directly onto the plastic, replaced paper licenses.

11 AUTOMOBILE LICENSE-PLATE MILESTONES

1. 1905-1909

The state issued small metal "dashboard discs" and required auto owners to make their own plates for the rear of their vehicles. Most drivers made their license plates by stretching black leather on a metal frame on which they then painted white numbers.

2. 1907

The state required, for the first time, two license plates — one on the rear and one on the front of automobiles.

3. 1910-1914

Steel plates with a glazed porcelain-like finish were issued by the state.

4. 1915

Stamped metal plates, with an aluminum state seal riveted to them, were issued.

5. 1926

The state department licensed the millionth Michigan automobile.

6. 1944

Single plates were issued.

7. 1957

Two plates were again issued.

8. 1964

Michigan licensed its two millionth vehicle.

9. 1971

Motorists were able to both order their license plates by mail and pay by check for the first time.

10. 1973

Motorists were allowed, for a $25 fee, to personalize their license plates by choosing, within limitations, their own combinations of six letters and numbers.

11. 1977

Single plates again were issued.

7 MOST COMMON
LICENSE-PLATE COLORS

The seven most-common color combinations of Michigan automobile license plates since the state began issuing metal plates in 1910.

1. BLACK & WHITE	14

This color combination, because of its high visibility, is the most popular with police.

2. GREEN & WHITE	10
3. BLUE & WHITE	10
4. RED & WHITE	8

11 SIGNS AND SIGNALS

1. 1911

The first traffic lines to designate road lanes were painted in white on River Road near Trenton.

2. 1912

By banding telephone poles with different colors and numbers, William Bachman (Detroit), one of the founders of the American Automobile Association, created, in Michigan, the first systematic road-marking system in the country.

3. 1914

Michigan's first traffic signal, a lamp atop an iron pipe held upright by a cement-filled bicycle wheel, was used at the corner of Woodward Avenue and Grand Boulevard in Detroit.

4. 1917

Michigan's first stop sign was erected at the corner of Cass and Temple at Detroit by William Bachman (see number 2).

5. 1917

The nation's first centerline on a rural state highway was painted on the Marquette-Negaunee Road (state trunkline 15) in Marquette County.

6. October 9, 1917

Detroit installed the nation's first "Crowsnest" traffic tower at the intersection of Woodward and Michigan avenues. A traffic officer, who stood in the nest about six feet off the street, operated semaphore arms that displayed stop and go messages during the day and used red and green lights at night.

7. 1918

The first three-way traffic signal in Michigan was placed at Detroit's Michigan and Monroe streets.

8. October 1920

The world's first four-way traffic-signal tower was placed at the Woodward and Michigan avenues intersection in Detroit. The tower, which was manually operated, had 12 lamps, three in each direction.

9. 1924

The state highway department placed 10,000 metal signs along Michigan highways that marked, for the first time, railroad crossings, danger points, route markers, and mile posts.

10. 1927

The state highway department painted the first yellow "no passing" lines on curves and hills of Michigan highways and also posted, for the first time, speed limits at dangerous curves. The following summer, the highway commissioner also had to post signs on highways entering Michigan that informed out-of-state visitors what the yellow lines meant.

11. 1973

The highway department installed Michigan's first metric highway sign beside northbound US-27 near Dewitt.

4 SIGNIFICANT BUCKLING UPS

1. As of 1982, Midland County residents fastened their automobile safety belts at a rate higher than anyone else in the nation — 21 percent compared to a 12 percent national average.

2. In February 1984, Detroit-area Farmer Jack stores became the first in the state to install seat belts for children in grocery carts.

3. In April 1982, Michigan passed a law requiring parents to place babies under the age of one in a restraint seat while traveling in an automobile. The same law also required children aged one to four to be restrained if riding in the front seat and to be belted or restrained if riding in the back seat.

During the law's first year, traffic deaths for babies younger than one year old dropped 40.2 percent, and casualties for children ages one to four were down 24.8 percent.

4. In February 1985, Michigan became the fourth state to pass a mandatory seat-belt law. The law, which took effect July 1, 1985, provides for a fine of $10 for anyone who, in the process of being stopped for another traffic violation, is observed not wearing a seat belt.

3 UNIQUE
MACKINAC BRIDGE CROSSINGS

1. The BIGGEST SINGLE DAY of traffic was July 1, 1978, when 24,569 vehicles crossed the bridge.

2. The LARGEST ONE-DIRECTION CROSSING in a 24-hour period occurred on November 11, 1966, when 17,351 vehicles, most carrying deer hunters, crossed into the Upper Peninsula.

152

3. The SLOWEST SINGLE TRAFFIC DAY day in the bridge's history was January 26, 1978, when only 274 vehicles crossed the bridge.

2 MACKINAC BRIDGE COLORINGS

1. Mackinac Bridge designer David Steinman insisted that the Mackinac Bridge towers be painted ivory and the spans green.

2. To appease University of Michigan partisans, yellow and blue night lighting is used on the bridge.

3 EXTANT COVERED BRIDGES

The only three original 19th-century wooden covered bridges left in Michigan. The barn-like structures, some built decades before the auto was invented, were so constructed because the roof protected the bridge floor and underpinning against the decaying effects of rain, snow, and sun. (See photo, page 154)

1. FALLASBURG

The single-span bridge was erected over the Flat River near Lowell in 1871 by Jarel Bresee at a cost of $1,500.

2. LANGLEY

The bridge, constructed in 1887, stretches 282 feet across the backwater of the St. Joseph River to Sturgis Dam near Centreville.

3. WHITES BRIDGE

Constructed in 1867 over the Flat River in Ionia County southwest of Smyrna.

5 UNIQUE BRIDGES

1. The Keystone Bridge, a series of arches across the Black River near Ramsay, was built in 1891 with hundreds of limestone blocks — but no mortar. Constructed on a solid rock foundation in the manner of old Roman architecture, each arch has a center keystone at the top that "locks in" the whole structure. Over the past 94 years, though millions of tons of mining materials, logs, and, rail freight have passed over the bridge, not a single stone has moved.

2. Michigan's 10,000th highway bridge, a $3.5-million project with 13 separate spans, opened December 21, 1966, and began carrying Eight-Mile-Road traffic over the Lodge Expressway at the Detroit-Oak Park city limits.

3. The Sixth Street Bridge in Grand Rapids, constructed over the Grand River in 1884, is the state's and perhaps the nation's oldest wrought-iron span. (See photo, page 154)

Whites Bridge (See story, page 153)

Fallasburg Bridge (See story, page 153)

Langley Bridge (See story, page 153)

Grand Rapids' Sixth Street Bridge

(See story, page 153)

Holz-Brucke Bridge (See story, page 155)

4. Zehnder's Holz-Brucke (Wooden Covered Bridge) at Frankenmuth, which opened in 1980, is the largest wooden covered bridge built in this century. (See photo, page 154)

5. The first hot-dip galvanized bridge in the nation, dedicated August 31, 1966, replaced a 61-year-old span over Stearns Bayou near Grand Haven.

8 SOO LOCKS MILESTONES

1. June 4, 1853

Excavation began on the canal and locks that would eventually connect Lake Superior and Lake Huron at the rapids of the St. Mary's River near Sault Ste. Marie.

2. May 31, 1855

A one-mile-long canal and two solid masonry locks at Sault Ste. Marie officially opened and marked the completion of one of the most spectacular engineering feats of the era. The $999,802 two-year project conquered the rapids that drop 22 feet from Lake Superior to Lake Huron and removed the last barrier to development of the Upper Peninsula's mining resources.

3. June 18, 1855

The side-wheeler *Illinois*, flags flying and whistle blowing, made the first passage through the canal and locks.

4. August 17, 1855

The Brig *Columbia*, laden with ore from Marquette, became the first ore ship to pass through the locks.

5. June 9, 1881

The State of Michigan turned over ownership of the Soo locks and canal to the United States and made passage free to all vessels. From the canal's opening until 1877, Michigan had collected first a four-cent then a three-cent-per-ton toll except from U.S. government ships.

6. January 1945

Four seagoing freighters, just completed at Duluth, Minnesota and Superior, Wisconsin shipyards, made the first-ever midwinter passage through the locks.

7. April 2, 1975

A 384-foot Canadian tanker *Saturn* fought its way through the ice-clogged St. Marys River and passed through the MacArthur lock, marking the first time in history that shipping on the upper Great Lakes had completed 365 days without interruption.

8. July 13, 1980

For the first time in history, because of shipping slowdowns caused by an economic downturn, two of the four Soo locks were temporarily closed.

6 FIRST FERRIES

1. BOB-LO (June 20, 1898)

The first excursion ferry, a steamer from Detroit, arrived at Bois Blanc (Bob-Lo) Island.

2. ISLE ROYALE (August 4, 1929)

A 20-passenger ferry, the *Water Lily*, began service from Copper Harbor to Isle Royale, and Michigan residents could, for the first time, travel by boat directly to their great wilderness island in upper Lake Superior. Prior to the Michigan runs, all Isle Royale visitors traveled by boat from either Duluth, Minnesota, or Port Arthur, Ontario.

3. LAKE MICHIGAN (November 24, 1892)

The first railroad-car ferry in the world to navigate open waters (as opposed to crossing only rivers or narrow bodies of water) was placed in service by the Toledo, Ann Arbor and North Michigan railroad from the mouth of the Betsie River at Elberta across Lake Michigan to Kewaunee, Wisconsin.

4. MACKINAC ISLAND (1878)

The Arnold Transit Co. began the first passenger ferry service to Mackinac Island.

5. MACKINAC STRAITS (July 31, 1923)

The highway department opened ferry service across the Straits of Mackinac with one small wooden boat, the *Ariel*, which carried 10,351 cars during her first season. The ferry service expanded and, over the next 35 years until its closing, carried another 12 million vehicles and 30 million passengers.

6. ST. CLAIR RAILWAY (November 21, 1859)

The Chicago, Detroit, and Canada Grand Trunk Junction Railway connected Michigan to the Grand Trunk Railway of Canada via a ferry across the St. Clair River from Sarnia to Port Huron. Railway cars were slowly ferried across the busy waterway for 32 years until the St. Clair railway tunnel, the world's first underwater tunnel to join two countries, opened beneath the river.

8 UNIQUE LIGHTHOUSES

1. The FORT GRATIOT LIGHTHOUSE, just north of the Blue Water Bridge at Port Huron, is the oldest of Michigan's 50-plus lighthouses. The original light-

house was built during the late 1820s then replaced in 1861 with the present tower.

2. GREY'S REEF LIGHTHOUSE, 32 miles off Charlevoix, was the last manned offshore Great Lakes lighthouse. The lighthouse, which had housed a crew since 1891, became fully automated in October 1976.

3. The LITTLE SABLE LIGHTHOUSE, south of Pentwater, was the last kerosene-powered light on the Great Lakes, not being electrified until 1954.

4. The LIVINGSTON MEMORIAL LIGHTHOUSE, built in the Detroit River on the eastern tip of Belle Isle in 1930, is the only marble lighthouse in the country.

5. POINT BETSIE LIGHTHOUSE, near Frankfort, was the last manned lighthouse on mainland Michigan. The lighthouse, which had been operated manually since 1858, became fully automated in April 1983.

6. The ROCK OF AGES LIGHTHOUSE, three miles off the west end of Isle Royale in Lake Superior, with 4,500,000-candlepower lights that can be seen for 19 miles, is the most powerful beacon on the entire Great Lakes.

7. SPECTACLE REEF LIGHTHOUSE, built on the Straits of Mackinac in Lake Huron during the early 1870s, is considered the best specimen of monolithic stone masonry in the United States.

8. STANNARD ROCK LIGHTHOUSE, lying 23 miles southeast of Manitou Island in Lake Superior, is farther from shore than any other American lighthouse on the Great Lakes.

6 SPECIAL SHIPS AND BOATS

1. The *CALEDONIA* had the unique distinction of being used by both sides — British and American — in two separate attacks against Fort Mackinac (Mackinac Island) during the War of 1812. On July 17, 1812, British soldiers carried by the *Caldeonia* to the island captured the American fort. Later that year, the ship was captured by the Americans who then used it in 1814 in an unsuccessful attempt to recapture the island.

2. *CHAMPION*

In the first regular trans-Lake Michigan steamship service, the sidewheeler began carrying passengers in 1849 from Grand Haven to Milwaukee and other Wisconsin settlements.

3. *JOHN JACOB ASTOR*

With its launching by the American Fur Company near Sault Ste. Marie in 1835, the prefabricated schooner became the first American ship on Lake Superior.

4. *MACKINAW*

The U.S. Coast Guard cutter, homeported in Cheboygan, was commissioned in 1944 as the first true Great Lakes icebreaker designed specifically to extend the navigational season.

5. The *STRAITS OF MACKINAC* was the last of the State Highway Department's auto-ferry fleet to stay in service in Michigan waters. When the Mackinac Bridge knocked the auto ferries out of service in 1958, the coal-burning steamer was converted to a passenger ferry which ran until 1968.

6. *WALK-IN-THE-WATER*

The first steamboat to sail on the Great Lakes made its first Michigan arrival at Detroit on August 27, 1818. The vessel carried passengers at a fare of $18.00 each on biweekly Detroit-Buffalo round trips until October, when she was wrecked in a Lake Erie storm.

2 PRESIDENTIAL YACHTS

Two Michigan-built yachts were obtained for President Harry S Truman after World War II and used by subsequent presidents until sold during President Nixon's administration in 1970. They were:

1. The *PATRICIA*, formerly known as the *Honey-Fitz*, *Barbara Anne*, and *Lenore*, was built by the Defoe Shipyards (Bay City) in 1931.

2. The *JULIE*, formerly known as the *Patrick J.*, *Susie E.*, *Margie*, *Margaret T.*, and *Dol-lar* was built by the Fisher Boat works (Detroit) in 1940.

2 NOTABLE LOCOMOTIVES

1. FIRST (January 20, 1837)

The Erie & Kalamazoo Railroad put the first locomotive ever to run on Michigan tracks into service on their 33-mile Adrian-to-Toledo route. Prior to the locomotive's arrival, horses had pulled the railroad cars along the tracks.

2. LAST (October 23, 1965)

The last steam-operating locomotive in Michigan, owned by the Canadian National Railroad, traveled from Durand to Detroit on its final run.

5 SPECIAL RAILROADS

1. PONTIAC & DETROIT RAILWAY COMPANY

On July 31, 1830, at a time when not a single mile of track was yet in use anywhere in the United States, this company received Michigan's first railway charter. Eight years later, after reincorporating as the Detroit and Pontiac Railway, the railroad finally began to run trains.

2. The ERIE & KALAMAZOO RAILROAD began operation on October 1, 1836, as Michigan's first functioning railroad and the first in the country to be built west of the Allegheny Mountains. The train, whose cars were drawn by horses at a top speed of 10 m.p.h., ran 33 miles between Adrian and Toledo.

3. The YPSILANTI AND ANN ARBOR began operating in 1890 as Michigan's first interurban railroad. Within a few years, a network of the electric railways had spread over southern Michigan, but during the 1920s, the automobile, bus, and truck put them out of business.

4. The KENT, BARRY AND EATON (KBE) CONNECTING RAILWAY, which began running on 42 miles of track between Grand Rapids and Vermontville in 1979, was Michigan's and possibly the nation's first black-owned railroad.

5. The MICHIGAN NORTHERN RAILROAD, run by Beth Andrus, was, as of 1981, one of only three railroads in the country headed by a woman.

3 NOTABLE FIRE ENGINES

1. The first fire wagon in Michigan was imported from Montreal in February 1778 and was paid for by the British government.

2. The nation's first factory-built motorized fire engine officially went into service at Lansing on December 17, 1908. Nine months later, the engine skidded on wet pavement and, in the nation's first known accident involving an automobile fire engine, crashed into a hitching post.

3. On April 10, 1922, Detroit's last horse-drawn fire wagon made a five-minute ceremonial final run.

4 SNOWMOBILE MILESTONES

1. September 1, 1968

Michigan snowmobile owners were required, for the first time, to license their vehicles.

2. February 14, 1970

Thirteen members of an upper-peninsula snowmobile club crossed the Mackinac Bridge during a 400-mile cross-country expedition from Marquette to Cadillac. One lane of the bridge was closed during the snowmobile crossing, the first in the span's history.

3. November 3, 1972

   Mackinac Island residents passed a law allowing snowmobiles to be driven in areas outside the state-park boundaries, and the machines became the first motor-driven vehicles on the island since 1949.

4. 1973

   Michigan became the first state in the union to buy sound meters to enforce noise-level limits on snowmobiles. Under Michigan law, no snowmobile may make noise louder than 86 decibels.

2 DISTINCTIVE BICYCLE PATHS

1. Michigan's first state-financed bicycle path was built in 1973 next to M-99 between Hillsdale and Jonesvile.

2. An eight-foot-wide, 37-mile-long bicycle sidewalk built along I-275 from Monroe County to southern Oakland County in 1977 was the first in the country to be constructed along an interstate freeway.

Two turn-of-the-century "high-wheelers" participated in the dedication of Michigan's first state-financed bicycle path. (See story, above) *Michigan Department of Transportation photo*

5 SPECIAL AIRPORTS

1. The BALLOON CORPORATION OF AMERICA BALLOON PORT opened near Fenton in January 1985 as the first and only such licensed facility in Michigan. The 10-acre complex, in addition to serving as a base for hot-air balloons, also provides several "chase trucks" to retrieve balloons, pilots, and passengers.

2. In June 1929, the EMMET COUNTY AIRPORT became the first county field in Michigan to be dedicated under the newly created state Aeronautics Commission.

3. The FORD AIRPORT (Dearborn) in 1928 became the first in the nation to construct a concrete runway.

4. The KALAMAZOO MUNICIPAL AIRPORT became Michigan's first licensed municipal airport in December 1929.

5. The PONTIAC MUNICIPAL AIRPORT on February 11, 1930, became the first in the nation to receive the U.S. Department of Commerce's highest rating, A1-A.

15 FIRST FLIGHTS

1. August 16, 1858

Ira Thurston, a well-known and experienced balloonist, lifted off from Adrian and completed Michigan's first hot-air balloon flight by landing 17 miles away in Riga Township (Lenawee County). While releasing gas after landing, Thurston accidentally let go of one of the hold-down ropes, and the bag shot into the air with the hapless aeronaut desperately clinging to the top. Four hours later, the deflated bag came to earth without Thurston, and his bones were found years later only a few miles from the point of the unplanned ascent.

2. October 22, 1898

Augustus Moore Herring (Benton Harbor) may have flown the world's first airplane five years before the Wright brothers' famous flight. A reporter for the *Benton Harbor Evening News* reported the brief flight from Silver Beach (St. Joseph) but did not take an in-flight picture of the motorized chanute glider. In the absence of any conclusive proof that Herring's plane had left the ground under its own power, Orville and Wilbur Wright were given credit for the first manned flight in 1903.

3. October 17, 1909

Edwin Elton Smith (Traverse City) soared 600 feet at an altitude of 50 feet and completed the first successful flight of the first glider ever built in Michigan. Smith flew the craft, built by Charles Augustine (Traverse City), at a farm near Arbutus Lake, a few miles out of Traverse City.

4. July 14, 1910

The first airplane to fly in Detroit skies took off from the state fairgrounds.

5. September 3, 1911

The Wright brothers brought a biplane to the West Michigan Fair at Grand Rapids and gave that area's residents their first chance to fly.

6. 1900s

Philip Orin Parmelee (Matherton Michigan), who had joined a flying school run by Orville and Wilbur Wright, became the first pilot to transport merchandise, drop live bombs from a plane, and search from the air for criminals.

7. November 3, 1913

Toward evening, William E. Scripps (Detroit) took off in a pontoon plane from the Detroit Motorboat Club for a brief flight over Detroit. But, while circling over Grand Circus Park, Scripps developed engine trouble, landed on the Detroit River, completed repairs at dusk, then set out to taxi the plane down the river and Lake St. Clair to the club. As it got darker, however, Scripps feared he might strike a boat so he took off and completed the nation's first night airplane flight by successfully landing back at the club.

8. July 1, 1917

Jack Vilas made the first airplane flight across Lake Michigan, traveling from St. Joseph to Chicago in a Curtiss flying boat in one hour, 10 minutes.

9. July 1926

When Edward Stinson landed his airplane on the golf course in front of the Grand Hotel on Mackinac Island, it was the first time a gasoline-powered vehicle had ever entered the island.

10. July 10, 1928

Arthur A. Billings and George Frers flew from Muskegon to Milwaukee then, by returning to Muskegon, completed the first round-trip airplane flight across Lake Michigan.

11. January 7, 1929

Michigan pilots William Brock and Edward Schlee completed the first-ever nonstop Detroit-to-Miami, Florida airplane flight, making the trip in nine hours and 20 minutes.

12. February 20, 1929

In what was the state's first aviation junket, Governor Fred W. Green and 15 other state officials flew from Lansing to a conference in Kalamazoo.

13. August 19, 1929

The ZMC2, the nation's first all-metal dirigible, rose into the air from

Grosse Isle Airport. After the successful test flight, the navy purchased the ship from the manufacturer, the Detroit Aircraft Corporation.

14. August 10, 1946

The first jet airplane to fly in Michigan skies, a P-80, took off from Selfridge Field (Mount Clemens) during a Civil Air Patrol show.

15. July 20, 1948

Sixteen Lockheed Shooting Stars took off from Mount Clemens and completed the first west-to-east transatlantic jet flight by arriving at Odiham, England, 10 hours and 40 minutes later.

7 RECORD FLIGHTS

1. October 14, 1922

At a national airplane meet at Selfridge Field (Mount Clemens), Lt. Lester James Maitland flew an airplane faster than 200 m.p.h. for the first time in aviation history.

2. May 20, 1927

Detroit-native Charles A. Lindbergh completed the first nonstop solo flight across the Atlantic Ocean, flying 3,610 miles in the "Spirit of St. Louis" from New York to Paris in 33 hours.

3. June 25, 1930

Amelia Earhart, flying a Lockheed "Vega," set a women's speed record, 174.9 m.p.h., at Detroit. Seven years later, the famous aviatrix disappeared while attempting an around-the-world flight.

4. May 29, 1931

Detroit aviators Walter Lees and Frederick Brossy landed a diesel-motored monoplane at Jacksonville Beach, Florida, after staying aloft a world-record 84 hours and 33 minutes without refueling.

5. August 30, 1937

Two Jackson aviators landed after a 29-hour flight in a low-powered airplane during which they refueled 43 times by raising a two-gallon gas can by rope from a speeding auto. The pair then claimed a sustained-flight record but found that the American Aeronautical Association did not recognize flights in which refueling was done by automobile.

6. September 7, 1956

Captain Iven Kincheloe (Cassopolis) set a world's altitude record of 156,000 feet in a Bell X-2 rocket plane.

7. June 21, 1980

R. Steven Powell performed a record 2,315 5/8 "inside loops" in a Bellanca Decathalon over Almont.

3 FIRST FLYING-WOMEN

1. MRS. RUSSELL A. ALGER became first woman to ride in an airplane in Michigan skies when on June 19, 1911, she went up with aviator Frank Coffyn on one of the first of his 45 passenger-flying demonstrations from the Grosse Pointe Country Club golf course.

2. MARY E. VON MACH, the first woman in Michigan to own and fly a plane, became Michigan's first licensed female pilot in July 1928.

3. MARY LIVINGSTON (Manistique), in ceremonies held at Williams Air Force Base (Arizona) September 2, 1977, received her silver wings as Michigan's first female air-force jet pilot.

3 FORCED LANDINGS

1. On June 27, 1981, Joe Thorin crash-landed an experimental airplane on M-35 near Escanaba then collided with a utility pole. In a subsequent lawsuit, Thorin claimed that his car insurance policies should cover the damages since he was operating the airplane on a public highway. The court, however, dismissed his suit ruling that, in spite of the unique circumstances, auto-insurance laws were never intended to cover airplanes.

2. When the single engine of their Piper Cherokee Lance suddenly stopped running during a flight over northern Kentucky on July 15, 1983, the pilots, James Jabara (Plymouth) and Larry Edmondson (Romulus), headed the craft into a grove of trees, prevented an explosion by intentionally shearing off the wings which housed the fuel tanks, then landed without wings or wheels in a field. The two pilots and two passengers, who were traveling from Plymouth, Michigan, to Knoxville, Tennessee, received only minor injuries.

3. Charles Hess (Troy) took off from Big Beaver Airport (Troy) in his 1974 Piper Cherokee on November 12, 1984, and headed for a business appointment Cleveland. Six minutes later, when carburetor icing caused the plane's engine to stall, Hess calmly landed the plane on a section of I-696 under construction in Royal Oak.

4 HELICOPTER MILESTONES

1. August 21, 1917

Robert E. Frederick (Rogers City) received a patent for "new and useful improvements in Flying Machines," which turned out to be a forerunner of helicopters.

2. February 12, 1931

The first autogiro in the nation to be used commercially was delivered to the *Detroit News*, which used the small half-helicopter, half-airplane to gather news and take aerial photographs.

3. June 21, 1965

A helicopter carrying Lt. Governor William G. Milliken and James Ramsey, director of the state Department of Aeronautics, made the first landing on a heliport, Michigan's first, located on top of the National Lumberman's Bank Building, Muskegon.

4. March 1967

The R.J. Enstrom Company (Menominee) delivered Michigan's first state-owned helicopter to the conservation department, which used it to spot forest fires, count deer, check timber, and nab game-law violators.

3 AIRCRAFT-CONSTRUCTION FIRSTS

1. L.M. Driver constructed a 78-foot-long, 17-foot-in-diameter dirigible, the first built in Michigan, at the Drihopa Airship Company (Detroit) in July 1906.

2. The Brooks Aeroplane Company (Saginaw), which began operation in 1909, was Michigan's first manufacturer of airplanes.

3. The eight-passenger Ford Trimotor, built at Dearborn during the 1920s, was the nation's first airplane specifically designed for commercial passenger service.

5 FLIGHT ORGANIZATIONS

1. Forty-four prominent Detroiters met at the Ponchartrain Hotel (Detroit) on December 16, 1909, and with the help of guests Orville and Wilbur Wright, organized Michigan's first aero club. The following day, the members conducted Detroit's first airport survey — by car.

2. The first meeting of the Women's National Aeronautic Association was held April 7, 1929, at the Hotel Statler (Detroit), and Mrs. Orra Heald Blackmore (Detroit) was elected as the group's first president.

3. On May 20, 1929, the legislature created the Michigan Board of Aeronautics to regulate licensing of pilots, standardize aviation schools, investigate air accidents, and control airport construction and operation.

4. The Michigan wing of the Civil Air Patrol, a volunteer civilian auxiliary of the U.S. Air Force, was formally activated January 1, 1942.

5. Sixty-two charter members met at Capitol City Airport (Lansing) on September 14, 1946, and organized the Michigan Flying Farmers.

4 FIRST PLANE TOURS AND SHOWS

1. Forty manufacturers exhibited 63 different aircraft during the nation's first aircraft show, held at Detroit's convention center in April 1928.

2. Forty-two planes carrying 125 people left Pontiac on June 10, 1929, in the state's first organized air tour, a five-day trip to 32 Michigan cities.

3. Three seaplanes took off from Lake St. Clair on August 8, 1930, and began the nation's first air-water tour. The members of the Detroit Flying Club, organizers of the nine-day trip, visited 26 Great Lakes towns and cities in six states and Ontario.

4. Thirty pilots took off from Traverse City in September 1946 on Michigan's first air color tour, which took them to Manistique, Crystal Falls, Marquette, and Blaney Park.

3 COMMERCIAL-FLIGHT FIRSTS

1. The United States Aero Club in March 1917 named Grand Rapids and Detroit as two Michigan cities to be included in the nation's first four main transcontinental airways.

2. The Thompson Airline Company began Michigan's first inter-city commercial airfreight service on August 1, 1919, by carrying 200 pounds of auto parts from Detroit to Saginaw via Lansing.

3. The Ford Motor Company in 1961 became the first Michigan business firm to purchase a jet.

6 PASSENGER SERVICES

1. August 1, 1926

Ford Airport opened the nation's first airline passenger depot, and Stout Air Services began the nation's first regularly scheduled passenger service with one round trip per day from Detroit to Grand Rapids.

2. June 27, 1929

The Detroit Auto Club opened Michigan's first consolidated air-travel ticket office.

3. December 11, 1929

Stout Airlines (see number 1) became the nation's first airline to carry

100,000 passengers and in doing so, traveled 900,000 miles over three years with a perfect safety record. The airline was later absorbed by United Air Lines.

4. 1931

The Dearborn Inn, the world's first hotel designed and built for the air traveler, opened. The inn was also the first hotel in the country to provide air conditioning and the first in Michigan to offer in-room telephones.

5. April 30, 1954

Following several ceremonial speeches, a London-bound DC6B "Great Lakes Clipper" sped down a lone runway past a skinny control tower and climbed into sunny skies as the first passenger flight to lift off from Wayne Major (now Metropolitan) Airport. There was no restaurant at the time, so an enterprising entrepeneur showed up with coffee and doughnuts for the ceremonies.

6. 1984

Simmons Airlines, headquartered at Marquette, is the only Michigan-based passenger airline.

8 ORIGINAL PASSENGER INSTRUCTIONS

Passengers who embarked on Stout Air Services (see numbers 1 and 3 in the preceding list) flights in 1926 were handed instructions which advised in part:

1. Don't worry. . . . If there's any worrying to be done, let the pilot do it; that's what he's hired for.

2. . . . an airplane is tilted when making a perfect turn. Take the turns naturally with the plane. Don't try to hold the lower wing up with the muscles of the abdomen . . .

3. The atmosphere . . . supports the plane. . . . put your hand out the window and feel the tremendous pressure.

4. . . . swallow once in a while . . . so that the pressure on both sides of the eardrums will be equalized.

5. There is no discomfort in looking downwards while flying because there is no connection with the earth; only a sense of confidence and security, similar perhaps, to what birds feel.

6. Owing to altitude you may think you are moving very slowly, although the normal flying speed of the Stout-Ford plane is ninety-five miles an hour.

7. Under no occasion, attempt to open the cabin door, until the plane has come to a full stop.

8. An expert motor and plane mechanic flies every trip and is also trained as an alternate pilot.

4 BUSIEST AIRLINES

Four busiest airlines based on the number of daily flights to or from Michigan, as of May 1, 1983.

1. REPUBLIC		167
2. SIMMONS		93
3. NORTHWEST ORIENT		38
4. UNITED		33

— Thanks to Ed Boucher, Michigan Department of State, for providing a great deal of research material from which portions of this chapter were written. —

8

LET US ENTERTAIN YOU

Sour Notes
2 ROCK CONCERTS GONE BAD

1. GOOSE LAKE ROCKS MICHIGAN (August 7, 1970)

The open sale and use of drugs at a three-day rock festival which attracted 200,000 young people to Goose Lake, a private park near Jackson, prompted a statewide anti-drug television address by Governor William G. Milliken. And legislators, outraged by several instances of nude bathing at the gathering, passed a law regulating such events.

2. GANGS ATTACK ROCK FANS (August 15, 1976)

Two hundred youth-gang members forced their way into a rock concert at Cobo Hall (Detroit) and beat, terrorized, and robbed members of the audience. The violence then spread outside, where at least one woman was reportedly raped on a sidewalk and several other persons were assaulted and robbed.

3 RECORD TICKET SALES

1. With more than three million people a year spending an average of $10 a ticket for family shows, rock concerts, and sporting events, Joe Louis Arena/ Cobo Hall is the number one entertainment-sports complex in the country, topping even New York's Madison Square Garden.

2. As part of a special "Emily & Pooh & Dominoes Too" five-mile fun run that ended with a lap around the Tiger Stadium warning track, the race's sponsors purchased 2,000 reserved seats — the largest single sale of tickets in the Detroit Tigers history — so that the runners could watch the team's September 16, 1984 game against Toronto.

3. Rock singer Madonna's May 25, 1985 Cobo Hall concert sold out all 12,000 tickets in a record 29 minutes.

4 OUTDOOR MUSIC THEATRES

1. CASTLE FARMS MUSIC THEATRE (Charlevoix) — Opened 1978.

2. MEADOW BROOK MUSIC FESTIVAL (Rochester) — Opened 1963.

3. PINE KNOB MUSIC THEATRE (Clarkston) — Opened 1972.

4. TIMBER RIDGE (Gobles) — Opened 1982.

PINE KNOB'S FIRST 2 ACTS

1. DAVID CASSIDY

At the outdoor theatre's grand opening, Sunday afternoon, June 25, 1972, pre-teen girls rushed the stage and hurled themselves at their heartthrob's feet.

2. ANDY WILLIAMS

Later that same evening, adults, who paid $7, $5, or $2.50 for tickets, watched Williams, Pine Knob's "official" opening act.

3 NOTABLE FIRST CONCERTS

1. Mr. Blisse, a Tyrolese singer, presented a formal concert, Michigan's first, at Detroit on June 21, 1832. Admittance to the performance, held at the Capitol Building, was 25 cents.

2. At the Detroit Opera House on February 26, 1914, the Detroit Symphony Orchestra presented its first concert.

3. On March 24, 1970, the Detroit Symphony Orchestra presented a concert at Northern Michigan University (Marquette), the first upper-peninsula performance in the symphony's 56-year history.

9 CLASSIC SONGS
WRITTEN BY MICHIGAN COMPOSERS

1. BILL BAILEY WON'T YOU PLEASE COME HOME — Hughie P. Cannon (Jackson)
2. DRIFTING IN DREAMLAND — Loyal Curtis (Fowlerville)
3. I WANT A GIRL JUST LIKE A GIRL (That Married Dear Old Dad) — Harry Von Tilzer (Detroit)
4. I'LL SEE YOU IN MY DREAMS — Isham Jones (Saginaw)
5. POPEYE THE SAILOR MAN (Sam Lerner) — Detroit
6. SLEEPY TIME GAL — Ange Lorenzo (Saginaw) and Joseph Reed Alsen (Grand Rapids)
7. THE SWEETHEART OF SIGMA CHI — Byron D. Stokes (Albion) and F. Dudleigh Vernor (Albion)

8. TOO-RA-LOO-RA-LOO-RA — James Royce Shannon (Adrian)
9. YOU GOTTA BE A FOOTBALL HERO — Buddy Fields (Detroit) and Al Lewis (Detroit)

2 SPECIAL PIANOS

1. The first piano was brought to Michigan in 1803 by Mrs. Solomon Sibley (Detroit) who had used the less-than-full-size instrument while attending school at Bethlehem, Pennsylvania, and had it transported on horseback to Detroit after her marriage.

2. E.S. Votey (Detroit) on May 22, 1900, patented the nation's first pneumatic player piano.

4 UNIQUE MUSIC MAKERS

1. JOHN CHALLIS (Detroit), during the 1950s, was the nation's top harpsichord maker. Challis, who manufactured 12 of his internationally famous instruments a year for music schools and musicians, moved to New York in 1965, when a freeway project forced him from his business location.

2. GENERAL DEVICES and FITTINGS CO., formerly the Thomas J. Nichols Co. (Grand Rapids), was, by 1930, the country's only remaining steam-calliope manufacturer. By World War II, every circus or carnival calliope in the U.S. had been made or serviced by the firm, and Grand Rapids was known as the calliope capital of the world.

3. GIBSON INC. (Kalamazoo)

During the 1960s, the guitar-making factory manufactured 1,000 guitars a day for hundreds of bands and performers, including B.B. King, Chet Atkins, Les Paul, and the Rolling Stones, who once even chartered a plane to pay homage to the home of their instruments. But in 1984, because of foreign competition and a shrinking guitar market, the plant, after 90 years of operation, closed.

4. RICHARD SCHNEIDER (Kalamazoo) builds hand-crafted guitars that incorporate the first major design-change in the instrument in 100 years. Schneider charges $6,000 to $20,000 each for his guitars, which are constructed with a radically different number and pattern of tone bars. Theodore Bikel and Les Paul have both purchased Schneider's creation, and classical guitarists Andres Segovia, John Williams, and Julian Bream have tried his instruments but have yet to play them in concert.

2 COLLEGE MUSIC-FIRSTS

1. The nation's first Bachelor of Music degree was granted in 1873 by Adrian

College to Mattie Pease Lowrie, who had completed a four-year course in vocal and instrumental music.

2. The University of Michigan and Michigan State marching bands in 1972 included female members for the first time in their history. The University of Michigan band accepted six coeds in its 210-member squad, and Michigan State added two women to its 225-member band.

5 NOTABLE THEATRES

1. Michigan's first theatre was set up in the top story of a government warehouse at Detroit in 1816. There, army officers from nearby Fort Shelby gave amateur performaces for their families and other civilians.

2. The CALUMET THEATRE opened in 1900 at Calumet as the first municipally owned theatre in America. During the copper boom, the 1200-seat facility, with its ultra-modern electric lighting, steam heating, and indoor lavatories, rivaled the stages of New York and San Francisco for elegance and quality of entertainment.

3. The CASINO THEATRE, Michigan's first theatre devoted exclusively to showing motion pictures, opened at Detroit in 1905.

4. The DETROIT OPERA HOUSE in 1896 installed Michigan's first motion-picture projector.

5. The FISHER THEATRE (Detroit) opened October 2, 1961, as one of the very few new legitimate playhouses built in the country since the Depression.

7 ENTERTAINMENT PERSONALITIES BORN IN MICHIGAN

Michillaneous, on page 21, lists 32 entertainment personalities who were born in Michigan (including one notable error — see page 279). The following seven personalities were not included in that list.

1. WALLY COX (Detroit, December, 1924)

   Actor best known for his portrayal of television's *Mr. Peepers*.

2. CHRISTOPHER GEORGE (Royal Oak, 1929)

   Tall, rugged leading man of film and television action dramas.

3. CASEY KASEM (Detroit, 1933)

   Host of radio's weekly *American Top 40* program.

4. TIM "COL. T.J." MCCOY (Saginaw, April 10, 1891)

   Screen and television actor, film director, and wild-west performer.
   — *Item contributed by Mrs. Raymond Chartrand, Saginaw* —

5. GILDA RADNER (Detroit, June 28, 1946)

Comedienne.

6. BOB SEGER (Ann Arbor, May 6, 1945)

Rock singer.

7. DEL SHANNON (Grand Rapids, December 30, 1939)

Rock star of the late 1950s and early 1960s.

2 MICHIGAN GIANTS

1. LOUIS "BIG LOUIE" MOILANEN (Hancock Township), who, at age 18, stood eight feet, one-inch tall and weighed over 400 pounds, traveled with the Ringling Brother's circus during the early 1900s as a sideshow freak called the "Copper Country Giant." Moilanen returned to the Hancock area, was elected justice of the peace, but died in 1914 at age 28.

2. CELESTA GEYER (Detroit)

In 1927 a carnival signed the 300-pound woman and billed her as the sideshow freak, "Dolly Dimples — The Entertaining Fat Girl." But at the height of her career and weight — 555 pounds — Geyer suffered a heart attack and was told to diet or die. Geyer began dieting and, at the rate of a pound a day, had, by 1950, trimmed down to 122 pounds.

5 MEMORABLE FIRST RADIO BROADCASTS

1. February 10, 1922

The Detroit Symphony Orchestra, conducted by Ossip Gabrilowitch, gave the nation's first complete symphony concert ever presented by radio. The *Detroit News* radio station (later called WWJ) broadcast the performance.

2. October 25, 1924

WWJ radio (Detroit), with Ty Tyson at the microphone, broadcast the first radio play-by-play of a University of Michigan football game. The broadcast generated so many ticket requests for Michigan's next game that coach Fielding H. Yost gave WWJ permission to broadcast all home games.

3. April 20, 1927

The Detroit Tigers opened their American League baseball season at their home Navin Field, and WWJ radio announcer Ty Tyson gave fans at their sets the first play-by-play account of a Tiger game direct from the field.

4. January 30, 1933

The Lone Ranger made its first public broadcast over Detroit radio station

WXYZ. By the end of the decade, more than 400 stations nationwide carried the popular program.

5. October 9, 1935

The Ionia Reformatory became the only prison in the world, at the time, to make radio service available to every inmate. Convict-laborers had run wires to each cell in the prison, and inmates who paid 25 cents a month for the privilege could plug headphone jacks into one of the three outlets, each of which was connected to one of the three major broadcasting networks.

3 NOTABLE RADIO STATIONS

1. WDTR (Detroit) went on the air January 8, 1948, as the state's first educational FM station.

2. WKAR (East Lansing)

The Michigan State University station went on the air August 18, 1922, as Michigan's first educational radio station.

3. WWJ (Detroit) received Michigan's first radio license on October 13, 1921; joined New York station WEAF and a small group of other stations in organizing the first radio network on February 13, 1925; and became Michigan's first FM station on May 9, 1941.

2 RADIO STATIONS RUN BY AUTO COMPANIES

Two Michigan radio stations that were owned and operated by automobile companies.

1. WWI (Detroit), owned and operated by the Ford Motor Company, went on the air March 25, 1922, and broadcast until 1926.

2. WREO (Lansing), owned by the REO Motor Car Company, went on the air in November 1, 1924, and broadcast until 1927.

6 FIRST TELEVISION BROADCASTS

1. March 4, 1947

Though less than 100 families in the area had receivers, the state's first television station, WWJ-TV (Detroit), began daily broadcasts consisting, at first, of test patterns and studio presentations.

2. Summer 1951

Color television first arrived in Michigan when Detroit television-set dealers were shown a preview of a show called *Mike and Buff*. The first color broadcast for the general public was a football game between Maryland and North Carolina the following October.

3. October 15, 1951

WWJ-TV (Detroit) sent its mobile unit and announcer Bud Lynch to Government Dock (Windsor, Ontario) and, in the world's first international television broadcast, featured live coverage of an informal reception given Philip, Duke of Edinburgh, and Princess Elizabeth of Great Britain. Four months later, Elizabeth became Queen of England.

4. April 1953

WPAG-TV (Ann Arbor) became the state's first UHF television station.

5. 1962

The first golf hole-in-one ever recorded on televison was made by Jerry Barber on the 17th hole of the Buick open (Grand Blanc).

6. 1981

In the first-ever live national telecast of a 500-mile Indy Car event, NBC televised the Michigan International Speedway's (Brooklyn) Michigan 500 Indy Car race.

7 NEWSPAPER FIRSTS

1. SUCCESSFUL NEWSPAPER (July 25, 1817)

The first issue of the *Detroit Gazette*, Michigan's first successful regularly issued newspaper, was published at Detroit. The paper was published weekly for 13 years at an initial subscription cost of $4 per year.

2. DAILY (1835)

The *Detroit Free Press* became the state's first daily newspaper.

3. TEACHERS JOURNAL (March 1838)

The *Monthly Journal of Education*, published by John D. Pierce, Michigan's first Superintendent of Public Instruction, was the first teachers' journal west of the Appalachians and one of the first in the United States to circulate to a whole school system.

4. FARM PAPER (January 19, 1841)

The first issue of Michigan's first farm-journal newspaper, the *Western Farmer*, was published at Detroit. The eight-page semi-monthly folio was subsequently renamed the *Michigan Farmer*, which has been published to this day.

5. SUNDAY PAPER (October 2, 1853)

The *Detroit Free Press* became the first Michigan newspaper to be issued regularly on Sunday mornings.

6. WOMEN'S SECTION (January 12, 1878)

The first women's section of the *Detroit Free Press*, called "The Household," rolled off the presses.

7. AERIAL PHOTOGRAPHS (June 17, 1912)

Detroit News photographer William A. Kuenzel, riding in a hydro aeroplane piloted by Walter Brookens, took pictures of the Detroit River. The *News* then printed Michigan's first newspaper aerial photographs.

4 SMALLEST DAILY NEWSPAPERS

The four smallest of Michigan's 51 daily newspapers, based on 1983 circulation.

1. *MARSHALL EVENING CHRONICLE*	2,327
2. *DETROIT LEGAL NEWS*	2,363
3. *DOWAGIAC DAILY NEWS*	3,110
4. *ALBION EVENING RECORDER*	3,616

— List idea Dennis Guerriero, Harrison —

6 SMALLEST WEEKLY OR SEMI-WEEKLY NEWSPAPERS

The six smallest of the approximately 250 regularly issued weekly papers or semi-weekly papers published in Michigan, based on 1983 circulation.

1. *OLIVET OPTIC NEWS*	226
2. *BELLEVUE GAZETTE*	420
3. *HANOVER HORTON LOCAL*	458
4. *GALESBURG ARGUS*	466
5. *CLARKSVILLE RECORD*	522
6. *FREEPORT NEWS*	578

— List idea, Dennis Guerriero, Harrison —

2 FEMALE NEWSPAPER FIRSTS

1. The MICHIGAN WOMAN'S PRESS ASSOCIATION, Michigan's first organization for female journalists, was formed July 22, 1890, at the Hotel Park Place, Traverse City.

2. KATHERINE LAUGHTON (Menominee) in 1913 became the first female managing editor of a daily newspaper in the nation.

3 READING MATTERS

1. FIRST BOOKSTORE AD (July 25, 1817)

Michigan's first known bookstore advertised in the first issue of the *Detroit Gazette* (see page 175). The owners of the bookstore, who also owned the newspaper, listed mostly works of fiction with many titles by Sir Walter Scott.

2. FIRST COPYRIGHT (May 5, 1824)

Philo E. Judd received a copyright, Michigan's first, for a map of the Territory of Michigan. Judd, however, submitted only the title and died before finishing the map itself.

3. LONGEST-RUNNING BOOK FAIR

The Children's Book Fair of Metropolitan Detroit, held annually since 1953, is the oldest continuous children's book fair in the country.

4 LIBRARY FIRSTS

1. Michigan's first library, the City Library of Detroit, incorporated on August 26, 1817. The library was, when completed, located in the building built for the forerunner of the University of Michigan, and the teachers of the university acted as librarians. Initial financing was obtained by selling 90 shares of stock at $5 a share to members of the organizing library society.

2. The Michigan territorial legislative council on June 16, 1828, established the Library of Michigan and later appointed William B. Hunt, at a $100 annual salary, as the first librarian.

3. Michigan, by stipulating in the constitution of 1835 that ". . . the legislature shall provide for the establishment of libraries, one at least in each township . . .," became the first state to mandate library services for its residents.

4. Members of the Michigan Library Association held their first formal meeting on September 1, 1891, at Detroit.

5 NOTABLE LIBRARIES

1. The AMASA COMMUNITY LIBRARY (Iron County), with 2,638 volumes, is Michigan's smallest.

2. The BENTON HARBOR PUBLIC LIBRARY in September 1969 became the

first Michigan city library to hire a black director.

3. The DETROIT PUBLIC LIBRARY, with 2.6 million volumes, is Michigan's largest.

4. The ELK RAPIDS LIBRARY is located on an island reached by board walkway over the Elk River.

5. The MICHIGAN STATE UNIVERSITY LIBRARY includes 16,000 comic books, the only cataloged collection of such publications in the nation.

2 FABULOUS FOUNTAINS

1. WORLD'S LARGEST MUSICAL FOUNTAIN (Grand Haven)

The 260-foot-long $150,000 fountain pumps 4,000 gallons of water per minute in a constantly changing blend of light, color, and music.

2. CASCADES (Jackson)

Two thousand gallons of water a minute, lit by 1,268 flashing colored lights, pour over 16 separate 60-foot-wide waterfalls.

3 NOTABLE CIRCUSES

1. One of the first circuses to tour Michigan was the "June, Titus and Angevine Company," which performed throughout the state during the summer of 1842.

2. Michigan's first advertisement for an electric light, which appeared in the May 18, 1879 *Detroit Post and Tribune*, announced the coming of a circus

whose tents would be "lighted with wondrous arc lights, worth traveling 500 miles to see."

3. On February 26, 1906, at Detroit's Moslem Shrine Temple,3,000 spectators watched the nation's first Shrine Circus. The one-ring show grew to become a major fund-raiser for Shrine temples throughout the country.

3 FORMER PLUSH RESORTS

1. BLANEY PARK (Schoolcraft County)

During the 1930s, 40s, and 50s, Michigan governors, Henry Ford, authors, actors, and even a few underworld kingpins flocked to the 17,000-acre playground for the wealthy which included an airstrip, golf course, dude ranch, stable, and the Blaney Inn, which seated 400 guests for exquisite meals prepared by European chefs.

2. GRANOT LOMA (Marquette)

The cavernous lodge, built in the 1920s on a rocky precipice overlooking Lake Superior by Louis G. Kaufman, a Marquette native who became a multimillionarie banker, had 70 rooms filled with hand-carved furniture, huge polar bear rugs, paintings, murals, and big-game tophies; 30 open fireplaces; balconies; card, billiard, and massage rooms; and sauna baths. The basement contained a massive storage area for pleasure boats, which were winched up from the lake along rails. At one time, the lodge even had its own railroad spur, by which entire Broadway troupes would arrive to entertain guests.

3. IDLEWILD (Lake County)

During the 1950s, thousands of midwestern blacks, unable or unwilling because of discrimination to visit white recreational areas, flocked to Idlewild to enjoy Paradise and Idlewild lakes by day and glamorous night life at places such as the Flamingo Club and Club Paradise at night.

But with the coming of integration during the sixties, blacks sought out other vacation and entertainment spots, and the resort area — which once had attracted such famous visitors as Della Reese, the Four Tops, Count Basie, Brook Benton, and Barbara McNair— faded into economic near devastation.

5 COUNTIES WITH
THE MOST VACATION HOMES

Five counties with the highest percentage of total housing units in 1980 consisting of seasonal or migratory dwellings. State average = 3.9%.

1. KEWEENAW		45.4
2. MACKINAC		42.6
3. CLARE		38.5

4. MONTMORENCY   37.1
5. OSCODA   36.2

6 MOST EXPENSIVE HOTELS

Based on the most expensive double-occupancy rate as listed in the 1984 *Mobil Travel Guide.*

1. GRAND HOTEL (Mackinac Island)* $290
2. WESTIN HOTEL-RENAISSANCE CENTER (Detroit) $130
3. HILTON INN NORTHFIELD (Troy) $125
4. PONTCHARTRAIN (Detroit) $119
5. HYATT REGENCY DEARBORN $113
6. AMWAY GRAND (Grand Rapids) $112

*Rate includes two meals per day.

— List idea contributed by Dennis Guerriero, Harrison and Mike Gregory, Battle Creek —

2 OLDEST HOTELS

1. The NATIONAL HOUSE INN (Marshall), built in 1835 as Calhoun County's first brick building, is the oldest operating inn in the state.

2. The BOTSFORD INN (Farmington) was built as a home in 1836 and converted into a tavern-hotel in 1841.

3 NUDIST CAMPS

1. FOREST HILLS CLUB (Saranac)
2. SUNSHINE GARDENS FAMILY NUDIST RESORT (Battle Creek)
3. WHISPERING OAKS (Oxford)

4 OVEREXPOSURES

1. During an October 1977 weekend promotion at Fairlane Towne Center (Dearborn), a Plymouth housewife asked to see muscleman Arnold Schwarzenegger's famous chest. When the actor, multiple winner of "Mr. Universe" bodybuilding titles, and author of the book, *Pumping Iron*, kiddingly said he would if she would do the same, the woman quickly whipped off her turtle neck sweater and bra. Schwarzenegger then lived up to his part of the bargain by removing his shirt.

2. The *Sexy Sixties* calendar, published annually since 1982 by Bill Baldwin, an East Lansing industrial consultant, features nude photos of men and women, all over age 60.

3. After the Detroit Tigers' 1984 World Series victory, Kirk Gibson, wearing only a towel, slipped into view of cameras as a television sportscaster was giving his wrap-up from the locker room. While lifting a bottle of champagne to pour over the sportscaster's head, Gibson inadvertently lifted his towel and briefly bared himself to viewers.

4. State Attorney General Wilbur M. Brucker on July 15, 1929, ruled that, since control over highways was vested in the state highway commission, Livingston County did not have the authority to prohibit women in bathing suits from riding in cars.

7 PARK FIRSTS

1. 1895

Twenty years after congress had established Mackinac Island as the nation's second national park, following Yellowstone, the federal government turned the fort and park over to Michigan, and the island became our first state park.

2. 1919

The newly created State Park Commission established its first state park, D.H. Day State Park, near Glen Arbor.

3. 1929

Spring Lake Campground, Michigan's first state forest campground, opened near Fife Lake. The system now includes over 150 campgrounds with 3,000 campsites on lakes and rivers throughout Michigan's state forests.

4. January 1972

Special senior citizens state park annual motor vehicle permits, the first of their kind in the nation, were made available.

5. 1972

The Department of Natural Resources opened the state's first cross-country ski trail in the 123,000-acre Fife Lake State Forest near Traverse City.

6. 1982

As part of a nationwide National Forest Service experiment to lower park maintenance and administration costs, the Sand Lake Recreation Area (Dublin) became Michigan's first privately operated U.S. park. Though still owned by the government, the park's campgrounds, beach, boat launch, and picnic areas were leased to a private concessionaire.

7. July 4, 1984

Autoworld (Flint) opened as the nation's first urban indoor theme park, with all rides, exhibits, animated and hands-on displays, shops, and restaurants designed to tell the story of the automotive industry and the role that Flint has played in it.

3 STATE PARKS WITH
THE MOST CAMPSITES

1. INTERLOCHEN (Interlochen)	550
2. HIGGINS LAKE SOUTH (Roscommon)	512
3. LUDINGTON (Ludington)	398

5 LARGEST STATE PARKS

In acres.

1. PORCUPINE MOUNTAINS	58,335
2. TAHQUAMENON FALLS	35,733
3. WATERLOO (Chelsea)	18,027
4. PINCKNEY (Pinckney)	9,994
5. HARTWICK PINES (Grayling)	9,238

4 NATIONAL PARKS

1. MACKINAC ISLAND NATIONAL PARK, the nation's second, following the creation of Yellowstone by only three years, was established by Congress on March 3, 1875. Twenty years later, the federal government turned the fort and park over to Michigan, and the island became our first state park.

2. ISLE ROYALE NATIONAL PARK was established August 27, 1946.

3. PICTURED ROCKS NATIONAL LAKESHORE, 35 miles of massive multicolored rock formations, sand dunes, beaches, and forests along the Lake Superior shoreline from Munising to Grand Marais, was dedicated October 6, 1972.

4. SLEEPING BEAR DUNES NATIONAL LAKESHORE became Michigan's last national park on October 21, 1970.

5 UNIQUE PARKS

1. GARDEN OF EDEN

An article in a 1939 Boston paper reported that a Massachusetts man had, after analyzing a biblical passage that described a river which parted into "four heads," concluded that the river in the description was the St. Mary's River, the four heads were the Great Lakes, and, therefore, the Garden of Eden was in southern Michigan.

2. ISLE ROYALE is the nation's only national park that is an island. Isle Royale is also the least visited of all the nation's national parks.

3. METROPOLITAN BEACH (Macomb County), with 3,000 feet of sand beach on Lake St. Clair, is the largest man-made beach in the world.

4. THE OLD MILL CREEK HISTORICAL PARK, a reconstructed late-18th-century water-powered sawmill east of Mackinaw City, opened June 15, 1984, as Michigan's newest state park.

5. PORCUPINE MOUNTAINS STATE PARK, with more than 58,000 acres, is the nation's largest state park.

10 MOST POPULAR VACATION AREAS

Ten areas most often used by AAA's "Triptik," as reported in *Michigan Living*, April 1985.

1. MACKINAW CITY
2. MACKINAC ISLAND
3. TRAVERSE CITY
4. DETROIT
5. FRANKENMUTH

6. PETOSKEY
7. HOUGHTON LAKE
8. CHARLEVOIX
9. HOLLAND
10. COPPER HARBOR

4 TOURISM TIDBITS

In Michigan in 1983:

1. $6.9 million was spent on tourism promotion.

2. The tourism industry took in $10.9 billion in revenues.

3. 142,000 Michigan people were directly employed and another 111,000 indirectly employed in travel-industry jobs.

4. Frankenmuth, with 2.5 million visitors, was the state's biggest tourist attraction.

5 FIRST HOLIDAYS

1. December 25, 1660

Father Rene' Menard, who had established a mission near Keweenaw Bay, held Michigan's first known Christmas celebration with, as he wrote, "all the fervor possible under the trying conditions of a primitive wilderness with a few French *coureurs-de-bois* (woods rangers) and a small group of Huron converts as companions."

2. November 25, 1824

By decree of territorial Governor Lewis Cass, who was influenced by the steady influx of New Englanders, Michigan celebrated its first official Thanksgiving.

3. May 29, 1869

Michigan observed Memorial Day for the first time. The origin of the holiday is disputed, but most versions agree that it began in the South in 1866 when Civil War widows gathered to place flowers on their husbands' graves.

4. April 15, 1876

Michigan celebrated its first Arbor Day, the tree-planters holiday, but most Michigan residents ignored the event.

5. February 5, 1974

Nine years before President Ronald Reagan signed a bill declaring a national holiday for Martin Luther King Jr., Governor William G. Milliken signed into law a bill designating the second Sunday in January as a legal Michigan holiday to honor the slain civil-rights leader.

11 FIRST CELEBRATIONS

1. October 1, 1839

Michigan's first agricultural fair was scheduled to take place at Ann Arbor. But the man in charge made no preparations and forgot to show up, only two exhibitors arrived, and Ann Arbor residents totally ignored the event.

2. September 25, 1849

The nation's first successful state fair, then called the Fair Michigan State Agricultural Society, began at Detroit and has been held annually since.

3. August 20, 1916

Oakland County began a week-long centennial celebration, the first staged by any Michigan county.

4. July 1926

Traverse City held its first-ever National Cherry Festival.

5. May 1929

Holland opened its first Tulip Festival. The colorful festival grew to become Michigan's largest and ranks just behind the Mardi Gras (New Orleans) and Rose Parade (Pasadena) in national popularity.

6. May 1954

The first Michigan Week celebration took place.

7. June 1959

The first Frankenmuth Bavarian Festival, begun by William Zhender to celebrate the grand opening of his Bavarian Inn, was held.

8. July 11, 1964

Kalkaska began its first annual Blueberry Festival.

9. July 2, 1966

Manistee began its first National Strawberry Festival.

10. August 20, 1971

After learning that the *Encyclopedia Brittanica* had credited an Oscoda native, *Detroit News-Tribune* reporter James MacGillivary, with being the first to write about the legendary lumberman Paul Bunyan, Oscoda staged its first annual Paul Bunyan Festival.

11. December 9, 1972

Grand Rapids became the first Michigan city to climax its traditional Christmas parade with the arrival of a black Santa Claus.

10 FIRST RESTAURANTS

Location and opening date of the first Michigan restaurant of the following ten chains.

1. A & W — W. Jefferson, Trenton (1937)

2. ARBY'S — W. Grand River Avenue, East Lansing (September 28, 1966)

3. BILL KNAPP'S — S.W. Capital Avenue, Battle Creek (June 21, 1948)

4. BURGER KING — Clio Road, Flint (August 10, 1965)

5. DAIRY QUEEN — W. Bristol Road, Flint (1945)

6. DOMINO'S PIZZA — Ypsilanti (1960)

   Was also the nation's first Dominos.

7. LITTLE CAESARS — Garden City (May 1959)

   Was also the nation's first Little Caesars.

8. MCDONALDS — N. Larch Street, Lansing (May 20, 1957)

9. RED LOBSTER — W. 12 Mile Road, Madison Heights (November 26, 1974)

10. WHITE CASTLE — E. Jefferson, Detroit (June 13, 1929)

9 BEST RESTAURANTS

From *Goodfood: The Adventurous Eater's Guide to Restaurants Serving America's Best Regional Specialities*, by Jane and Michael Stern. The Sterns traveled across Michigan some 10 times and tried about 50 different restaurants but only found nine they deemed worthy of including in their 1983 book.

1. CHERRY HUT (Beulah)

   Cherry pies, sundaes and floats.

2. THE DEARBORN INN (Dearborn)

   "Midwestern man food," planked steak and Lake trout.

3. EVERETT'S SMOKED FISH (Naubinway)

   Smoked salmon and menominee.

4. GREAT LAKES WHITEFISH AND CHIPS (Charlevoix)

Whitefish and walleye.

5. JUILLERET'S (Harbor Springs)

Planked whitefish.

6. FINLANDIA RESTAURANT (Marquette)

Pasties.

7. LAWRY'S PASTY SHOP (Ishpeming)

Pasties.

8. LONDON CHOP HOUSE (Detroit)

Perch and lamb.

9. MATTIE'S BAR-B-QUE (Detroit)

Soul food and ribs.

4 FAST-FOOD COUNTIES

Four counties with the most fast-food establishments per 10,000 residents in 1983. State average = 9.0.

1.	MANISTEE	25.6
2.	KEWEENAW	25.5
3.	ROSCOMMON	23.8
4.	MASON	23.1

5 SLOW-FOOD COUNTIES

Five counties with the fewest fast-food establishments per 10,000 residents in 1983. State average ⁻ 9.0.

1.	OSCEOLA	3.2
2.	MECOSTA	4.1
3.	TUSCOLA	4.4
4.	MENOMINEE	4.6
5.	BARAGA	4.7

4 SPECIAL FOOD DELIVERIES

1. The first oysters were shipped to Michigan in 1826.

2. The first pistachio nuts arrived in the U.S. at Detroit in 1924 when, according to Frank Germack, head of Germack Pistachio Company, his father and uncle began bringing in the nuts from the Middle East as part of their food import service.

3. Eleven Detroit-area White Castle hamburger restaurants in May 1983 filled an order for 102,000 hamburgers — to go. A private-school group in Albuquerque, New Mexico, had placed the order then, in a unique fund raiser, sold the bite-size burgers to former midwesterners in their city, which has no White Castle establishments.

4. Two hundred Domino's Pizza employees from 20 separate restaurants arrived in 60 vehicles with more than 30,000 slices of pizza for the 10,0000 participants who had finished a September 16, 1984 "Emily & Pooh & Domino's Too" five-mile fun run inside Tiger Stadium (see also page 169).

7 GORGINGS

1. Dizzy Densmore, whose name is enshrined on a small wood-grain plate at the Hot Dog Hall of Fame (Rockford), holds the unofficial world record for hot dog consumption — 42 in four hours. The unusual hall of fame, located in The Corner tavern, also displays the names of another 2,000 people — including the female record-holder, Sharon Sholten, who downed 20 — who have eaten a dozen or more hot dogs in four hours.

2. John VanDyke (Walker) ate '97 live nightcrawlers on March 30, 1985, in an unsuccessful attempt to beat a world record 206 worms eaten in one hour.

3. Seventy-three-year-old Fred Magel (Oak Park, Illinois), who said he hadn't eaten at home in 55 years, ate his 46,000th restaurant meal at Zehnders in Frankenmuth on June 22, 1983.

4. Detroiters are the national leader in potato chip consumption, devouring an average of seven pounds each annually compared to the average American intake of 4.3 pounds of chips per year.

5. Gaylord stages what they call the "World's Largest Coffee Break" during their annual summer Alpenfest.
   — Item contributed by Mary A. Flinn, Gaylord —

6. At the 1983 Battle Creek Cereal City Festival, more than 25,000 people sat down to free cereal and milk at what was billed as the world's largest breakfast table.

7. At the City of Flint's 1982 Fourth of July celebration, a local grocery store chain served the world's largest submarine sandwhich — a 1,000-foot-long bun piled with 2,600 slices of cheese, 3,300 slices of lunchmeat, 25 pounds of mustard, 1,000 pounds of shredded lettuce, and 100 pounds of chopped onions. (See photo, page 189)

5 DRINKS INVENTED IN MICHIGAN

1. The BULLSHOT — a mixture of vodka, bouillon, and ice cubes which is flavored with a special concoction made up of Worcestershire, Tabasco, Ango-

Though it took weeks to make, 6,000 Flint-area residents devoured a one-ton "world's largest subma-rine sandwhich" in only minutes. (See story, page 188)   *Flint Journal photo*

stura Bitters, and celery salt — was invented in 1952 at Detroit's Caucus Club by John Hurley. Hurley, a Detroit advertising man who had as one of his client's, the Campbell Soup Co., was trying to invent a drink that would boost sales of the company's beef bouillon soup.

2. COLD DUCK was invented in 1937 by Harold Borgman, then owner of the Pontchartrain Wine Cellers, who made the drink by combining one part dry California Bugundy with two parts New York State Champagne.

3. THE HUMMER, a mixture of Kahlua, rum, and ice cream, was concocted in 1970 by London Chop House bartender Farouk Elhaje and the restaurant's owner, Lester Gruber. In the course of their experimentation, they also invented seven or eight other ice cream drinks but none achieved the fame of the Hummer.

4. ICE CREAM SODAS were invented on a hot day in 1875 when a harassed clerk of the Sanders Store in Detroit, having run out of the usual sweet cream used for sodas, substituted ice cream. The new drink became a Sanders speciality during the 1880s and 1890s.

5. VERNORS, the nation's oldest soft drink, was made in 1866 by pharmacist James Vernor from a secret recipe no one has ever been able to duplicate.

3 TIPPLING TIDBITS

In 1984, according to the Michigan Liquor Control Commission, each Michigan resident over the age of 14 consumed an average of:

1. 2.40 gallons of wine.

2. 2.59 gallons of distilled spirits (hard liquor).

3. 29.35 gallons of beer.

3 UFO SIGHTINGS

1. According to the *Book of Lists III*, a Michigan woman named Jean Sheldon reported that on a 1966 summer evening a large silvery object descended from the heavens and drew her inside with a levitation beam. There, she was greeted by three naked male humanoids who telepathically transmitted the message, "My dear earthwoman . . . we wish to mate with you. It will be easier on your personality if you do this willingly."

The three aliens then stripped her, according to the report, and on a bedlike machine, made love to her for at least an hour. The woman said she found the experience exciting and stimulating but was somewhat ashamed of the unusual delight she felt.

2. Two hundred students, who were outside during a fire drill at Michigan State University on May 3, 1967, reported seeing a ball of fire with a writhing tail that passed over the campus. Ingham County Sheriffs also reported seeing the fireball as it whirled over the northern horizon.

3. An Owosso train conductor reported that on October 22, 1973, a "giant spotlight," so bright he couldn't look at it, had hovered 400 feet above his train for a few moments then sped away.

9

HONORABLE MENTIONS

19 EXTRAORDINARY SENIOR CITZENS

1. JESSIE BYRAM (Madison Heights, 1982), 98, became the oldest person in the United States ever to graduate from high school. Byram, who had left school after completing the tenth grade in 1883, resumed her studies in 1978 and completed her education through a senior-citizen-center program of high school courses.

2. DANIEL P. CASSIDY (Detroit, 1982), who still practiced law at age 100, had been a practicing attorney for 79 years, longer than anyone else in the history of the Michigan bar.

3. CULLEN and MILDRED CHILDS (Coloma, April 1985), ages 82 and 78 respectively, earned college diplomas from Lake Michigan College.

4. WILFIRD "BILL" DOYLE (Mackinac Island, 1982), 84, began his 50th year in state government which made him the longest-serving public official in the history of Michigan state government. Doyle was elected to the state Senate in 1932 then in 1939 was appointed to the Mackinac Island State Park Commission, on which, as of April 1985, he still serves.

5. REVEREND NORMAN A. DUKETTE (Flint, 1975), 85, who founded Flint's first black Catholic Parish in 1929, was honored as being the oldest living black priest in the United States.

6. ALICE ECKARDT (Mt. Morris, August 1982), 70, jumped 300 feet from a single-prop plane near Clio and became the oldest sky diver in Michigan history.

7. MINNIE FARMER (Howard City, 1974), 83, marked her 40th year as publisher of the weekly *Howard City Record*, circulation 1,000.

8. DOUGLAS FRASER (Detroit, May 1980) was elected to the Chrysler Corporation board of directors, and at age 63, became the first union officer in American labor history to sit on the board of a major American corporation.

9. DR. W.S. HINCKLEY (Hartford, 1968), 100, was the state's oldest practicing dentist. The general practitioner, who had graduated from the University of Michigan dental school in 1893, had, however, from age 85 on, limited himself to making dentures.

10. S.S. KRESGE actively headed the store chain he founded in Detroit in 1907 until his death in 1966 at age 99.

11. DAVID LOWENSTEIN (Detroit, 1983), who at age 83 had been hacking for 65 years, was Michigan's oldest-active and longest-serving cab driver.

12. LINA MARSHALL (Kalamazoo, 1980), an 84-year-old senior at Western Michigan University, joined the Phi Mu sorority.

13. JENNIE NELSON (Seney, 1980), 88, had served as the clerk or treasurer for the tiny upper-peninsula village since 1921, which made her, at the time, the longest-serving elected politician in Michigan and possibly the nation.

14. CECIL SINCLAIR (Grand Haven, April 1985), 97, made two takeoffs and landings and executed turns and other maneuvers as part of a a 10-minute flight check that protected his reputation as the world's oldest active licensed pilot.

15. HARRY SKEEGS (Dowagiac, 1974), 85, who had delivered the *Dowagiac Daily News* for 70 years, was the oldest newspaper carrier in the state, both in terms of age and years of service. Skeegs also had the distinction of being the state's oldest and longest-serving constable, having served in that position for 50 years.

16. RICHARD SULLIVAN (New Boston, 1982), 70, won the 21st Michigan House District seat and became the oldest freshman ever elected to the state legislature.

17. ELLA TUTTLE (Clinton, 1982) began writing for the *Clinton Local* newspaper and at age 102 became the oldest working newspaper columnist in the world.

18. LAWRENCE E. TAYLOR (Beulah, 1974), 90, compiled the state's unofficial safest-driving record. Taylor started driving at the turn of the century, got a ticket in 1905 because his vehicle scared a few horses, then drove for another 69 years before receiving another citation, this time for failing to yield the right of way on a turn.

19. MILDRED WEIL (Flint, 1983), 76, became the oldest person ever admitted to the Michigan bar.

14 JUNIOR ACHIEVERS

1. TIM BALZESKI (Grand Rapids), as a 16-year-old high school junior in 1982, won both the Greco-Roman and freestyle national wrestling champion-

ships of the Amateur Athletic Union and also the Greco-Roman world wrestling championship.

2. CHRIS BROWN (Albion, 1982), who began a business of selling hand-stamped personalized leather key tags to executives at Fortune-500 companies, became at age 16 the youngest known listee in Dun & Bradstreet, the nation's best known business credit-rating and listing service.

3. ETIENNE BRULE was 22 years old when, in the early 1620s, he became first white man to set foot on Michigan soil.

4. TY COBB (1907) and AL KALINE (1955) each won an American League batting championship at age 20.

5. JOHNNY GAEDERT (Vermontville, 1965), 16, took over as the editor-publisher of the *Vermontville Echo* and became the youngest newspaper editor in Michigan.

6. ANGIE GEMALSKY (Lansing, 1982), 10, became Michigan's youngest female competitive weightlifter.

7. JIMMY HOFFA (Detroit, 1930), as a 17-year-old freight handler at the Kroger Grocery and Baking Company, organized and won his first union strike.

8. AARON KRICKSTEIN (Grosse Pointe Woods)

Two weeks after turning pro at age 16, Krickstein, by winning the Israel Tennis Center Classic on October 15, 1983, became the youngest player ever to win a Grand Prix tennis title. A year later, Krickstein was named rookie of the year and in January 1985, as the number-11-ranked tennis professional in the world, became the youngest player ever to compete in the Masters Tournament.

9. CHRISTOPHER LAMB (Flint, 1982), a 23-year-old percussionist, became the youngest musician ever to play with New York's Metropolitan Opera Orchestra.

10. CHARLES LINDBERGH (Detroit) made his famous 1927 solo transatlantic flight at age 25.

11. MONICA McCLENDON, a 13-year-old freshman at Lansing Sexton High School, became the youngest gubernatorial appointee in Michigan history when in July 1984 she was appointed to a one-year term on a newly established Committee on Juvenile Justice.

12. ROBERT (Rockin' Robby) NAISMITH JR. (Pinconning, 1984), 5, was the host and disc jockey on a weekly top-40 radio program.

13. HERBERT (Todd) NEWHOUSE II (Grand Rapids, April 1983), an 18-year-old high school senior who took over his family's business, the Little Red Barn Theater, claimed that he was the youngest porno-theater operator in the world.

14. BARBARA PARDEE, 16, and CHARLOTTE ADAMS, 17, who had saved money from baby sitting, selling garden vegetables, and odd jobs, purchased the *Concord News* in 1970 for $1,500 and took over as publishers of the four-page weekly.

8 PROMINENT BLACKS

Michigan's eight most eminent and powerful blacks as listed in *Ebony* magazine's 1983 list of "The 100 Most Influential Black Americans."

1. RICHARD AUSTIN

Michigan Secretary of State.

2. REV. CHARLES BUTLER

President of the $2^1/2$-million-member Progressive National Baptist Convention.

3. JOHN CONYERS JR.

United States Representative, 1st Congressional District (Detroit).

4. REP. GEORGE CROCKET (Detroit)

United States Representative, 13th Congressional District (Detroit).

5. ROBERT GORDON

Grand polemarch of the Kappa Alpha Psi Fraternity, one of the nation's oldest fraternities.

6. DAMON KEITH

U.S. Appeals Court judge.

7. OTIS SMITH

General counsel for General Motors.

8. COLEMAN YOUNG

Detroit mayor.

2 MALE MOMS

1. ALLAN KERR (Detroit) in 1970 became the first bachelor in Michigan history to adopt a child, a son. A year later, Kerr adopted a second son.

2. KEITH H. WELLSTED (Flint) in 1983 became the first man to be named the Michigan State Fair's annual *Homemaker of the Year*.

3 DISTINCTIVE COOKS

1. BETTY D. ENGLES (Midland) has been selected six times to compete in the national Pillsbury Bake-off finals and has won $4,600 in cash, five stoves, five mixers, one microwave oven, one toaster oven, and all-expenses-paid trips to San Diego, Beverly Hills, Phoenix, San Francisco, Boston, and New Orleans.

2. DAN HUGELIER, executive chef at the Detroit Athletic Club, was one of four culinarians in the country chosen to make up a United States team to compete in the 1984 Culinary Olympics at Frankfurt, Germany.

3. The WHIRLPOOL CORPORATION (Benton Harbor), as the prime food contractor for NASA's 1969 Apollo missions, provided astronauts Neil Armstrong and Edwin Aldrin with the first meal — bacon squares, peaches, sugar cookie cubes, pineapple-grapefruit drink, and coffee — ever eaten on the moon.

2 PRESIDENTIAL DESSERTS

1. The Hawkins Bakery (Traverse City) baked a three-foot-in-diameter 42-pound cherry pie then on August 18, 1926, hand-delivered the special dessert to President and Mrs. Calvin Coolidge and several guests, who were attending a distinguished dinner party at the president's summer white house in the Adirondack Mountains of New York.

2. Since January 1983, when President Ronald Reagan first sampled Tom's Mom's Cookies, Tom Kneeland, owner of Tom's Cafe and Bakery (Charlevoix), has sent 15 dozen of his chocolate-chunk specialities to the White House each week.

2 SPECIAL WEIGHT WATCHERS

1. GEORGE KULCHESKY (Hamtramck), who, from 1970 to 1972, dropped from 397 pounds to 190 pounds, was the first Michigan person and one of only a few in the nation to lose more than 200 pounds through the Weight Watchers of America program.

2. FLORINE MARK (Southfield), whose organization conducts more than 1,350 weekly Weight Watchers classes in seven states and Mexico, owns the largest group of Weight Watchers franchises in the world.

3 FIRST ARCHITECTS

1. EMILY BUTTERFIELD (Pontiac) became Michigan's first female architect in 1929.

2. ALDEN DOW (Midland), designer of the Ann Arbor City Hall, Ann Arbor Public Library Kalamazoo Nature Center, Grace A. Dow Memorial Library

(Midland), McMorran Auditorium and Sports Arena (Port Huron), and Northwood Institute (Midland), was named in 1983 as the first Architect Laureate of Michigan.

3. DONALD FRANK WHITE (Pontiac) in 1938 became Michigan's first black licensed architect.

3 GREAT MICHIGAN ARCHITECTS

1. ALBERT KAHN (Detroit), who designed the General Motors Building in 1920, is considered one of the greatest factory architects in history.

2. ELIEL SAARINEN (Bloomfield Hills) designed the Tribune Tower (Chicago) and the Cranbrook School and Institute of Science.

3. EERO SAARINEN (Birmingham), Eliel's son, designed the Dulles Airport (Washington, D.C.) and the Columbia Broadcasting System Building (New York City).

5 SINGULAR STRUCTURES

1. The AMYWAY GRAND HOTEL (Grand Rapids) in 1984 became the first Michigan hotel ever to receive a Five Diamond Award from the American Automobile Association, which assigns the honor to a select few properties judged to provide superior service, facilities, and amenities.

2. DEARBORN TOWERS (Clearwater, Florida), an eight-story apartment building bought by the city of Dearborn in 1967 to house 200 Dearborn retirees, is believed to be the only out-of-state retirement building owned by any city in the nation.

3. THE DE ZWAAN WINDMILL (Holland, Michigan), moved some 15 years ago from the Netherlands, is the largest reconstructed windmill in the world.

4. FORT MIAMI (St. Joseph), built in November 1679 by French explorer Robert Cavalier de la Salle, was the first non-Indian post in the Lower Peninsula.

5. The HOTEL BANCROFT (Saginaw) in March 1881 featured the first incandescent electric lamps in the state.

2 OLDEST HOUSES

1. The recently discovered and restored McGulpin House on Mackinac Island, built as early as 1740, is thought to be the oldest existing structure in Michigan.

2. The oldest freestanding house that remains in private hands is the Tucker House, located along the Clinton River about 25 miles east of Detroit. Though built in 1784, it has a deceivingly 1950s appearance since the original logs were bricked over.

Michigan's first Civil War monument. (See story, page 199)

6 UNIQUE MONUMENTS AND MARKERS

1. Michigan's first Civil War monument, a simple sandstone shaft costing $1,500, was placed in the cemetery at Tipton (Lenawee County) and dedicated July 4, 1866. (See photo, page 198)

2. At the village of Three Oaks on October 17, 1899, President William McKinley dedicated a cannon captured by Admiral George Dewey during the Spanish-American War's battle of Manila. Three Oaks had won the war trophy by raising the largest per-capita contribution of any U.S. community for a memorial to the men of the *Maine*, sunk in Havana Harbor in 1898.

3. A monument at Initial Point, on the Ingham County-Jackson County boundary east of US-127, marks the point from which all land surveying in Michigan has been done since 1812.

4. On October 22, 1955, at East Lansing, the Michigan Historical Commission dedicated the first official marker in their program to register and mark state and local historic sites. The Registered Historic Site No. 1 commemorates the founding of Michigan State University, the first agriculutral college in the nation.

5. A cross standing on a 100-foot-high bluff at Cross Village (Emmet County) has overlooked Lake Michigan for 200 years.

6. The Michigan Historical Commission on February 1, 1968, presented their 2,500th "Centennial Farm" marker to Kenneth and Edna Morrow (Bridgeport Township). In 1948 the commission began the program to certify Michigan farms that have been owned by the same family for at least 100 years and through 1983, had placed 5,068 markers.

3 FIRST MEDAL-OF-HONOR WINNERS

1. OWEN HAMMERBERG (Flint), who died February 17, 1945, when he dove into Pearl Harbor to rescue two other sailors, was the first Michigan sailor ever to receive the Medal of Honor.

2. DWIGHT JOHNSON (Detroit), who killed 12 enemy soldiers while rescuing a fellow officer near Dak To, Vietnam, in 1968, is the only Michigan Congressional Medal of Honor winner from the Vietnam War.

3. ALEXANDER MACOMB (Grosse Pointe), who led a small army of volunteers to victory over 1,500 British soldiers at Plattsburg, New York, during the War of 1812, was Michigan's first Medal of Honor winner.

4 NOTABLE SOLDIERS

1. JOHN COHANSKI (Ironwood) and Adam Blazikowksi (Milwaukee, Wisconsin) captured the first German soldier taken by the U.S. Army in World War I.

2. PRIVATE ROGER CUTSINGER (Banfield) became a national celebrity in 1979 after he had become the first soldier ever to publicly admit his homosexuality and attempt to remain in the army.

But in a bizarre twist of events, Cutsinger, while fighting his discharge, moved into a Seattle apartment with another man, took out a $500,000 insurance policy on his roommate's life, then, according to later court testimony, fatally shot him. On February 22, 1980, Cutsinger was convicted of first-degree murder and sentenced to life in prison.

3. ORLANDO LEVALLEY (Caro), who died in 1948 at the age of 107, was the last surviving Civil War veteran of a Michigan unit.

4. THOMAS WILLIAMS (Detroit) in 1836 became the first Michigan resident to be appointed to West Point.

9 COMBATIVE WOMEN

1. LEE ALVERSON (East Tawas) in 1973 was one of the first two female crew members ever to fly on a navy anti-submarine mission.

2. In 1976, DONNA BUEFER and 3. MARY TUOHEY, who had graduated together from Utica Eisenhower High School, became the first Michigan female Marines to attend the U.S. Naval Academy, Annapolis, Maryland.

4. DONNA JEAN GODFREY (Redford Township) in 1974 became the first Michigan woman to join the Coast Guard.

5. In 1974, CYNTHIA R. GONYEA (Trenton), an R.O.T.C. cadet at Western Michigan University (Kalamazoo), became the first female R.O.T.C. commander on any U.S. campus.

6. JULIA KEEFER (Jackson) in 1974 became the first woman to join the Michigan National guard.

7. MATTIE V. PARKER assumed command of the Armed Forces Examining and Entrance Station at Detroit in May 1975 and became the nation's first female recruiting-station commander.

8. ROSELYN ROBERT (Menominee), a former WAC who served as a physical therapist during World War II, was elected on July 19, 1964, as the Michigan American Legion's first female vice-commander.

9. HAZEL STIMSON (Flint) responded to a pamphlet that invited her to "work side by side with the men of the Marine Corps" and on September 18, 1918, became the first Michigan woman to enlist in the Marines during World War I.

4 RECENT WOMEN OF THE YEAR

1. HELEN J. CUERCIO (Grosse Pointe Park), a legal secretary who success-

fully worked to repeal unjust labor practices shown to female municipal workers, was one of 17 women, 40 or older, named as 1983 *Wonder Women of the Year* by the Wonder Woman Foundation (New York).

2. LUELLA DAVIDSON (Sylvan Lake), who, in 1976, founded Grandparents Anonymous to fight for visitation rights for grandparents who, when their own children divorced, could not see their grandchildren, was named national *Grandparent of the Year* in 1982.

3. AGNES MARY MANSOUR (Lansing) joined Helen J. Cuercio (see number 1) as one of the Wonder Woman Foundation's 1983 *Wonder Women of the Year*. As director of the Michigan Social Services Department, which administers funds for abortion, Mansour, a nun, was ordered by the Vatican in May 1983 to resign but, instead, left her religious order, the Sisters of Mercy (Farmington Hills).

4. MARY SINCLAIR (Midland), who led the fight against a proposed Consumers Power nuclear power plant in her city (see page 269), joined Democratic vice-presidential candidate Geraldine Ferraro and Olympic marathon runner Joan Benoit as one of *Ms. Magazine's* 12 1985 *Women of the Year*. Sinclair, who because of her crusade, was, at one time, a virtual outcast in her own home town, was also profiled in the *Wall Street Journal*, appeared on television's *Today Show* and *60 Minutes*, and was named one of 10 *Michiganians of the Year* by the *Detroit News*.

6 FIRST WOMEN

1. JEANNETTE A. CHAMPLIN (Belding), who graduated from Michigan State University in 1972, became the first woman in Michigan to get a degree in construction.

2. HELEN CLAYTOR, who was elected president of the Grand Rapids Y.W.C.A. in 1949, became the first black woman in the nation to hold that office.

3. MARIE COMSTOCK (Detroit — 1900) is credited with being Michigan's first female driver.

4. In 1977, KAREN FARMER (Detroit) became the first black member of the Daughters of the American Revolution, a national group that requires its members to trace their ancestry to men or women who served in the American military or government during the Revolutionary War. Farmer joined the group after she had learned that her maternal grandmother, a white woman who had married a black man, had had an ancestor who served in the Continental Army.

5. MARY LIVINGSTONE (Livonia), during the early 1920s, became the first female member of the Detroit Symphony Orchestra's violin section.

6. MARY A. RIPLEY (Sault Ste. Marie) in 1934 became the first female postmaster of a Michigan first-class office.

2 FIRST AUTOMOBILE SALESWOMEN

1. LILLIAN REYNOLDS WAGNER (Detroit) in 1915 became Michigan's first female automobile salesperson.

2. CANDY DYKSTRA (Eaton Rapids) in 1977 became the first Michigan woman to be awarded a Ford dealership.

3 FEMALE AUTO EXECUTIVES

The only three women, as of January 1984, who had reached the level of vice president at any of the Big Three automakers.

1. BETSY ANCKER-JOHNSON

Head of the General Motors environmental activities staff.

2. HELEN PETRAUSKAS

In charge of Ford Motor Company's Environmental and Safety Engineering Department.

3. MARINA VON NEUMANN WHITMAN

General Motors' chief economist.

4 FIRST FEMALE GOVERNMENTAL APPOINTEES

1. KATHY BEZOTTE became Michigan's first female conservation officer in 1977.

2. CINDY NIEWADA (Grand Ledge) in 1972 became the first female page in state-senate history.

3. In 1983, GLORIA SMITH became the first woman, the first nurse, and the second non-physician to head the Michigan Department of Public Health.

4. JOAN L. WOLFE (Belmont) in January 1977 became the first female chairperson of the Michigan National Resources Commission. In accepting her appointment, Wolfe also became the first woman in state history to chair a major state commission and the the first woman in the country to head a resources commission.

3 HAIR RAISERS

1. BEVERLY ANN BAECKER (Milford) in October 1983 sued the manufacturer of a creme rinse she claimed had matted and tangled her hair so badly that she was forced to cut off more than five feet of the blond locks that had taken nearly 16 years to grow.

2. CINDY CHRISTIAN (East Lansing), a 28-year-old who hadn't trimmed her hair for 15 years, had, as of 1983, hair 74$^1/_2$ inches long.

3. JACKIE WALLS (Detroit)

While being advertised by the hair tonic company that employed her during the 1920s as, "the girl with the longest hair in the United States," Walls traveled the country in a custom-built green-and-pink Packard to exhibit her 7-foot, 4-inch-long hair at fairs, store openings, and parades.

3 FEMALE RHODES SCHOLARS

It took an act of English Parliament to do it, but in 1976 women were allowed to compete, for the first time, for Rhodes Scholarships, which had been awarded since 1902. Since then, three female Michigan natives have won the scholarship for study at prestigious Oxford University in England. They are:

1. DENISE THAL (Huntington Woods)

On December 18, 1976, the Harvard University senior became one of the world's first 13 women to receive a Rhodes Scholarship.

2. MOLLY BRENNAN (Waterford)

The Michigan State University student received the award in 1981.

3. DENA SKRAN (Saginaw)

The Michigan State University student received the award in 1982.

3 SPECIAL SCHOLARS

1. DAN BRESCOLL (Birmingham) — 1984

Out of 1.4 million high school students nationwide who took the National Merit Scholarship qualifying test, the 16-year-old Detroit Country Day junior was one of only 15 test takers to get a perfect score.

2. DAN LEE (Houghton) — 1982

The 12-year-old seventh grader scored a perfect 800 out of 800 points on the math component of the Scholastic Aptitude Test, a national college-aptitude exam normally taken only by high school juniors and seniors.

3. MICHIGAN STATE UNIVERSITY holds the distinction of turning out more Rhodes scholars — 10 in the last 13 years — than any other public university in the nation.

4 FIRST COLLEGE PRESIDENTS

1. JOHN MONTEITH on September 8, 1817, was named as the first president of the University of Michigania at a salary of at $25 a year. The university at

Detroit did not become a reality but was the forerunner of the University of Michigan at Ann Arbor.

2. In 1852, HENRY PHILIP TAPPAN became the first permanent president of the University of Michigan at Ann Arbor.

3. C.R. WHARTON JR, who took charge as the 14th president of Michigan State University on January 2, 1970, became the first black in the country to preside over a predominantly white major college.

4. JOSEPH R. WILLIAMS (Constantine), a prominent politican, manufacturer, and Harvard graduate, was appointed on January 14, 1857, as the first president of the Michigan Agricultural College, forerunner of Michigan State University.

2 RECORD-SETTING SERMONS

1. In a final appearance before leaving his Birmingham Unitarian church congregation, Rev. Robert Marshall on January 3, 1976, set a Guinness Book world record by preaching for 60 hours and 31 minutes.

2. On November 18, 1982, Rev. M. Gregory Gentry, pastor of the Canton Calvary Assembly of God church, preached a 97-hour sermon, breaking a Guinness Book world record by four hours.

3 ROYAL VISITORS

1. BEATRIX WILHELMINA ARMGARD, Queen of the Netherlands, visited Grand Rapids and Holland, Michigan, on June 26, 1982.

2. ALBERT EDWARD, the first British Prince of Wales ever to visit the United States, arrived at Detroit, his first stop, on September 20, 1860.

3. CARL GUSTAV, 29-year-old King of Sweden, arrived in Detroit on April 20, 1976, for a 1$^1/_2$-day visit.

9 DISTINCTIVE VISITORS

1. AMELIA BLOOMER, originator of Bloomer undergarments, lectured in Detroit's Firemen's Hall October 13, 1853, on the subject of *Women's Rights*.

2. FATHER FRANCOIS DOLLIER de CASSON and 3. FATHER RENE BREHANT de GALINEE, while paddling from Lake Erie to Sault Ste. Marie in 1670, headed their canoe toward an Indian stone idol they had spotted on the northwest shore of the Detroit River. The two Sulpician priests then became the first known white visitors to the Detroit area when they landed their canoe, demolished the idol with a consecrated axe, and, as they continued on their journey, sank the pieces in the middle of the river.

4. WINSTON CHURCHILL visited Detroit twice, once in 1901 as a 26-year-old heroic veteran of four wars and again, in 1932, as the former British First Lord of the Admirality.

5. Two SOVIET COSMONAUTS, Maj. Gen. Georgy Beregovoy and Konstantin Feoktistov, as part of a national tour, arrived in Detroit on October 30, 1969.

6. WILLIAM H. HARRISON was the first future president to visit Michigan. Harrison, as governor of the Indiana territory, first came to Detroit May 10, 1803, then visited Michigan three more times before becoming president in 1841.

7. ABRAHAM LINCOLN, then an obscure Illinois lawyer, spoke at an August 27, 1856 rally held in Kalamazoo's Bronson Park for the newly formed Republican Party. Lincoln's speech, in support of the party's presidential candidate, was his first and only Michigan appearance.

8. PRESIDENT JAMES MONROE arrived at Detroit on August 13, 1817, and the city's residents hosted a five-day celebration for the first president ever to visit Michigan while in office.

9. ALEXIS de TOCQUEVILLE, French historian and political theorist whose study of American democracy was one of the most original and influential works of the 19th century, arrived at Detroit July 20, 1831, for a three-day visit.

7 AREAS OFF LIMITS TO RUSSIANS

Seven Michigan areas designated by the United States State Department as off limits to visiting Soviets.

1. ARENAC COUNTY
2. CHARLEVOIX COUNTY
3. DETROIT
Detroit and Houston are the only two American cities with populations of more than one million that are closed to the Soviets.
4. EMMET COUNTY
5. IOSCO COUNTY
6. MACOMB COUNTY
7. MARQUETTE COUNTY

2 ORIENTAL RECOGNITIONS

1. When, during the summer of 1983, a busload of Oklahoma tourists, who had paid thousands of dollars apiece to visit a place no Americans supposedly had ever been to, pulled into a remote village in Inner Mongolia, China, they were greeted by a high-ranking local official who wore a *Say Yes to Michigan* button. The official, as it turned out, had received his button from a Michigan bicyclist, who had traveled through the area with a tour group the week before.

2. In 1970, Shiga Prefecture, Michigan's sister state in Japan, designated the third week of May as *Michigan Week* in their state and sent a 49-member delegation to Detroit to commemorate the occasion.

15 FIRST ASSOCIATIONS

1. Michigan's first BIBLE SOCIETY was organized at Detroit on November 4, 1816, by Territorial Governor Lewis Cass; future congressman and governor William Woodbridge; and Protestant missionary John Monteith. During its first year, the society, which sold Bibles and used the proceeds to distribute Bibles to those who couldn't afford them, received $146.

2. The HISTORICAL SOCIETY OF MICHIGAN organized at Mansion House in Detroit on July 3, 1828. The first president and lecturer before the society, which later became the Pioneer and Historical Society then the current Michigan Historical Commission, was territorial Governor Lewis Cass.

3. The HOUSEWIVES LEAGUE, the first organization in the country to attempt to minimize the effect of the depression on black business people, was started at Detroit on June 10, 1930, by Mrs. Fannie Peck. Later, a national housewives association formed with Mrs. Peck as its president.

4. The world's first KIWANIS was chartered at Detroit on January 21, 1915.

5. The nation's first LADIES (SOLDIERS) AID SOCIETY organized at Detroit November 6, 1861, to supply comfort to Civil War soldiers at hospitals, camps, and battlefields.

6. The LADIES LIBRARY ASSOCIATION (Kalamazoo), informally begun in 1844 as a reading club, officially organized in January 1852 as the first women's club in Michigan and only the third in the United States.

7. The LODGE OF MASONS, NO. 1, Michigan's first Masonic Lodge and the oldest west of the Alleghenies, organized at Detroit on April 27, 1764.

8. The MICHIGAN AUDOBON SOCIETY met for the first time on February 27, 1904, at Detroit.

9. The MICHIGAN STATE ARCHAEOLOGICAL SOCIETY was formed January 17, 1924.

10. The MICHIGAN STATE ASSOCIATION OF ARCHITECTS, Michigan's first architectural society and forerunner of the Michigan Chapter, American Institute of Architects, was founded October 26, 1887.

11. The MICHIGAN STATE FIREMEN'S ASSOCIATION was formed at Battle Creek on April 13, 1875.

12. The MICHIGAN STATE MEDICAL SOCIETY formed at Detroit on June 5, 1866.

13. The NATIONAL RED CROSS, MICHIGAN BRANCH was formed in Detroit on June 15, 1905, by nine Detroit citizens and one delegate from Kalamazoo. The first recorded activity of the group was the collection and donation of $65,107.87 to the victims of the great 1906 San Francisco earthquake.

14. The ORDER OF THE ODD FELLOWS, Michigan Lodge No. 1, organized at Detroit on December 4, 1843.

15. Michigan's first ROTARY CLUB formed in Detroit in 1910.

2 BICENTENNIAL AWARD-WINNERS

1. In 1974, Macomb County became the first county in the nation to have all of its government entities (12 cities, 12 townships, and three villages) officially recognized as bicentennial communities. All 27 units of government had met the official bicentennial criteria by planning historical exhibits and adopting an English town with which information and exhibits were later exchanged.

2. Michigan's red-white-and-blue bicentennial license plates were voted the best designed for 1976 by the Automobile License Plate Collectors Association.

4 SPECIAL OLYMPICS PARTICIPANTS

1. HORNER FLOORING (Dollar Bay) supplied the basketball floor used during the 1984 Summer Olympics at Los Angeles.

2. JAMES LEMSON (Grant) operated one of 17 official tow trucks during the 1980 Winter Olympics held at Lake Placid, New York.

3. In February 1985, MARQUETTE won official designation as the country's third official Olympic training site.

4. SNOW MACHINES INC. (Midland), the largest manufacturer and supplier of snowmaking equipment in America, provided 22 snowmaking machines for the 1984 Winter Olympics in Yugoslavia.

7 SPECIAL FLAG-RAISINGS

1. July 10, 1796

American troops, sent to occupy former British forts in the Northwest Territory, raised, at Monroe, the first American flag to fly over Michigan.

2. February 22, 1837

The state of Michigan's first governor, Stevens T. Mason, presented Michigan's first official state flag to the Brady Guard at Detroit.

3. July 4, 1866

General O.B. Willcox and a procession of the survivors of decimated Michigan Civil War regiments formally presented 23 battle-stained and bullet-marked flags to Governor H.H. Crapo. The flags are still on display at the state capitol.

4. April 29, 1911

The legislature adopted Michigan's current official state flag, a blue field upon which is delineated the state coat of arms.

5. November 11, 1923

The J.L. Hudson Company, as a beginning to their annual Thanksgiving Day parade, displayed for the first time a 90-by-123-foot American flag on the front of their Detroit headquarters. In 1949 the company replaced the "world's largest flag" with an even larger 235-by-104-foot stars and stripes, made from 2,038 yards of shrink-proof wool, 5,500 yards of thread, 57 yards of heavy canvas, and over a mile of rope. On June 14, 1976, Hudsons unfurled the flag for the last time before donating it to the Smithsonian Museum.

6. April 14, 1982

Michigan astronaut Col. Jack Lousma presented Governor William G. Milliken with a small United States flag he had carried on an eight-day Columbia space shuttle that flew 3.8 million miles while making 129 trips around the world.

7. April 28, 1984

Davison (Genesee County) became the first and only Michigan city to permanently fly the flags of all 50 states.
— *Item contributed by David Horton, Davison* —

14 MICHIGAN STAMPS

Fourteen stamps issued by the U.S. Post Office that have commemorated Michigan subjects.

1. May 1, 1901

An eight-cent violet and black stamp, issued at Buffalo, New York, as part of a Pan American Exposition issue, featured the canals and locks at Sault Ste. Marie.

2. November 1, 1935

Michigan's centennial stamp, a three-cent purple stamp featuring the Michigan state seal, was issued at Lansing as a first-day issue. A total of 176,962 "first-day covers" were mailed from Lansing, breaking all previous records.

3. July 24, 1951

A three-cent blue stamp, issued at Detroit, commemorated the 250th anniversary of the landing of Cadillac at the city.

4. February 12, 1955

A three-cent green stamp, issued at East Lansing, commemorated the founding of Michigan State University, the first land-grant college in the nation.

5. June 28, 1955

A three-cent blue stamp was issued at Sault Ste. Marie to mark the 100th year of the Soo locks.

6. June 25, 1958

A three-cent bright greenish blue stamp, postmarked *Mackinac Bridge, Michigan*, featured the Mackinac Bridge.

7. November 1, 1966

The nation's official Christmas stamp, a five-cent multi-colored depiction of the Madonna and child, was issued at Christmas, Michigan.

8. July 30, 1968

A 12-cent stamp, issued at Dearborn, celebrated Henry Ford's birthdate 105 years earlier.

9. September 20, 1968

Three hundred years after Father Jacques Marquette founded Michigan's first white settlement near the rapids of the St. Mary's River, a six-cent black, apple-green, and orange-brown stamp was issued at Sault Ste. Marie honoring the explorer and missionary.

10. February 15, 1976

A 13-cent stamp commemorated the 50th anniversary of the first contract air mail flight — Dearborn to Cleveland — in the U.S.

11. February 23, 1976

A 13-cent stamp, issued at Washington, D.C., featured the Michigan state flag.

12. October 18, 1978

The nation's official Christmas stamp, a child on a hobby horse, was issued at Holly, Michigan.

13. October 31, 1980

The nation's official Christmas stamp, featuring a pile of toys, was issued at Christmas, Michigan.

14. April 14, 1982

Two 20-cent stamps, one featuring the Michigan state bird (robin) and the other the state flower (apple blossom), were issued simultaneously at Lansing and Washington, D.C.

— List idea contributed by Dennis Guerriero, Harrison —

6 MICHIGAN MEDIANS

Six areas in which Michigan ranks exactly in the middle, i.e. 25th, of the 50 states.

1. Percent of population composed of Presbyterians — 2.1%.

2. Size of state legislature — 148 (110 representatives plus 38 senators).

3. Voter turnout as a percent of the voting population — 58.3%.

4. Physicians per 100,000 population — 149.

5. Juvenile drug arrests per 100,000 people — 2.7.

6. Percent of total population for which English is the mother tongue — 83.9%.

7 MICHIGAN ALMOST MEDIANS

Seven areas in which Michigan ranks almost in the middle, i.e. 23rd through 27th of the 50 states.

1. Michigan was the 26th state admitted to the union.

2. Total land area — 37.3 million acres (23rd).

3. Alcohol consumption per capita — 2.7 gallons (23rd).

4. Percent of white collar workers in the work force — 47.6% (27th).

5. Dentists per 100,000 population — 50 (26th).

6. Deaths from hypertension per 100,000 population — 2.7 (26th).

7. Average number of years of school completed per resident — 12.2 (23rd).

10
ATHLETE FEATS

9 LADIES' FIRSTS

FIRST FEMALE:

1. LITTLE LEAGUER — CAROLYN KING (Ypsilanti)

When the 12-year-old took the field May 8, 1973, as the first girl in the nation to play in the Little League, national Little League officials revoked the Ypsilanti team's charter. The city of Ypsilanti, on behalf of King, then retaliated with a sex-discrimination suit, but before the case made its way through the legal system, the U.S. Division of Civil Rights ordered the national Little League to drop its boys-only policy.

2. FOOTBALL PLAYER ON A BOYS' HIGH-SCHOOL TEAM — SHEILA GRIGSBY

The 17-year-old senior assisted on one tackle while playing on Covert High school's defensive line during her first game, an October 20, 1984 loss to Michigan Lutheran.

3. RUNNER IN A BOYS' HIGH SCHOOL TRACK MEET — SUE PARKS (Ypsilanti)

The 16-year-old finished fifth in the 880-yard run in her first competition, a May 9, 1972 dual meet.

4. TO SCORE A BASKET DURING A BOYS' HIGH SCHOOL TOURNA- MENT BASKETBALL GAME — MARY JOHNSON (Grand Marais), who sank a 28-foot shot during her team's March 1983 tournament loss to Engadine.

5. ON A MEN'S MICHIGAN COLLEGIATE SOCCER TEAM — SUE DEMARCO and SUE STONE, who made Kalamazoo College's 1975 team.

6. IN THE I-500 SNOWMOBILE RACE — DIANE MILLER (Flushing)

The eight-year veteran of snowmobile racing and Michigan's overall high-point driver in 1975 qualified 30th out of the 94 drivers who attempted to enter the February 1977 Sault Ste. Marie race but had to pull out after only 48 miles because of mechanical failure.

7. JOCKEY— MARY BACON, who in 1969 became the first female rider at the Detroit Race Course and in 1971 became the first jockette to ride a winner at Hazel Park Raceway.

8. IN THE MICHIGAN GOLF HALL OF FAME — DOTTIE HIGBIE (1984)

Higbie won the women's Michigan state amateur championship five times and the Women's District Golf Association title six times during the late 1920s and early 1930s.

9. TO COMPLETE THE NEWBERRY DOG-SLED RACE — DONNA PARKER (Flint), who in March 1978 finished the longest dog-sled race of its kind in the United States, a rugged 325-mile round trip through the pines of the Upper Peninsula.

4 GREATEST FEMALE ATHLETES

Four Michigan women included in the book, *100 Greatest Women in Sports*.

1. MAXINE "MICKI" KING (Pontiac)

1972 Olympic diving gold medalist.

2. MARION LADEWIG (Grand Rapids)

Eight-time winner of the Bowling Proprietors Association of America's All-Star tournament, including the first five from 1950; first winner of the PWBA tournament (1960); and first woman to enter the Michigan Sports Hall of Fame.

3. SUE NOVARA REBER (Flint)

World-champion bicyclist and state indoor-speedskating champion during the 1970s.

4. SHEILA YOUNG (Detroit)

The first American to win three medals in one winter Olympics (1976) and the first athlete ever to win world championships in track bicycling and speed skating in the same year (1973).

5 MICHIGAN
1984 OLYMPIC GOLD-MEDAL WINNERS

1. STEVE FRASER (Hazel Park)

The Washtenaw County sheriff's department deputy won the first gold medal in American history in Greco-Roman wrestling.

2. KARCH KIRALY (Jackson and Ann Arbor)

Captained the American men's volleyball team.

3. STEVE MCCRORY (Detroit)

Won the flyweight boxing championship.

4. PAM MCGEE (Flint)

American women's basketball team starter.

5. FRANK TATE (Detroit)

Won the light-middleweight boxing championship.

4 MICHIGAN
1984 OLYMPIC SILVER-MEDAL WINNERS

1. JUDI BROWN (East Lansing)

Finished second in the women's 400-meter hurdles.

2. LORI FLACHMEIER (Detroit)

The Michigan native, who grew up in Texas, was on the American women's volleyball team which made it to the finals against China.

3. DAVE GRYLLS (Grosse Pointe)

As the 4,000-meter team-pursuit cycling race began, the toe strap on Grylls' pedal snapped, leaving him at the starting line, but his three teammates managed to finish in second place without him.

4. BRUCE KIMBALL (Ann Arbor)

Won the silver medal in platform diving with his final dive.

9 MICHIGAN
1984 OLYMPIC BRONZE-MEDAL WINNERS

1. GREG BARTON (Homer)

Won the first medal in history by an American man in Olympic kayak racing.

2. BRIAN DIEMER (Grand Rapids)

Won his medal in the 3,000-meter steeplechase.

3. BOB ESPESETH (Grand Blanc)

Member of the American rowing team.

4. DOUG HERLAND

The Oregon native, who moved to Ann Arbor to be rowing coach at the University of Michigan, won a bronze medal as the coxwain in the pairs-with-coxwain event.

213

5. EARL JONES (Inkster)

Earned his medal in the men's 800-meter run.

6. RON MERRIOTT

The University of Michigan student won a bronze in springboard diving competition.

7. KIM TURNER (Detroit)

Won her medal in the 100-meter hurdles in a photo finish.

8. CHRIS SEUFERT (Chelsea)

Springboard diving.

9. WENDY WYLAND (Jackson)

Women's platform diving.

5 RECORD RUNS

1. Scott Welland (Union Lake) ran the entire 26.2 miles of the 1982 Detroit Free Press Marathon backwards and went into the Guinness *Book of World Records* as the first to accomplish the feat.

2. The annual Detroit Press Marathon is the world's only marathon that takes runners underwater (through the Windsor Tunnel).

3. The annual Emily-Midas 6.2-mile run through downtown Detroit is Michigan's largest and the nation's fifth-largest foot race, attracting more than 20,000 runners each year.

4. Jim Ryun ran professional track's first sub-four-minute mile at Cobo Hall (Detroit) during an April 1973 meet of the short-lived International Track Association.

5. The National Collegiate Athletic Association (NCAA) held its first-ever indoor track-and-field championship meet at Cobo Hall (Detroit) on March 12, 1965.

7 MARATHON WALKS

1. Ginny Broersma (Grand Rapids), a 47-year-old housewife, hiked 2,700 miles from Grand Rapids to San Francisco, California, in 1983 to raise $100,000 for a hunger-relief program.

2. After a two-year unsuccessful job hunt in several southern states, 34-year-old Harold Bedell (Gaines Township) in February 1983 put all of his belongings and his dog into a shopping cart at St. Petersburg, Florida, and pushed them 1,100 miles back to Michigan.

3. U.S. Senate candidate William S. Ballenger III (Lansing) tied his 1982 primary election hopes to a 1,037-mile campaign walk from Sault Ste. Marie to Detroit. The 41-year-old Republican hopeful, who began his hike on January 18 in 17-degree-below-zero weather and finished August 6 in 83-degree weather, finished second in a four-man contest but lost to the front-runner, Philip E. Ruppe, by more than 130,000 votes.

4. After receiving word that his supply-ship *Griffin* had disappeared, French-explorer Robert Cavalier de la Salle in 1680 hiked 1,000 miles from Illinois across Michigan to Fort Frontenac at the eastern end of Lake Ontario. At one point on the journey, the first by a white man across the interior of the Lower Peninsula, LaSalle had to set prairie grass on fire to hinder hostile Indians who were following his party.

5. Barbara Fisher (Byron) walked the length of the Lower Peninsula and the breadth of the Upper Peninsula. The 42-year-old educator began the more than 600-mile trek September 1983 at Adrian and, hiking only on weekends and during vacations, ended in July 1984 at Copper Harbor.

6. In 1982, Dave Krupa (Flint) hiked the entire upper-peninsula shoreline of Lake Superior. The 26-year-old began the 600-mile solo walk July 4 from the Wisconsin/Michigan border and finished August 31 at Sault Ste. Marie.

7. In October 1963, 64-year-old Marion Pearson (Grand Rapids) hiked 385 miles from Sault Ste. Marie to Sylvania, Ohio, to dramatize the growth of the Mackinac Trail from a footpath to what was then the nation's longest toll-free expressway, a border-to-border route composed of I-75, US-23, US-10, and US-27.

4 UNUSUAL VOYAGES

1. David Rude (Muskegon) crossed Lake Michigan while suspended from a 14-by-16-foot kite towed by a 17-foot boat with a 200-horsepower engine. The 18-year-old completed the July 16, 1964, 81-mile journey from Grand Haven to Milwaukee, Wisconsin, in three and one half hours.

2. On August 16, 1982, 24-year-old Dave Braddock (Sawyer) left Sawyer on a 12-foot sailboard and, six and a half hours and 58-miles later, completed, at Milwaukee, the first known solo sailboard crossing of Lake Michigan.

3. During the Michigan territorial period, Pierre Godfroy, a descendant of the French at Detroit, reportedly bet a fellow settler that he could cross the Detroit River in a wooden wheelbarrow. Godfrey then grabbed a canoe paddle and successfully floated and paddled the wheelbarrow to a visit with his girlfriend at Windsor.

4. On July 19, 1976, three Belleville college students ended an 800-mile trip down the east coast in an 18-foot replica of a Viking ship by sailing around the Statue of Liberty.

2 REMARKABLE CANOE TRIPS

1. In December 1983, Verlen Kruger (Lansing) and Steven Landick (Lansing) completed the world's longest canoe trip, a three-and-one-half-year 28,043-mile voyage that took the pair through 44 states, Canada, part of Mexico, all five Great Lakes, and three oceans.

2. During the summer of 1984, John Buckley (Mt. Pleasant) became the first person to paddle a canoe alone across all five Great Lakes. On June 25, the 42-year-old canoe-livery owner launched his partially covered 17-foot canoe at Milwaukee and, over the next three weeks, made the following crossings: Lake Michigan — Milwaukee to Muskegon, 85 miles in 23 hours; Lake Superior — Houghton to Thunder Bay, Ontario, 77 miles in $19^{1}/_{2}$ hours; Lake Huron — Harbor Beach to Goderich, Ontario, 55 miles in $11^{1}/_{2}$ hours; Lake Erie — Point Pelee, Ontario, to Lorain, Ohio, 45 miles in 11 hours; and Lake Ontario — St. Catharines, Ontario, to Toronto, Ontario, 35 miles in eight hours.

4 FANTASTIC FEATS

1. Two "human flies," using special gripping devices, scaled the outside of the 73-story Westin Hotel at Detroit's Renaissance Center on July 4, 1983 . At the conclusion of the $6^{1}/_{2}$-hour climb, police arrested Kenneth Rick (Lake Orion) and Ronald Broyles (Los Angeles, California) for trespassing and disorderly conduct.

One year earlier, 32-year-old Rick had scaled the RenCen's 39-story 300 Tower and, on another occasion, had parachuted from the catwalk on the Ambassador Bridge into the Detroit River.

2. Kirt Barnes, skating at Ann Arbor's Fuller Ice Skating Rink on February 26, 1971, covered 100 miles in five hours, 34 minutes, 1.45 seconds, making him the first ice skater in the world to cover that marathon distance in less than six hours.

3. Jim Brandenburg (Mount Clemens), a 52-year-old family counselor, spent seven days in July 1982 running from Detroit 305 miles on back roads though small communities to Mackinaw City as a charity fund-raiser.

4. At the Olympic Stadium track at Montreal in March 1985, 19-year-old Mike Secrest (Flint) set a world record for the most distance pedaled on a bicycle in a 24-hour period — 516 miles, 419 yards — breaking the old record by more than 14 miles.

5 UNUSUAL SPORTING EVENTS

1. BULLFIGHTING (Detroit) — September 23, 1978

Four thousand spectators at Cobo Hall watched what was billed as the Midwest's first bloodless bullfight, an event in which matadors did not torment bulls with lances or darts and, instead of killing the animals, placed a single red rose between the animals' horns as a sign of victory.

2. SLINGSHOOTING

The Multi-Lakes Conservation Association (Oakland County) was the only place in the country, as of 1983, with organized slingshooting leagues. There, about 100 participants, using wooden or metal slingshots with surgical rubber tubing or flat rubber strips, compete by shooting half-inch ball bearings at paper targets for accuracy and velocity.

3. SPEEDBALL

Genesee County, as of 1982, had the only high school speedball league in the nation, with seven teams playing the game, which combines elements of football, soccer, and basketball.

4. TOUGHMAN CONTESTS

In 1980-81 a Bay City entrepeneur gained national attention by staging *Toughman* contests, amateur elimination matches which featured adult males weighing betweeen 175 and 400 pounds wildly flailing away at each other for prizes up to $50,000. The Toughman tourneys were short lived, however, and effectively ended in 1981 when a Lansing contestant suffered serious injuries, prompting the state Athletic Board of Control to pass strict rules governing the events.

5. TUG-A-WAR

As part of the area's annual Historic Festival activities, a rope several miles long is stretched across Little Traverse Bay, and the world's longest tug-a-war is then held between Stafford's Bay View Inn (Petoskey) and Harbor Inn (Harbor Springs).

3 SPECIAL SKI JUMPS

1. Crowds of spectators gathered at Ishpeming on February 25, 1888, to watch professional jumpers compete for cash prizes as Michigan's first ski club sponsored its first public ski-jumping meet.

2. On February 27, 1970, Ironwood hosted the Western Hemisphere's first tournament for ski "flyers," who jump more than 500 feet through the air, nearly 200 feet more than the best ski "jumpers."

3. The largest man-made ski jump in the western world sits atop 364-foot Copper Peak, northeast of Ironwood. The 469-foot-long slide juts 241 feet above the peak's summit and is designed to permit leaps of 500 feet and more.

4 SPEEDBOAT RACES

Michigan is the current capital of offshore boat racing with four of the

American Power Boat Association's 10 championship races being held in the state. Those races are:

1. THE STROH'S THUNDERFEST, held on the Detroit River, is the oldest continuous race on the offshore championship circuit.

2. THE DOWNRIVER CHAMPIONSHIP (Wyandotte)

3. THE CORAL GABLES RACE (Saugatuck)

4. An unnamed race held at the head of Grand Traverse Bay at Northport.

2 HORSE-RACING RECORDS

1. Shiaway Moses, a sleek nine-year-old trotter owned by a South Haven family, holds a world record that U.S. Trotting Association officials say may never be broken — 117 consecutive race losses, as of January 1985.

2. On a sunny and mild 1965 Memorial Day, 28,726 people — the largest recorded audience ever to view a horse race in Michigan — squeezed into the Hazel Park Race Course.

2 DISTINCTIVE HORSE-RACING WINNERS

1. BRIAN RUNNING (Lapeer), at age 17 in 1978, became the youngest person in the state to win a race at a Michigan parimutuel track (Hazel Park).

2. THUMBSUCKER (Detroit)

On June 18, 1983, the four-year-old became the first Michigan-bred horse to win the state's richest and most prestigious horserace, the Detroit Race Course's 35-year-old "Michigan Mile."

3 WINNING DRIVERS

1. SHIRLEY MULDOWNEY (Mount Clemens)

The 43-year-old grandmother: (1) in 1976 became the first woman to win an NHRA drag championship; (2) had, as of 1983, reigned as the National Hot Rod Association's (NHRA) World Champion a record three times; and (3) in 1982 led the voting for the 1982 All-American Racing Team.

2. JAY SPRINGSTEEN (Lapeer) had, as of June 1984, won 38 national dirt track motorcycle racing championships, seven more than any other rider in history. The 25-year-old also had recorded the most one-mile dirt-track wins and the most half-mile triumphs since the American Motorcycle Association began keeping records.

3. GORDON JOHNCOCK (Hastings and Coldwater), who won the Indianapo-

lis 500 in 1973 and 1982, is the only Michigan-born Indy-500 winner. John-cock, who won the 1976 national driving championship, is also the only driver to win both the Indy and Michigan 500s.

— Item contributed by Jan Shaffer, Public Relations Director, MIS Speedway, Brooklyn —

4 NATIONAL SOAPBOX-DERBY WINNERS

1. THOMAS D. FISHER (Detroit)	1940
2. GREG CARDINAL (Flint)	1979
3. RUSSELL YORK (Flint)	1979
4. MICHAEL BURDGICK (Flint)	1983

— List contributed by Todd Benson, Fenton —

5 MOST POPULAR
HIGH SCHOOL BOYS SPORTS

Five boys sports sponsored by the Michigan High School Athletic Association with the most participating schools, as of the 1983-84 school year.

1. BASKETBALL	702
2. TRACK	652
3. BASEBALL	635
4. FOOTBALL	634
5. CROSS COUNTRY	489

5 LEADING HIGH SCHOOL GIRLS SPORTS

Five girls sports sponsored by the Michigan High School Athletic Association with the most participating schools, as of the 1983-84 school year.

1. BASKETBALL	697
2. TRACK	642
3. SOFTBALL	617
4. VOLLEYBALL	607
5. CROSS COUNTRY	396

12 NATIONAL HIGH SCHOOL RECORD HOLDERS

As listed in the National Federation of State High School Association's official *National High School Sports Record Book, 1984*.

1. KEN BEARDSLEE (Vermontville)

Highest per-game career baseball strikeout record — 452 strikeouts in 25 games for an 18.1 per game average (1947-49).

2. JEFF BOWMAN (Clinton)

Most baseball grand slams in consecutive at bats — 2, set during a game against Napoleon on April 25, 1983.

3. KELLY FISHER (New Lothrop)

Most runs scored during a softball career — 151 (1979-82) and most stolen bases during a season — 71 (1982).

4. GROSSE POINTE UNIVERSITY LIGGETT

Most consecutive state boys tennis championshps — 1972-83.

5. AMY HUME (Chelsea)

Most RBIs during a softball season — 71 (1981 and 1982).

6. LIVONIA LADYWOOD

Most rebounds in a girls basketball season — 1,653 (1980-81); most rebounds per game, season average — 68.9 (1980-81); and most rebounds, one team/one game — 116 vs. Riverview Gabriel Richard on October 4, 1979.

7. KIM TURNER (Detroit Mumford)

110-yard low hurdles — 13.6 (1979).

8. AMY UNTERBRINK (Chelsea)

Most softball strikeouts during a season — 262 (1982).

9. DELISA WALTON (Detroit McKenzie)

880 yard run — 2:07.7 (1978).

10. CARRIE WENDLNG (New Lothrop)

Most softball hits, season — 52 (1982).

11. LAURIE WENDLING (New Lothrop)

Most career softball hits — 128 (1979-82) and most career RBIs — 122 (1979-82).

12. BRENDA YACKLIN (New Lothrop)

Most triples during a softball season — 10 (1983).

3 DISTINCTIVE COLLEGE CHAMPIONS

1. ALMA COLLEGE, one of the smallest schools in the Michigan Intercollegiate Athletic Association (MIAA), has won more league football championships, 21, than any other school in its conference.

2. MICHIGAN STATE UNIVERSITY beat Indiana State 75-64 on March 26, 1979, and became the first Michigan college to win the NCAA Division I

basketball championship. State has also won more NCAA cross country team titles, eight, than any other college in the nation.

3. THE UNIVERSITY OF MICHIGAN hockey team has won more NCAA tournaments, seven, than any other college in the country. Michigan has also appeared in that tournament more times (13) than any other school except Boston University (also 13).

4 WINNING COLLEGE COACHES

1. ISTVAN DANOSI, Wayne State University's head fencing coach from 1957 to 1982, recorded more victories, 238, than any other coach in the history of college fencing.

2. JOHN MACINNES, while coaching Michigan Tech's hockey team from 1956 to 1982, won 555 games, more than any other coach in college-hockey history.

3. BENNIE OOSTERMAN in 1948 became the first and only first-year college football coach to lead his team, the University of Michigan, to an undefeated season and a national championship.

4. BO SCHEMBECHLER in 1983 became only the third football coach, following Woody Hayes, Ohio State (152) and Amos Alonzo Stagg, University of Chicago (113), to win more than 100 Big Ten games.

3 CONSPICUOUS PROFESSIONAL ATHLETES

1. THOMMIE BERGMAN

The 24-year-old defenseman was the first European hockey player ever signed by the Detroit Wings. Bergman came to Detroit from the Swedish National Team in 1972 and played 246 games for the Wings over five seasons.

2. BOB LANIER

The former Detroit Piston, who wears a size-22 shoe, holds the NBA record for largest feet.

3. TOM OWENS

When the Indiana Pacers traded Owens to the Detroit Pistons in September 1982, it was his tenth change of uniforms, an unofficial pro-basketball record.

4 PROFESSIONAL WINNING STREAKS

Club-record winning streaks for Michigan's four major professional teams.

1. The LIONS won 10 straight in 1934 and again from November 7, 1953, to October 16, 1954.

2. The PISTONS won nine straight from October 14 to October 28, 1970.

3. The RED WINGS didn't lose for 15 straight games, including nine regular season games and six playoff games, from February 27 to April 5, 1955.

4. The TIGERS won 14 straight in 1909 and again in 1934.

7 MEMORABLE SUSPENSIONS

1. May 15, 1912

The American League suspended Tiger star Ty Cobb, who had assaulted a heckling New York fan. Three days later, in support of their teammate, the rest of the Tigers refused to play but, faced with a $100-per-day fine and at the request of Cobb, ended baseball's first strike after missing one game and forcing the rescheduling of another. Cobb returned to play May 26.

2. April 17, 1963

The National Football League suspended Detroit Lion tackle Alex Karras and Green Bay's Paul Hornung for betting on NFL games and associating with gamblers. The league also fined five other Detroit players $2,000 each. Karras was reinstated eleven months later.

3. February 8, 1966

For the first time in their history, the Detroit Lions suspended a player. Coach Harry Gilmer suspended veteran end Gail Cogdill indefinitely for making detrimental remarks about the team and coaches during an off-season personal public appearance. In August, Cogdill returned with the rest of the team to the Lions' pre-season training camp.

4. February 19, 1970

Baseball Commissioner Bowie Kuhn suspended Detroit Tiger pitcher Denny McLain indefinitely for his involvement with bookmakers. McLain, the first major-league ball player suspended since 1924, was permitted to join the Tigers the following July, but on August 28, Tiger management suspended the Cy Young award-winner for dousing a sportswriter with water. Two weeks later, Commissioner Kuhn again suspended McLain, this time for carrying a gun, and on October 9, the Tigers traded their former star to the Washington Senators.

McLain spent three more unspectacular years as a player then quit. In 1985, McLain's long tumble from baseball's summit ended when he was sentenced to 23 years in prison for cocaine possession, racketeering, conspiracy, and extortion.

5. August 31, 1973

American League President Joe Cronin suspended Billy Martin for three days after the Detroit Tiger manager had ordered his pitchers to throw illegal "spitballs" then told newsmen about it. Two days later, the Tigers fired Martin.

6. January 25, 1976

    The National Collegiate Athletic Association (NCAA) placed the Michigan State University football program on probation for three years and also banned the team from appearing on any televised games or participating in post-season play during that period. The sanctions resulted from an investigation into 70 alleged recruiting violations involving the MSU football coaching staff.

7. November 4, 1976

    Detroit Red Wing defenseman Bryan "Bugsy" Watson, who had fractured the jaw of Chicago's Keith Magnuson in a hockey brawl during a late-October game, was suspended by NHL President Clarence Campbell for 10 games, the longest suspension ever incurred by a Red Wing. Less than a month later, the Wings traded Watson to Washington.

3 RETIRED NUMBERS

    Michillaneous in 1982 listed the only three athletes from Michigan professional sports teams — Larry Aurie, Gordie Howe, and Al Kaline — who had had their numbers officially retired. Since then, three more athletes have had their numbers retired. They are:

1. DAVE BING, #21, became the first Detroit Piston to have his number retired (March 18, 1983).

2. CHARLIE GEHRINGER — #2, Detroit Tigers (June 12, 1983)

3. HANK GREENBERG — #5, Detroit Tigers (June 12, 1983)

6 RECENTLY DEFUNCT PROFESSIONAL SPORTS TEAMS

1. THE DETROIT COUGARS of the North American Soccer League disbanded in September 1968 after only six months in operation.

2. THE DETROIT LOVES, one of 16 teams in a women's professional World Team Tennis League, moved to Indianapolis, Indiana, in November 1974 after five months of financial difficulties and lack of interest.

3. DETROIT WHEELS

    Thirty-four people paid $50,000 each to be owners of the Detroit entry into the World Football League, formed in 1974 to rival the National Football League. The Wheels, after asking their players to live in tents during tryouts and training camp, began their season with 10 straight losses. During that time, the team once had to call off practice because it couldn't afford to pay a laundry bill and also ran out of tape to patch up players.

    The Wheels situation got so desperate that the league assessed the other 11 teams $50,000 each so that Detroit could pay its players. But instead of meeting their payroll, the Wheels used the money to pay tax bills then declared bankruptcy. On October 11, 1974, the World Football League cut the Detroit Wheels from the remainder of its schedule.

4. THE LITTLE CAESARS softball team, which included former Detroit Tigers Mickey Stanley, Jim Northrup, and Norm Cash, played in a 12-team Professional Slow Pitch Softball League during the late 1970s.

5. In July 1983, THE MICHIGAN PANTHERS won the newly created United States Football League's first championship. The Panthers played a mediocre second season then in November 1984 left Michigan to merge with the Oakland Invaders.

6. THE MICHIGAN STAGS, formerly the World Hockey Association Los Angeles Sharks, came to Detroit in 1974. By February 1975, the Stags, mired in last place, plagued by poor attendance, and $250,000 in debt, were taken over by the league and moved to Baltimore, where they finished out the season then folded.

4 PROFESSIONAL ARRIVALS

1. THE DETROIT TIGERS

The Detroit Baseball Company, forerunner of the Detroit Tigers, was organized on November 29, 1880, played in the National League from 1881 to 1888, then on November 23, 1893, joined the Western Baseball League, which later changed its name to the American League.

2. THE DETROIT RED WINGS

On September 25, 1926, a group of Detroit businessmen purchased an NHL franchise and imported the Victoria Cougars of the Western Canada League to represent the Motor City. The team later changed its name to Falcons, then Red Wings.

3. THE DETROIT LIONS

On June 30, 1934, G.A. Richards, owner of Detroit radio station WJR, purchased a Portsmouth, Ohio football franchise for $15,000, moved the team to Detroit, and renamed them the Lions.

4. THE DETROIT PISTONS

In 1957, Fred Zollner, an Indiana piston manufacturer, moved his NBA basketball team from Fort Wayne to Detroit.

6 STADIUM CAPACITIES

1. UNIVERSITY OF MICHIGAN
   FOOTBALL STADIUM   101,701

2. PONTIAC SILVERDOME (football)	80,638
3. MICHIGAN STATE UNIVERSITY FOOTBALL STADIUM	76,000
4. TIGER STADIUM	52,687
5. PONTIAC SILVERDOME (basketball)	22,366
6. JOE LOUIS ARENA	19,275

2 TOP NHL CROWDS

As of December 1, 1983, the two largest crowds ever to watch National Hockey League games have been at the Joe Louis Arena (Detroit).

1. 21,019

Detroit Red Wings vs. Pittsburgh, November 25, 1983

2. 21,002

NHL All Star Game, January 17, 1982

4 BEST RED WINGS SEASONS

Based on season point totals.

1. 1950-51

101 points (44 wins, 13 losses , 13 ties)

2. 1951-52

100 points (44 wins, 14 losses, 12 ties)

3. 1954-55

95 points (42 wins, 17 losses, 11 ties)

4. 1969-70

95 points (40 wins, 21 losses, 15 ties)

5 SPECIAL RED WING GAMES

1. November 18, 1926

The Wings, then called the Cougars, played their first National Hockey League game, losing to the Boston Bruins 2-0. Construction of Olympia Stadium had just begun, so the team played all home games of their first season at Border Cities Arena, Windsor.

2. November 22, 1927

The Cougars lost to the Ottawa Senators 2-1 in the first National Hockey League game played at their new rink, Olympia Stadium.

3. April 11, 1936

   The Red Wings defeated Toronto 3-2 to win their first National Hockey League Stanley Cup.

4. December 16, 1979

   The Wings tied Quebec 4-4 in their final National Hockey League game at Olympia Stadium. The Wings had treated fans to 11 regular-season championships and seven Stanley Cups during their 52 years on Olympia's ice.

5. December 27, 1979

   The Wings lost to St. Louis 3-2 in their first game at Joe Louis Arena.

2 IMPORTANT RED WING COURT CASES

1. Under National Hockey League free-agency rules, an arbitrator in 1978 awarded Detroit Red Wing center Dale McCourt to the Los Angeles Kings as compensation for the Wings' signing of former Kings' goalie Rogie Vachon.

   McCourt, however, refused to report to his new team and appealed his case through the judicial system to the U.S. Supreme Court. But before the Supreme Court heard the case, the Kings and Wings negotiated a settlement, and McCourt stayed with Detroit until 1981 when he was traded to Buffalo.

2. In the first civil case of its kind involving National Hockey League players, a Detroit federal jury in 1982 awarded Detroit Red Wing Dennis Polonich $850,000 in damages for facial injuries he suffered during a 1978 game when, according to the suit and several witnesses, Wilf Paiement of the Colorado Rockies hit him with his stick in a baseball-bat-type swing.

6 NHL RECORDS HELD BY THE RED WINGS

1. Longest winning streak including playoffs

   15 games, 1955.

2. Most consecutive goals in one game

   The Wings scored 15 unanswered goals in a January 23, 1944, 15-0 win over the New York Rangers at Olympia Stadium.

3. Fewest ties in one season (minimum 70 game schedule)

   4 (1966-67).

4. Most penalties, both teams, one game

   In a March 31, 1976 game played at Detroit between the Wings and the Toronto Maple Leafs, referee Lloyd Gilmour handed out a record 48 penalties to both teams, most of them during a second-period bench-clearing brawl.

5. Most goals, both teams, one period

Toronto scored six times and Detroit four during the third period of a March 17, 1946 game.

6. Fastest five goals, both teams

Toronto scored twice and Detroit three times in only one minute, 39 seconds of the third period of a November 15, 1944 game.

5 PLAYOFF RECORDS
HELD BY THE RED WINGS

1. Longest playoff overtime — 116:30 (March 24-25, 1936)

Detroit beat the Montreal Maroons 1-0 and went on to win not only the semifinal series, but also their first Stanley Cup.

2. Fastest two play-off goals — 5 seconds (April 11, 1965)

Both scored by Norm Ullman.

3. Fewest goals, both teams in a seven-game series — 18 (1945)

Toronto and Detroit each scored only nine goals in the final series won by Toronto 4 games to 3.

4. Most power play goals, both teams one game — 6, (March 23, 1939)

Detroit scored four and Montreal two.

5. Most shorthanded goals, both teams, one game — 3 (April 5, 1947)

Toronto had two and Detroit one.

3 PISTON SINGLE-GAME CLUB RECORDS

1. Points — 56

Kelly Tripucka, (January 29, 1983)

2. Rebounds — 33

Bob Lanier (December 22, 1972)

3. Assists — 25

Kevin Porter (March 9, and April 1, 1979) and Isiah Thomas (February 13, 1985)

3 PISTON SINGLE-SEASON CLUB RECORDS

1. Points — 2,213
   Dave Bing (1970-71)

2. Assists — 1,123
   Isiah Thomas (1984-85)

3. Rebounds — 1,205
   Bob Lanier (1972-73)

3 PISTON CAREER CLUB RECORDS

1. Points — 15,488
   Bob Lanier (1970-1980)

2. Assists — 4,330
   Dave Bing (1966-75)

3. Rebounds — 8,033
   Bob Lanier (1970-80)

2 PISTON NBA SCORING CHAMPIONS

1. GEORGE YARDLEY
   2,001, 27.8 per game average (1957-58)

2. DAVE BING
   2,142, 27.1 per game average (1967-68)

2 AWARD-WINNING PISTONS

1. DAVE BING
   Rookie of the year (1966-67)

2. RAY SCOTT
   Coach of the year (1973-74)

3 LARGEST PISTON CROWDS

1. 43,816 (An all-time NBA record crowd, February 16, 1985)

2. 35,407 (March 31, 1984)

3. 35,364 (February 11, 1984)

2 UNIQUE PISTON GAMES

1. The Pistons and the Denver Nuggets played the highest-scoring game in NBA history, a December 13, 1983 contest at Denver, which Detroit won in triple overtime 186-184.

2. When the Pistons beat the New York Nicks 129-115 at the Silverdome on October 18, 1979, it marked the first time in NBA history that teams composed entirely of black players competed against each other in a regular season game.

5 MEMORABLE MOMENTS
From Michigan vs. Michigan State basketball series

1. In 1909, Michigan State, then known as the Michigan Agricultural College, won the first two games in the rivalry by scores of 24-16 and 45-25.

2. In MSU's first gym, the backboards were attached to brick walls and the overhead beams were so low that players on both sides often looped shots over the girders.

3. In a 1923 game, Michigan made only nine of 69 field goal attempts but won 24-19.

4. Michigan holds the longest winning streak in the series, 11 games from 1921 to 1928.

5. On February 2, 1963, Michigan cleared the boards of an incredible 77 rebounds against State.

5 TOP-SCORING
HIGH SCHOOL BASKETBALL PLAYERS

Figures represent career totals and year of graduation.

1. JAY SMITH (Mio)   2,844 (1979)
2. RICHIE JORDAN (Fennville)   2,208 (1966)
3. RICK BAILLERGEON (Maple City Glen Lake)   2,144 (1977)
4. DOM JOCABETTI (Negaunee St. Paul)   2,140 (1965)
5. JIM MANNING (Ewen-Trout Creek)   2,137 (1961)

5 *MR. BASKETBALLS*

The five best male high school basketball players, selected annually since 1981 by the Basketball Coaches Association of Michigan.

1. SAM VINCENT (Lansing Eastern)   1981
2. ROBERT HENDERSON (Lansing Eastern)   1982
3. ANTOINE JOUBERT (Detroit Southwestern)   1983
4. DEMETREUS GORE (Detroit Chadsey)   1984
5. GLEN RICE (Flint Northwestern)   1985

3 *MISS BASKETBALLS*

Michigan's three best female high school basketball players, selected annually since 1982 by members of the Basketball Coaches Association of Michigan.

1. JULIE POLAKOWSKI (Leland)   1982
2. SUE TUCKER (Okemos)   1983
3. MICHELE KRUTY (Manistee)   1984

3 HIGH SCHOOL FOOTBALL PLAYOFF MILESTONES

1. Pontiac beat Plainwell 6-5 at Ann Arbor on November 23, 1899, in the first high school championship football game ever played in Michigan. No formal playoff setup had been developed or established, so both teams, as the only unbeaten teams in the state, had simply agreed to meet to determine the unofficial state championship.

2. On November 22, 1975, Livonia Franklin (Class A), Dearborn Divine Child (Class B), Ishpeming (Class C), and Crystal Falls (Class D) won the first official MHSAA-sponsored state high school football championship games ever played.

3. Escanaba, which lost 32-7 to Detroit Catholic Central in the 1979 Class A championship game, was the first upper-peninsula Class A team to play in the MHSAA football playoffs.

19 BIG TEN FOOTBALL CHAMPIONSHIPS

1.-15. THE UNIVERSITY OF MICHIGAN won solo championships in 1947, 1948, 1950, 1964, 1971, 1980, and 1982 and was co-champion in 1943, 1949, 1969, 1972, 1973, 1974, 1977, and 1978.

16.-19. MICHIGAN STATE UNIVERSITY won outright championships in 1965 and 1966 and tied for the championship in 1953 and 1978.

230

7 ROSE-BOWL-WINNING YEARS

1. 1902 — Michigan (49) vs. Stanford (0)
2. 1948 — Michigan (49) vs. Southern California (0)
3. 1951 — Michigan (14) vs. California (6)
4. 1954 — Michigan State (28) vs. UCLA (20)
5. 1956 — Michigan State (17) vs. UCLA (14)
6. 1965 — Michigan (34) vs. Oregon State (7)
7. 1981 — Michigan (23) vs. Washington (6)

7 ROSE-BOWL-LOSING YEARS

1. 1966 — Michigan State (12) vs. UCLA (14)
2. 1970 — Michigan (3) vs. Southern California (10)
3. 1972 — Michigan (12) vs. Stanford (13)
4. 1977 — Michigan (6) vs. Southern California (14)
5. 1978 — Michigan (20) vs. Washington (27)
6. 1979 — Michigian (10) vs. Southern California (17)
7. 1983 — Michigan (14) vs. UCLA (24)

3 COLLEGE-FOOTBALL STREAKS

1. EASTERN MICHIGAN UNIVERSITY holds the national record for consecutive games lost, 27, from September 13, 1980, to November 6, 1982.

2. MICHIGAN STATE UNIVERSITY'S longest winning streak is 28 games, 1950-53.

3. THE UNIVERSITY OF MICHIGAN'S longest winning streak is 29 games, 1901-03.

5 UNIQUE COLLEGE FOOTBALL GAMES

1. September 14, 1974

The University of Michigan used pompon girls at a football game for the first time in the school's history. Only two years before, when women were allowed to join the band, had the school broken the 94-year monopoly held by men on all on-the-field activites.

2. January 1, 1982

The University of Michigan trounced UCLA 33-14 in the Blue Bonnet Bowl at the Houston Astrodome, one of the nation's first enclosed stadiums. The game was the first the Michigan squad had ever played in Texas and the first they had ever played indoors.

3. September 18, 1982

Clusters of portable 6000-watt 150-foot lights, developed by an Iowa-based firm, illuminated Notre Dame Stadium as Notre Dame beat Michigan 23-17 in the first major sporting event ever lit by such a traveling light show.

4. December 22, 1984

Michigan State lost to Army 10-6 in the first post-season bowl game ever played in Michigan, the Cherry Bowl held at the Pontiac Silverdome.

5. 1985

Alma College was chosen to represent the United States in the first Arctic Bowl, an overseas competition scheduled for June 1985 that matches the 40-player Alma squad against two Finnish All-Star teams.

3 UNIQUE MEDIA COVERAGES
OF COLLEGE FOOTBALL GAMES

1. RUSSIANS SCORE UM FOOTBALL

"Wall Street encourages bloodthirsty football games . . . to work up a war-like mood in the U.S.," charged Moscow radio in an August 10, 1950 radio broadcast that also said that players in Michigan football games, "are often carried from the field to the hospital . . . or cemetery."

The next day, the Voice of America offered a season pass to University of Michigan games to any Soviet correspondent who wanted to see whether "flowers and wreaths (really) are in order there."

2. PRESSED IN

An historic November 19, 1966 showdown at Spartan Stadium for the nation's number-one ranking between the undefeated Michigan State University and Notre Dame football teams attracted what is believed to be a record media turnout — 745. The teams tied 10-10, but Notre Dame was ranked national champion at the season's end.

3. NO NUMBER — NO GLORY

An October 1910 *Michigan Daily* editorial strongly requested that University of Michigan football players be identified during future games by sewing numbers on their jerseys. But Coach Fielding H. Yost vetoed the idea, saying he feared it would interfere with teamwork by singling out the efforts of individuals, and University of Michigan players were not assigned numbers until the 1916 season.

3 DISTINCTIVE COLLEGE
FOOTBALL PLAYERS

1. TOM HARMON is the only player from a Michigan college ever to win the

Heisman trophy, an award presented annually since 1935 to the nation's outstanding college football player. Harmon, who won the award in 1940, averaged nearly six yards per carry during his three years at the University of Michigan and also led the nation in passing and rushing in 1939-40.

2. DENNIS FRANKLIN, who started at quarterback for the University of Michigan from 1972 to 1975, was the first black quarterback in the team's history.

3. JESSE LAKES

In October 1971 the Flint native and Central Michigan University running back became the first Michigan college-football player ever to gain over 3,000 career-rushing yards. Lakes ended his college football career later that season with a total of 3,639 rushing yards.

3 UNUSUAL FOOTBALL ALL-AMERICANS
Oh Brother

Three Michigan brothers, all tackles who played football for the University of Michigan, hold the distinction of being one of only two sets of brothers in college-football history who have played for the same school and made all-american. The UM brothers are:

1. FRANCIS WISTERT		1933
2. ALBERT WISTERT		1942
3. ALVIN WISTERT		1948 and 1949

16 DETROIT LION HEAD COACHES

NAME	YEARS	RECORD
1. POTSY CLARK	1934-36,40	30-15-3
2. DUTCH CLARK	1937-38	14-8-0
3. GUS HENDERSON	1939	6-5-0
4. BILL EDWARDS	1941-42	4-9-1
5. JOHN KARCIS	1942	0-8-0
6. GUS DORAIS	1943-47	20-31-2
7. BO MCMILLAN	1948-50	12-24-0
8. BUDDY PARKER	1951-56	47-23-2
9. GEORGE WILSON	1957-64	53-45-6
10. HARRY GILMER	1965-66	10-16-2
11. JOE SCHMIDT	1967-72	43-34-7
12. DON MCCAFFERTY	1973	6-7-1
13. RICK FORZANO	1974-76	15-17-0
14. TOMMY HUDSPETH	1976-77	11-13-0
15. MONTE CLARK	1978-84	43-61-1
16. DARRYL ROGERS	1985-	

5 NOTABLE LION GAMES

1. FIRST NFL GAME (September 23, 1934)

The Lions beat the New York Giants 9-0 at the University of Detroit Stadium before a crowd of 12,000.

2. FIRST NFL CHAMPIONSHIP (December 9, 1935)

vs. the New York Giants

3. FIRST BRIGGS (TIGER) STADIUM GAME (September 9, 1938)

4. LAST NFL CHAMPIONSHIP (December 28, 1957)

vs. Cleveland

5. FIRST SILVERDOME GAME (August 23, 1975)

3 NFL RECORDS HELD BY THE LIONS

1. LONGEST PASSING PLAY

During the fourth quarter of a Lion 45-14 loss at Baltimore on October 16, 1966, Detroit quarterback Karl Sweetan took the snap at his own one-yard line, dropped back into his end zone, and threw a pass to Pat Studstill. Studstill gathered in the throw on the dead run at the Lion 45 and completed the National Football League's longest passing play (99 yards) by running for a touchdown.

2. LONGEST INTERCEPTION RETURN

During the fourth quarter of a November 24, 1949 game against the Chicago Bears at Detroit, Detroit defensive-back Bob Smith ran back an interception an NFL-record 102 yards for the Lions' only touchdown in the 28-7 loss.

3. MOST KICKOFF-RETURN YARDAGE

On October 29, 1950, Wally Triplett returned four kickoffs for an NFL-record 294 yards, but in spite of his feat, the Lions were trounced by Los Angeles 65-24.

3 RECORD LION HOME ATTENDANCES

1. REGULAR SEASON OPENER — 80,642 (October 6, 1975 vs. Dallas)

2. THANKSGIVING DAY — 80,638 (November 26, 1981 vs Kansas City; November 27, 1980 vs. Chicago; and November 27, 1975 vs Los Angeles)

3. PRE-SEASON — 62,094 (August 23, 1975 vs Kansas City)

234

3 CROWDED DETROIT TIGER YEARS

Three highest Detroit Tiger yearly attendance totals.

1.	2,704,794	1984
	The second largest total in American league history.	
2.	2,031,847	1968
3.	1,951,474	1950

2 SMALLEST MODERN-DAY TIGER CROWDS

1. 3,507

   September 22, 1977 vs Boston

2. 5,868

   May 19, 1983 vs Texas

4 RECORD TIGER CROWDS

1. LARGEST CROWD — 58,369

   July 20, 1947 vs. New York, doubleheader

2. LARGEST OPENING-DAY CROWD — 54,089

   April 6, 1971 vs. Cleveland

3. LARGEST SINGLE-GAME CROWD — 57,888

   September 26, 1948 vs. Cleveland

4. SMALLEST CROWD — 404

   September 24, 1928 vs. Boston

6 BEST TIGER YEARS

Six years with the highest team winning percentages.

1.	1934	.656 (101-53)
2.	1915	.649 (100-54)
3.	1909	.645 (98-54)
4.	1984	.642 (104-58)
5.	1968	.636 (103-59)
6.	1961	.623 (101-61)

6 WORST TIGER YEARS

Six years with the lowest team winning percentages.

1. 1952	.325	(50-104)
2. 1975	.358	(57-102)
3. 1902	.385	(52-83)
4. 1953	.390	(60-94)
5. 1931	.396	(61-93)
6. 1920	.396	(61-93)

4 MOST LOPSIDED TIGER WINS

1. 21-0 vs. Cleveland, September 15, 1901.

2. 21-2 vs. Philadelphia, July 17, 1908.

3. 18-0 vs. St. Louis, April 29, 1935.

4. 19-1 vs. New York, June 17, 1925.

3 TIGER RUN RECORDS

1. The Tigers scored a major-league-record 36 runs in a doubleheader against the St. Louis Browns on August 14, 1937.

2. The Tigers scored 13 times in the sixth inning, the highest single-inning scoring in their history, en route to beating New York 19-1 at Yankee Stadium on June 17, 1925.

3. On June 18, 1953, at Boston, the Red Sox scored the most runs ever scored in one inning against the Tigers, 17 in the bottom of the seventh inning, and went on to pound Detroit 23-3.

4 TIGER GAME-FIRSTS

1. AMERICAN LEAGUE GAME (April 25, 1901)

In the first American League game ever played, the Tigers rallied for 10 runs in the bottom of the ninth inning to beat the Milwaukee Brewers 14-13 at Bennett Park. The Tigers' home field had been created by spreading two inches of loam over cobblestones that dated back to when the site had served as the town hay market.

2. WORLD SERIES GAME WIN (October 12, 1908)

The Tigers beat the Chicago Cubs 8-3 at Chicago but lost the series four games to one.

236

3. WORLD CHAMPIONSHIP (October 7, 1935)

The Tigers won their first-ever world championship with a 4-3 seventh-game victory over the Chicago Cubs at Briggs Stadium.

4. NIGHT GAME (June 15, 1948)

The Tigers beat Philadelphia 4-1 at Briggs Stadium in the first night professional-baseball game ever played at Detroit.

6 FRIDAY THE 13TH TIGER HAPPENINGS

On Friday the 13th, 1984, during a game against Boston at Boston:

1. The Tigers sent 13 men to the plate in the top of the first inning.

2. All three outs in the first inning were made by Lance Parrish, who wears jersey number 13.

3. The Tigers scored eight times and the Red Sox five times in the first inning for a total of 13 runs.

4. The Tigers won the game 13-9.

5. Parrish, jersey number 13, scored the 13th run.

6. Larry Herndon, jersy number 31, got the game-winning RBI.

2 TIGER HAPPENINGS
THAT PROMPTED RULE CHANGES

1. On August 19, 1951, St. Louis owner and showman Bill Veeck sent 3'7" midget Eddie Gaedell in as a pinch hitter for the Browns' leadoff batter. Gaedell, wearing number 1/8, walked on four straight pitches, but the Tigers retired the rest of the side and went on to win 6-2. Following the game, major-league rules were hastily rewritten to prevent the situation from recurring.

2. Herman "Germany" Schaefer, a Tiger secondbaseman from 1905-1909, who was blessed with both speed and finesse, would often steal second base then steal first. The unorthodox practice drove opposing players crazy and drove the league to write a rule-change prohibiting base-theft in reverse.

5 GAMES FORFEITED TO THE TIGERS

1. May 2, 1901

When rain began to fall at Chicago after the Tigers had taken the lead, the White Sox, in spite of the umpire's warnings, tried stalling to get the game washed out. Finally, the exasperated umpire declared Detroit the winner, and the Tigers won the first forfeit in American League history.

2. May 31, 1901

When Detroit scored in the bottom of the ninth on a close play at home to tie the game 5-5, Baltimore players charged out of the dugout en masse to protest. As the umpire turned to walk away, one in the crowd of Baltimore players threw a bat at him and another whipped a ball in his direction. But the umpire calmly continued walking to a bench, sat down, pulled a watch out of his pocket, and when Baltimore didn't clear the field in time, awarded a forfeit to Detroit.

3. August 21, 1901

With Detroit leading 7-4 and Baltimore batting in the bottom of the fourth inning, the umpire called a Baltimore player out on a close play at first base. Several Baltimore players rushed out of the dugout to protest the call, and when one spit in the umpire's eye, the offended official awarded a forfeit to Detroit, whereupon members of the crowd, several of whom were arrested, joined players in physically attacking the ump.

4. August 8, 1903

With Detroit leading 6-5 and two out in the bottom of the 11th, Cleveland batter Nap Lajoie complained to the umpire that the ball was so dirty it couldn't be seen. When the umpire wouldn't put a new ball in play, Lajoie, at the urging of a fan, tossed it over the fence, whereupon the umpire awarded the game to Detroit.

5. July 12, 1979

The Tigers won the second game of a doubleheader against the Chicago White Sox, at Chicago, by forfeit when an estimated 5,000 to 10,000 people, who swarmed out of the stands during a between-games, anti-disco music promotion, made the field unplayable.

2 GAMES FORFEITED BY THE TIGERS

1. August 22, 1905

With the score tied 1-1 in the top of the 11th, two out, and Washington at bat, the Tigers ran onto the field en masse to protest a go-ahead run scored on a close play at home. When the Tigers didn't clear the field as ordered, the umpire awarded the game to Washington.

2. June 13, 1924

When Tiger pitcher Bert Cole hit Yankee Bob Meusel with a pitch, Meusel charged the mound, precipitating an on-the-field brawl that incited the 18,000 Detroit hometown fans to riot and cause the Tigers to lose by forfeit.

4 TIMELY TIGER GAMES
The long and short of it

1. July 16, 1909

At Detroit the Tigers and Senators battled for 18 scoreless innings before darkness called a halt to the longest scoreless game in American League history.

2. August 8, 1920

The Tigers shut out the New York Yankees 1-0 in one hour and 13 minutes of playing time, the quickest nine-inning game in American League history.

3. June 24, 1962

The Tigers played the longest game in baseball history, a 22-inning game against New York that took seven hours to play. Yankee outfielder Jack Reed hit a two-run homer, the only one of his 222-game major-league career, in the top of the 22nd inning to beat the Tigers 9-7.

4. June 17, 1967

The Tigers played the longest doubleheader, nine hours and five minutes of playing time, in the club's history. Detroit beat Kansas City 7-6 in the first game, which was rain-delayed, then lost 6-5 in a 19-inning second game.

2 UNIQUE TRADES

1. On January 28, 1958, the Tigers, in a trade with the San Francisco Giants, obtained infielder Ozzie Virgil, the first black ever to play for Detroit. Virgil played with the team until the middle of the 1960 season when he went to Kansas City.

2. In one of the most unusual trades in baseball history, the Cleveland Indians on August 3, 1960, sent their manager, Joe Gordon, to the Tigers in return for their manager, Jimmy Dykes, the first and only time in major-league history two managers were traded for each other.

3 OUTSTANDING TIGER TRADES

1. Spring 1984

Detroit obtained Willie Hernandez and Dave Bergman in a trade which sent Glenn Wilson and John Wockenfuss to Philadelphia. The acquisition of Hernancez, who won the American League's Cy Young and MVP awards, is generally credited as being *the* reason the Tigers became world champions in 1984.

2. April 12, 1960

In what is generally regarded as the best trade in Tiger history, Detroit acquired first baseman Norm Cash from Cleveland for third baseman Steve

Demeter. Cash hit 373 home runs in a 15-year career at Detroit while Demeter barely played for Cleveland before being sent to the minors.

3. May 18, 1946

The Tigers sent outfielder Barney McCosky to the Philadelphia Athletics and in return obtained George Kell, who became the greatest third baseman in Tiger history.

2 TIGER BROTHERS-TOGETHER

The only two sets of brothers who have played together on Tiger teams.

1. FRANK AND MILT BOLLING

Frank was Detroit's regular second baseman from 1954 to 1960. Older brother Milt appeared in 24 games in 1958 after coming from Washington.

2. JACK AND EDDIE ONSLOW

Eddie played first base, 1912-13, and Jack caught in 31 games in 1912.

2 BROTHER-AGAINST-BROTHER ACTS

1. On July 3, 1973, for the first time in American League history, two brothers, Jim Perry (Detroit) and Gaylord Perry (Cleveland) started a regular-season game as opposing pitchers. Neither finished the game, played at Cleveland and won by the Tigers 5-4.

2. Graig Nettles (New York) hit a first-inning home run and his brother Jim (Detroit) hit one in the second inning of a September 14, 1974 Tiger 10-7 loss.

8 TIGER OWNERSHIPS

1. JAMES BURNS (1901)

A hotel owner and Wayne County Sheriff.

2. SAMUEL ANGUS (1902)

An insurance man.

3. WILLIAM HOOVER YAWKEY (1904)

The son of a lumber and ore magnate bought the team for $50,000.

4. FRANK NAVIN (1907)

The Tigers' bookkeeper was given a part-interest in the team for helping arrange the sale to Yawkey then bought out Yawkey's half-interest for $40,000.

5. WALTER BRIGGS SR. (1935)

An auto industrialist.

6. JOHN FETZER, FRED KNORR, KENYON BROWN and eight other radio-television men bought the team from Briggs' estate for $5.5 million in 1956.

7. In 1961, JOHN FETZER bought the interest held by Knorr's estate after buying out Brown a year earlier.

8. THOMAS MONAGHAN (1983)

The founder of Domino's Pizza, the nation's second-largest pizza chain, purchased the Tigers from Fetzer for a reported $55 million, the highest price ever paid for any sports franchise.

10 1984 SEASON HIGHLIGHTS

1. April 7

Jack Morris became only the fourth pitcher in Detroit Tiger history and the first since 1958 to pitch a no-hitter as the Tigers shutout the Chicago White Sox, 4-0.

2. April 13

The Tigers beat the Boston Red Sox 13-9, at Boston, for the best start — 8 wins, no losses — in the club's history.

3. April 30

Detroit concluded the first month of baseball with an 18-2 record.

4. May 24

Detroit tied the major league record for most consecutive road victories with 17.

5. May 24

The Tigers got off to the best 40-game start in baseball history, 35-5, then lost three straight to Seattle.

6. September 29

The club finished the regular season with 104 wins, the most in the team's 84-year existence.

7. October 5

Detroit won the American League pennant by sweeping Kansas City in three straight games.

8. October 14

At Tiger Stadium, in the fifth game of the World Series against San Diego, two home runs by Kirk Gibson and one by Lance Parrish helped the Tigers clinch their fourth world championship.

9. October 30

Ace Reliever Willie Hernandez became only the second Tiger and only the third relief pitcher to win the American League Cy Young Award..

10. November 6

Willie Hernandez was voted the American League's most valuable player.

5 NATIONAL YOUTH BASEBALL CHAMPIONS

1. ALPENA (1982)

Won the Babe Ruth World Series for 16-to-18 year olds.

2. EDISON POST (Detroit) (1959)

Won the American Legion national title.

3. GAYLORD (1979)

Won the World Series of Little League girls' fastpitch softball.
— *Item contributed by Scott Rich, Gaylord* —

4. HAMTRAMCK (1959)

Won the national Little League crown.

5. HAMTRAMCK (1961)

Won the national Pony League crown.

11

MICHIGAN ELECTIVES

11 ELECTION MILESTONES

1. FIRST ELECTION — July 16, 1792

Though Michigan had, by treaty, become a part of the United States nine years earlier, the British, who still occupied Michigan forts, included Michigan in a scheduled legislative session of the Provincial Assembly of Upper Canada. In August, in the first election ever held in (present-day) Michigan, voters selected representatives to that English assembly.

2. FIRST AMERICAN ELECTION — December 17, 1798

Michigan's first participation in an American election began at Detroit with each voter verbally announcing his choice for a delegate to the Northwest Territory Assembly.

3. FIRST CONGRESSIONAL ELECTION — February 16, 1819

Citizens of the Territory of Michigan sent William Woodbridge to the U.S. House of Representatives as Michigan's first congressman.

4. FIRST PRESIDENTIAL ELECTION — November 8, 1836

Michigan citizens voted for the first time in a U.S. presidential election and helped place Martin Van Buren in the oval office.

5. FIRST AMENDMENT RATIFIED — 1865

The first U.S. constitutional amendment ratified by Michigan was the 13th, which prohibited slavery and involuntary servitude except for the punishment of a crime.

6. FIRST BLACK VOTE — November 8, 1870

Negroes voted for the first time in a Michigan state election.

7. FIRST SECRET BALLOT — 1891

The secret ballot was initiated in Michigan.

8. FIRST MACHINE VOTE — 1893

Voting machines were first authorized for use.

9. FIRST PRIMARY ELECTION — 1910

10. FIRST TO APPROVE WOMEN'S VOTE — June 10, 1919

Five days after the U.S. Congress passed the 19th constitutional amendment, Michigan became the first state to ratify the women's suffrage amendment.

11. FIRST PUBLIC FUNDING — December 31, 1976

Governor William G. Milliken signed a law which allowed Michigan residents to contribute $2 to a gubernatorial campaign fund through a checkoff provision on their state personal income-tax forms, and Michigan became the first state in the nation to provide partial public funding of governor's elections.

3 NATIONAL POLITICAL CONVENTIONS HELD IN MICHIGAN

1. July 6, 1854

At an oak grove in Jackson, 1,500 Michigan Whigs, Democrats, and Abolitionists, rebelling against slavery and other prevailing policies of their day, organized the nation's first Republican Party.

2. August 1922

The American Communist Party held its first national convention on a farm near St. Joseph.

3. July 14, 1980

The 32nd Republican National Convention opened at Detroit and, before nominating Ronald Reagan as its presidential candidate, brought 20,000 delegates, 8,000 journalists, and almost $40 million to the city.

3 NOTABLE DELEGATES

1. KATE ENGLISH (Saginaw), in 1914, became the first female delegate to a Michigan political convention.

2. OLIVIA P. "LIBBY" MAYNARD (Flint), on October 13, 1979, became the first woman to be elected state Democratic Party chairperson.

3. ADDISON G. PROCTOR (St. Joseph), who died at the age of 86 on February 16, 1925, was the last surviving member of the 1860 Republican convention that nominated Abraham Lincoln for president.

4 UNUSUAL ELECTIONS

1. On election day in 1823, the winning congressional candidate from Michigan, Father Gabriel Richard, was locked in the county jail, having been arrested on a body writ by one of his parishioners, who claimed the priest had slandered him from the pulpit. Richard made bond, however, and on December 8, took his seat as the first Roman Catholic priest ever to serve in the U.S. Congress.

2. Governor Luren Dickinson, having been nominated for re-election by the Republican Party in 1939, refused to campaign and even asked that voters not support him. Voters honored his request and placed Murray Van Wagoner in office.

3. In 1947, at a time when females were a rare participants in governing bodies at any level, the voters of Grass Lake (population 800) elected six women to their nine-member village council. The following year, a young-mens' ticket launched a rival campaign, but after a record turnout of 175 voters, female candidates captured all nine seats by a two-to-one margin.

4. After being pressed for months to enter the Republican race for Michigan governor, George W. Romney, a devout Mormon, made national news by announcing on February 8, 1962, that he would not reach a decision until he had concluded a 24-hour fast and session of personal prayer. Two days later he threw his hat into the ring and in November won the election.

2 MAYORS OUT OF A HAT

1. After an April 4, 1983 election for the part-time post of mayor of Bangor (Van Buren County) had resulted in a 148-vote two-way tie, the county Board of Canvassers ordered that the matter be settled by a drawing. A week later, two slips of paper, one containing the word, "elected" and the other, "not elected" were placed in a wooden jury box. Ed Waite, the 74-year-old incumbent, drew first, unfolded the paper, and happily reported that he had just been re-elected.

2. Tabulations of a November 1983 mayoral election in Mt. Morris (Genesee County) gave a two-vote victory to Allen J. LaFurgey, allowing him to reclaim the title he had lost in 1981 to Frank E. Goodroe. Goodroe asked for a recount, which resulted in a tie with 388 votes each. Eight days later, LaFurgey won the $600-a-year part-time job when Goodroe, in front of local and national media who had gathered in the Genesee County Clerk's office, drew a "not elected" slip of paper from a box.

2 FAMILY RIVALRIES

1. When Councilman James P. Green ran for mayor of Kalkaska in March 1984, one of his most active opponents was his wife of 16 years, Geri Sue. Geri Sue supported her husband's opponent by making phone calls, ringing door bells, placing an ad in the local newspaper and, according to published reports, even

defacing one of her husband's poltitical banners with a can of spray paint. Geri Sue said she campaigned against her husband, who lost by a vote of 203 to 139, because he had "become obsessed with power."

2. In 1982, Jack and Pat Conley (Davison), husband and wife for 31 years, both filed in the primary election — he as a Democrat and she as a Republican — for the 82d District seat in the Michigan House. A family rivalry in the general election was avoided, however, when Jack finished a distant third in his party's primary. Pat, a narrow winner in her primary, lost by a wide margin in the general election.

4 ALL-IN-THE-FAMILY ELECTIONS

1. George Montgomery Sr. (20th District — Detroit) and his son George Jr. (21st District — Detroit) were, on November 3, 1964, both elected to the Michigan House of Representatives.

2. When on November 3, 1970, Rep. Lucille McCollough (Dearborn) won re-election to the Michigan House of Representatives and her son Patrick (Dearborn) was elected to the state senate, they became the first mother-son legislative team in the state's history.

3. When Representative John Engler (Mt. Pleasant) and Representative Colleen House (Bay City) married in 1975, they became Michigan's first and only husband-wife lawmaking team.

4. With the swearing in of the 98th U.S. Congress in January 1983, Michigan had a brother team among those making the laws of the land. Democratic Senator Carl Levin began his fifth year in the U.S. Senate and his brother Sander Levin began his first year in the House of Representatives.

3 DEMOCRATIC SENATORIAL COUNTIES

The only three Michigan counties that have voted for the Democratic U.S. Senate candidate in every election since 1964.

1. ALGER
2. LAKE
3. WAYNE

5 REPUBLICAN SENATORIAL COUNTIES

The only five Michigan counties that have voted for the Republican U.S. Senate candidate in every election since 1964.

1. LEELANAU
2. MISSAUKEE
3. OSCEOLA

246

4. OTTAWA
5. SANILAC

2 DEMOCRATIC PRESIDENTIAL COUNTIES

The only two Michigan counties that have voted for the Democratic U.S. presidential candidate in every election since 1960.

1. DELTA
2. WAYNE

3 REPUBLICAN PRESIDENTIAL COUNTIES

The only three Michigan counties that have voted for the Republican U.S. presidential candidate in every election since 1960.

1. MISSAUKEE
2. OTTAWA
3. SANILAC

6 NOTABLE OFFICE-HOLDERS

1. CHARLES DIGGS won election as representative of the 13th District (Detroit) on November 2, 1954, and became Michigan's first black U.S. Congressman.

2. COLLEEN HOUSE (Bay City), on July 1, 1974, was sworn in at age 22 as the youngest female member in the history of the Michigan House of Representatives.

3. ORVILLE HUBBARD, Michigan's longest-serving mayor, completed his last term in 1978 after serving as the city of Dearborn's chief executive for 16 consecutive terms over 35 years.

4. GOVERNOR HARRY F. KELLY was the last statewide holder of elective office who had served in World War I.

5. FLOYD J. MCCREE, by a vote of the Flint City Commission in 1966, became the first black to preside as mayor of a large U.S. city.

6. LUDWIK WESOLOWSKI, on November 4, 1862, was elected as the Macomb County surveyor which made him, according to *Enduring Poles*, the first person of Slavic extraction to become an elected official anywhere in the U.S.

4 NOTABLE UNSUCCESSFUL CANDIDATES

1. LEWIS CASS, the Democratic presidential nominee in 1848, became the first person from Michigan to run for the nation's highest office. But because of the presence of a third party, the former Michigan territorial governor and U.S. senator lost the election to Zachary Taylor.

2. CHARLES A. FORREST III (Birmingham)

After being charged 25 cents to take out a book when he forgot his library card, the 13-year-old decided to correct what he felt was the unfair practice by filing to run in an election for a seat on the public library board. After city officials, a circuit court judge, and a three-judge appeals court panel all ruled Forrest ineligible because of his age, the determined youth launched an unsuccessful write-in campaign.

3. ROBERT J. GARNER

Two months after the age of majority was lowered from 21 to 18, Garner became the first 18-year-old to run for office in Michigan but lost in his bid for the Independence Township (Pontiac) clerk's job.

4. MICHELLE (FORMERLY OSCAR) STROM

The 27-year-old Jackson woman, who admitted undergoing a sex-change operation in 1978 , declared her candidacy in the 6th Michigan Congressional District 1980 Republican primary but did not gain the nomination.

3 SORE LOSERS

1. During Michigan's first American election, held at a Detroit tavern in December 1798, each voter was required to verbally announce his choice — James May or Solomon Sibley — for delegate to the Northwest Territory Assembly. After the election, May, the loser, accused Sibley, the winner, of bribing voters with liquor and ordering soldiers armed with clubs to threaten anyone who planned to vote for May.

2. According to newspaper reports of the day, W.W. Wedemery, an Ann Arbor U.S. congressman, was so despondent over losing a re-election bid in 1912 that he suffered a complete mental breakdown and attempted to jump off a boat into the sea while en route from New York to Panama.

3. In the 1918 Michigan primary election for a vacant U.S. Senate seat, auto magnate Henry Ford's name was placed on both the Republican and Democratic ballots, which at that time was possible. Ford won the Democratic nomination with only token opposition, but Truman Newberry, who campaigned vigorously, won the Republican nomination. Ford, however, who had expressed little interest in becoming senator, spent no money and did not campaign and, as a result, lost the November general election to Newberry by nearly 8,000 votes.

But then, in one of the most celebrated and controversial moves in Michigan political history, Ford attempted to prevent Newberry from taking the Senate seat by accusing him of violating campaign spending limits. After a long legal battle, Newberry was found guilty of violating the Federal Corrupt Practices Act and was sentenced to two years in prison. Newberry appealed; in May 1921 the Supreme Court overturned his conviction; and on January 12, 1922, 38 months after his election, Newberry took his seat in the Senate only to resign ten months later, when his opponents threatened to reopen the case against him.

5 FEMALE STATE SENATORS

Only five women have ever served in Michigan's 38-member upper chamber. They are:

1. EVA M. HAMILTON (Grand Rapids) — 1920-24
2. CORA BROWN (Detroit) — 1953-57
3. N. LORRAINE BEEBE (Dearborn) — 1966-70
4. CONNIE BINSFELD (Maple City) — 1983-
5. LANA POLLACK (Ann Arbor) — 1983-

8 POLITICAL FIRST LADIES

1. CORA ANDERSON (L'Anse) was elected without opposition on November 24, 1924, as Michigan's first female state representative.

2. LUCILE AVERY (Pontiac), in 1924, became the first Michigan woman to win a county-wide election when she became the Register of Deeds for Oakland County.

3. CORA BROWN (Detroit), who was overwhelmingly elected to the Michigan Senate on November 4, 1952, became the first black woman in any state senate.

4. MARTHA GRIFFITHS served as Michigan's first and only U.S. Congresswoman from 1955 to 1974 and in 1982 became Michigan's first elected female lieutenant governor.

5. EVA M. HAMILTON (Grand Rapids), on November 2, 1920, was elected by an 8,872-vote majority to the state senate and became the first female state legislator in Michigan history.

6. GRACE SANDERS (Stephenson), in 1930, became the first female village president in Michigan history.

7. HARRY LEE SCOTT (New Haven), who was elected in 1980 to a two-year term as mayor of the village of New Haven, became the first black woman mayor in Michigan history.

8. MATILDA DODGE WILSON (Rochester)

Lt. Governor Luren Dickinson, who had become governor when Frank D. Fitzgerald died in office on March 16, 1939 (see page 251), appointed Wilson as his successor. But Michigan's first female lieutenant governor served only the 45 days remaining in Fitzgerald's unexpired term.

2 SPECIAL SEATS OF GOVERNMENT

1. In November 1982 Muskegon became the nation's capital of the Ottawa Indian government.

2. Until January 1983, the municipal building in Fruitport, a 12-by-16-foot brick structure with no running water, was Michigan's smallest seat of government.

22 PLACES THAT ALMOST BECAME THE STATE CAPITAL

In 1847 the legislature, for a variety of reasons, decided to move the state capital out of Detroit. The legislators than spent a great deal of time and argument trying to decide where the new capital should be. Places that received votes, some seriously, some not so seriously, for the site were:

1. ALBION
2. ANN ARBOR
3. BATTLE CREEK
4. BYRON
5. CALEDONIA
6. CHARLOTTE
7. COPPER HARBOR
8. CORUNNA
9. DETROIT
10. DEWITT
11. DEXTER
12. EATON RAPIDS
13. FLINT
14. GRAND BLANC
15. JACKSON
16. LYONS
17. MARSHALL
18. ONONDAGA
19. OWOSSO
20. PONTIAC
21. SAGINAW
22. UTICA

4 CAPITOL DEVELOPMENTS

1. May 5, 1828

The territorial legislature met, for the first time, at Michigan's first **capitol** a 60-by-90-foot building constructed at Detroit at a cost of $24,500.

2. December 25, 1847

The state government was unceremoniously moved from Detroit to a new capitol consisting of temporary buildings that had been erected at a wilderness site on the banks of the Grand River near (present-day) Lansing.

3. January 1, 1879

The present domed state capitol building at Lansing was formally dedicated and occupied.

4. January 27, 1893

Michigan's first capitol building, which had been used by the Detroit Board of Education since 1848, burned in a fire.

11 GUBERNATORIAL FIRSTS

1. FIRST STATE GOVERNOR
Stevens T. Mason (1835-1839)

2. FIRST REPUBLICAN GOVERNOR
Kingsley S. Bingham (1855-1858) was Michigan's and the nation's first Republican governor.

3. FIRST NATIVE-BORN GOVERNOR

David J. Jerome (1881-1882), born November 17, 1829, at Detroit.

4. FIRST FOREIGN-BORN GOVERNOR
Fred M. Warner (1905-1910), born July 21, 1865, at Hickling, Nottinghamshire, England.

5. FIRST GOVERNOR TO CAMPAIGN IN AN AUTOMOBILE
Fred M. Warner (1905-1910)

6. FIRST GOVERNOR TO SERVE 3 CONSECUTIVE TERMS
Fred M. Warner (1905-1910)

7. FIRST (AND ONLY) GOVERNOR TO DIE IN OFFICE
Frank D. Fitzgerald (1935-1936 and January-March, 1939)

8. FIRST CATHOLIC GOVERNOR
Frank D. Murphy (1937-1938)

9. FIRST GOVERNOR INAUGURATED AT LANSING
Epaphroditus Ransom (1848-1849)

10. FIRST GOVERNOR TO RECEIVE A PRESIDENTIAL CABINET APPOINTMENT
Robert McClelland (1851-1853), while serving as governor of Michigan, resigned on March 4, 1853, to become Secretary of the Interior in the Administration of President Franklin Pierce.

11. FIRST (AND ONLY) GOVERNOR FROM THE UPPER PENINSULA
Chase M. Osborn (1911-1912), from Sault Ste. Marie.

3 OLDEST GOVERNORS

Based on age when taking office.

1. LUREN DICKINSON (1939-1940) 79 almost 80
2. JOSIAH W. BEGOLE (1883-1884) 67 almost 68
3. EDWIN B. WINANS (1891-1892) 64

3 YOUNGEST GOVERNORS

Based on age when taking office.

1. STEVENS T. MASON (1835-1839) 24
2. JAMES W. GORDON (1841) 32
   When Governor William Woodbridge was elected to the U.S. Senate, Gordon, as lieutenant governor, became acting governor at the age of 32.
3. JOHN B. SWAINSON (1961-62) 35

3 FOREIGN-BORN GOVERNORS

1. FRED M. WARNER (1905-1910) was born July 21, 1865, in Hickling, Nottinghamshire, England, and arrived in the United States at the age of three months.

2. GEORGE W. ROMNEY (1963-1969) was born July 8, 1907, at Chihuahua, Mexico, and came to Michigan in 1939.

3. JOHN B. SWAINSON (1961-62) was born July 31, 1925, at Windsor, Ontario, and moved with his family to Port Huron when he was an infant.

11 GOVERNORS BORN IN MICHIGAN

Of the 43 men who have served as Michigan's governor since 1835, only 11 have been born in the state of Michigan. They are:

1. DAVID H. JEROME (1881-1882)
   Born November 17, 1829, at Detroit.
2. ALEXANDER J. GROESBECK (1921-1926)
   Born November 7, 1873, at Warren Township (Macomb County).
3. FRED W. GREEN (1927-1930)
   Born October 20, 1872, at Manistee.
4. WILBER M. BRUCKER (1931-1932)
   Born June 23, 1894, at Saginaw.
5. WILLIAM A. COMSTOCK (1933-34)
   Born July 2, 1877, at Alpena.

6. FRANK D. FITZGERALD (1935-1936 and January-March, 1939)
   Born January 27, 1885, at Grand Ledge.
7. FRANK MURPHY (1937-1938)
   Born April 13, 1890, at Harbor Beach.
8. MURRAY D. VAN WAGONER (1941-42)
   Born March 18, 1898, at Kingston.
9. G. MENNEN WILLIAMS (1949-1960)
   Born February 23, 1911, at Detroit.
10. WILLIAM G. MILLIKEN (1969-1982)
    Born March 26, 1922 at Traverse City.
11. JAMES J. BLANCHARD (1984-)
    Born August 8, 1942 at Detroit.

5 LIEUTENANT GOVERNORS
WHO BECAME GOVERNOR

1. JAMES W.GORDON became governor in 1841 when William Woodbridge was elected to the U.S. Senate.

2. WILLIAM L. GREENLY became governor on March 4, 1847, when Governor Alpheus Felch was elected to the U.S. Senate.

3. ANDREW PARSONS became governor March 4, 1853, when Robert McClelland accepted an appointment as the U.S. Secretary of Interior.

4. LUREN D. DICKINSON became governor on March 16, 1939 following the death of Governor Frank D. Fitzgerald.

5. WILLIAM G. MILLIKEN became governor on January 22, 1969, when George Romney resigned in mid-term to become secretary of housing and urban development in the adminstration of President Richard M. Nixon.

4 GOVERNORS WHO SERVED MORE
THAN 2 CONSECUTIVE TERMS

1. FRED M. WARNER (1905-1910) — Three two-year terms.

2. ALEXANDER J. GROESBECK (1921-1926) — Three two-year terms.

3. G. MENNEN WILLIAMS (1949-1960) — Six two-year terms.

4. WILLIAM G. MILLIKEN (1969-1982) — Finished out the term of George Romney, then elected to three four-year terms.

5 LEGISLATIVE MILESTONES

1. July 9, 1805

A governing body composed of a governor and three judges passed and published the new Michigan territory's first law, which described and adopted an official territorial seal.

2. June 7, 1824

The first legislative council of the Territory of Michigan convened at Detroit. Father Gabriel Richard opened the session by praying that the "legislators may make laws for the people, and not for themselves."

3. November 1, 1835

The first legislature of Michigan under state constitution convened at Detroit, met only one day, passed only seven laws, then adjourned until February 1, 1836.

4. January 2, 1837

The first regular ongoing session of the legislature of the state of Michigan began at Detroit.

5. March 17, 1847

The state legislature met for the final time at Detroit before moving permanently to Lansing.

4 CONSTITUTIONS

1. By an overwhelming majority of 6,752 to 1,374, voters, on October 5, 1835, approved Michigan's first state constitution, which created a bicameral legislature (House and Senate) and specified that state officials, with the exception of governor, lieutenant governor, representatives and senators, be appointed.

2. Michigan's second constitution was adopted by a vote of the people on November 5, 1850. The new constitution established the governor's salary at $1,000 and changed the secretary of state, state treasurer, supreme-court justice and other principal state officials from appointed to elected positions.

3. In 1908 voters approved Michigan's third constitution, which was basically a rewrite and updating of the 1850 constitution.

4. On April 1, 1963, Michigan voters narrowly approved Michigan's fourth and latest constitution, which streamlined and modernized the 1908 constitution and changed the term of governor from two to four years.

2 MEMORABLE RECALLS

1. Detroit Mayor Charles Bowles, whom many residents blamed for the unchecked corruption and loose law enforcement that plagued their city during the Prohibition era, became, on July 21, 1930, the nation's first large-city mayor ever to be recalled.

2. On November 22, 1983, state Senator Philip O. Mastin, a Democrat from Pontiac, became the first state legislator in Michigan history to be recalled. The recall stemmed from Mastin's support of a 38 percent temporary income tax increase. A week later, Senator David M. Serotkin (D-Mount Clemens) was similarly recalled.

3 MOST INFLUENTIAL
STATE-GOVERNMENT LOBBYING FIRMS

1. GOVERNMENTAL ASSOCIATES, INC. (Bobby Crim and Robert Vanderlaan)

Major clients include: Chrysler Corporation, Allstate Insurance Company, City of Grand Rapids, Consumers Power Company, Ferris State College, Mobil Oil, and the 3M Company.

2. JAMES H. KAROUB ASSOCIATES (James Karoub)

Major clients include: Allied Supermarkets, Associated Food Dealers of Greater Detroit, Blue Cross/Blue Shield of Michigan, Delta Dental Plan, the Detroit Lions, Inc., Fraternal Order of Police, Michigan Association of Community Bankers, Michigan Automobile Dealers Association, Michigan Cable Television Association, Michigan Savings & Loan League, Pontiac Stadium Authority, and the Wine Institute.

3. PUBLIC AFFAIRS ASSOCIATES, INC. (Jerry Coomes)

Major clients include: Detroit Edison Co., Health Care Association of Michigan, John Hancock Mutual Life Insurance Co., Meijer Corporation, Michigan Association of CPAs, Michigan Chiropractic Council, Motion Picture Association of America, Shell Oil Company, State Bar of Michigan, and Teachers Insurance & Annuity Association.

12
MICHTAKES

4 BOTCHED PRACTICAL JOKES

1. THE BUTT OF THE JOKE I (Oscoda) — October 22, 1983

A Linden man, in an attempt to scare his Flint hunting companion who was sitting on a tent-enclosed portable toilet, aimed a .44-magnum revolver at the ground next to the facility and fired. But instead of striking the ground, the bullet pierced the canvas tent and the toilet, traveled through the Flint man's right buttock, and, after missing all "vital organs" according to authorities, lodged behind his knee.

2. THE BUTT OF THE JOKE II (Lakeland, Florida) — March 2, 1982

Detroit Tiger outfielder Kirk Gibson did the old pull-out-a chair trick just as pitcher and teammate Dave Rozema was about to sit in it. When Rozema hit the floor, a bottle of medicine he carried in his back pocket shattered, causing a derriere wound that took 11 stitches to repair.

3. PLAYING DEAD (Lansing) — May 1983

After leaving a party, four young people, as a joke, lay down in the middle of a street to scare motorists. After one or two cars had dodged around the youths, three of them got up and walked back to the curb. The fourth, a 19-year-old Haslett man, remained on the pavement to carry on the prank and was run over and killed by the next car that came down the street.

4. DIDN'T THINK AHEAD (Kansas City) — April 8, 1982

As six Detroit Tiger baseball players stood at a bar rail, pitcher Dave Rozema playfully pushed the back of shortstop Alan Trammel's head. The jolt smashed Trammel's head into a goblet, and the shattered glass caused a deep cut two inches above the all star's eye that required 40 stitches to close.

4 SELF-INFLICTED WOUNDS

1. PONTIAC SILVERDOME (September 27, 1981)

A Detroit man, who called himself the "Renaissance Cat," accidentally set his bright-blue cat costume ablaze as he carried a smoke bomb down an aisle toward the field to celebrate a Detroit Lion touchdown. The 28-year-old man not only suffered second and third-degree burns over much of his body, but also was arrested and convicted for placing a "foul, offensive or injurious substance" in the stadium "with the intent to alarm."

2. GRASS LAKE (August 23, 1984)

A 31-year-old Ohio man, after hearing a voice he thought was "the Lord's," punctured his eyes with an unidentified sharp object and blinded himself. The man, who was attending a week-long church camp, later said he realized it wasn't the Lord talking to him after all.

3. SAULT STE. MARIE (February 9, 1982)

A 19-year-old Lake Superior State College student who fired a .22-caliber rifle at his chest to demonstrate a bullet-proof vest to his friends was hospitalized when the bullet pierced the fabric and made a hole three-quarters of an inch deep in his chest. The student had tried the same stunt once before but had suffered only bruised ribs.

4. LANSING (January 1974)

While playing tennis, Lieutenant Governor James Brickley hit himself in the lip with his racket and took 25 stitches.

3 GASTRONOMIC GAFFES

1. BATTLE CREEK (July 1981)

A 23-year-old woman, who was considering suicide, mixed strychnine with pancake flour but reconsidered and threw the box into a kitchen waste basket. The next morning, the woman's mother, thinking that the nearly full box had been accidentally thrown away, retrieved the mix and used it to make breakfast for her husband and two other daughters. The family members, however, all complained that the pancakes were bitter tasting and fed them to the family dog, who dropped dead later that day.

2. SOUTH LYON (November 1984)

A 40-year-old woman died of liver failure after eating several poisonous mushrooms she had picked from her front yard.

3. LANSING (1973)

At a dinner to celebrate the state fisheries department's 100th anniversary, steak was served.

5 MEDICAL MISTAKES

1. CAN I HELP, DAD (Chelsea) — March 22, 1983

A 48-year-old surgeon allowed his curious 14-year-old son to not only

257

watch a gall bladder operation on a 50-year-old woman at Chelsea Community Hospital, but also to insert his gloved hand inside the patient's abdomen and put in two stitches. The doctor, who later admitted his "error in judgment," was suspended for two weeks by the Michigan Board of Medicine for "allowing an unlicensed, non-medical person to participate in a gall bladder operation."

2. NO LAUGHING MATTER (Benton Harbor) — October 1977

A maintenance man working in the operating room of Mercy Hospital inadvertently switched lines carrying nitrous oxide, commonly known as "laughing gas," and lines carrying oxygen. As a result, over the next two months, three people, who received the laughing gas instead of oxygen during surgery, died.

3. DEAD WRONG (Detroit) — November 22, 1981

Two Detroit Emergency Medical Services (EMS) technicians arrived at the home of a heart attack victim then left after refusing to take the man to the hospital because they said he was already dead. Another crew was called and took the 64-year-old victim, still alive, to the hospital where he died a short time later.

4. KEEPING PACE (June 1974)

The General Electric Corporation recalled 161 potentially malfunctioning pacemakers, eight of which had been surgically implanted in Michigan residents, and offered to "install" replacements free of charge.

5. LOST AND FOUND (Cadillac) — April 1985

A three-week-old baby, wo was being treated for pneumonia at Mercy Hospital, was accidentally stuffed with her bedding into a laundry cart and taken to to a basement laundry room where she remained on a concrete floor under a foot-high pile of dirty linen until being found 90 minutes later.

3 UNIQUE TRAFFIC ACCIDENTS

1. DETROIT (September 2, 1902)

George W. Bissell, a well-to-do lumberman, became Michigan's first known automobile-accident fatality when his carriage was hit by a car.

2. FLINT (July 31, 1969)

As a driver's-education student drove down a suburban street, an approaching car suddenly veered across the center line and smashed into the training car. The instructor was seriously injured in the crash, the first major accident involving a driver's-training vehicle since the education program began in 1955.

3. HAMBURG (Livingston County) — February 11, 1985

A tow-truck driver, who had been ordered by a policeman to remove one of two vans that had been involved in a head-on crash, towed the vehicle from the accident scene to his company's lot. There he discovered that the dazed and injured driver, a 37-year-old woman evidently forgotten by the police officer, was still in her wrecked van.

4 MOST-MISSED DRIVER'S-TEST QUESTIONS

The four most frequently missed questions on the Michigan written driving test. All four are missed by about 30 percent of test takers.

1. Whenever construction work or surveying blocks all or part of a lane on a highway, the speed limit is (a) 55, unless posted lower, (b) 45, unless posted lower, (c) 35, unless posted lower.

2. When there is a fatal highway accident, a drinking driver is involved about (a) 25 percent of the time, (b) 50 percent of the time, (c) 75 percent of the time.

3. Having one or two drinks before driving (a) has little or no effect on a person's driving ability, (b) affects the judgment of most people, (c) is illegal.

4. When you see this sign (a rectangle that looks like the side of a house with the outline of two children superimposed over it) you should (a) stop at the cross-walk unless a crossing guard signals you to go, (b) be prepared to stop for schoolchildren, or (c) stop when school buses are moving.
— *List contributed by Ed Boucher, Michigan Department of State, Lansing* —

·(q) sı suoıʇsǝnb ɹnoɟ ʅʅɐ oʇ sɹǝʍsuɐ ǝɥꓕ

4 MISTEACHINGS

1. NORTHERN MICHIGAN UNIVERSITY (Marquette) — September 1, 1983

On the first day of school, an Army Green Beret Sergeant-Major introduced himself to his 13 military science students while carrying a live chicken, then suddenly bit off the bird's head and drank its blood. The department chairman immediately suspended the instructor, who explained that his unorthodox teaching method was designed, "simply to get their attention, not to prove any particular point."

2. MIO (October 1983)

A junior high school student swatted a fly then asked his social studies teacher, who had told the class that his philosophy was, "you eat what you kill," if he was supposed to eat it. The 32-year-old man responded that the students knew what his policy was, whereupon the boy replied that he wouldn't eat uncooked meat. The teacher then, according to complaints, toasted the fly with a match and handed it back to the boy, who ate it.

The teacher, who denied forcing the student to eat the fly, was suspended without pay for the remainder of the school year.

3. DETROIT (September 1983)

A substitute custodian for Redford High School, who didn't know where he was supposed to report for work, went to the school's office and was sent by a secretary to a social studies class as a substitute teacher. After teaching two social studies classes and two study halls, the custodian told school personnel, who still hadn't discovered their error, that, though he had enjoyed his classroom experiences, he really didn't think he had been correctly assigned.

4. ROSEVILLE (April 1984)

A teacher paddled a 12-year-old student, who had been chewing gum in class, then encouraged and allowed 23 of her 26 classmates to line up and, one at a time, also paddle her. Several months later, the Roseville Board of Education awarded the girl $16,000 for "physical and emotional trauma" suffered during the incident.

6 SLIPS OF THE PEN

1. In his haste to meet a filing deadline for the 1982 U.S. senatorial election, Republican candidate Phil Ruppe's (Houghton) campaign manager forged his boss's signature on an affidavit then had a woman whose commission had expired nearly a year earlier notarize the signature. As a result, the Board of State Canvassers refused to certify Ruppe's candidacy, but the Michigan Supreme Court restored him to the ballot.

During the same election, Ruppe's campaign consultants sent out 2,000 fund-raising letters that asked — "Who is best suited to handle the future energy problems the United States faces — Phil Ruppe or (his opponent) Don Riegle?" — then answered, "Don Riegle, of course."

Ruppe lost to Riegle in the general election by more than 600,000 votes.

2. A proposed 1973 obscenity ordinance did not make it through the Sterling Heights City Council because councilmen said it was too obscene to read in public.

3. Because a scheduled launch of a *Columbia* space shuttle was so close to their deadline, the *Detroit News* prepared and printed their November 4, 1981 edition with a page-one story announcing a successful take-off of the craft. Shortly after 30,000 of the papers had been released for delivery, however, the mission was postponed, and the *News* ended up launching the space shuttle eight days before NASA did.

4. During the 1982 gubernatorial race, candidate James Blanchard's campaign workers sent out a mailing with envelopes stamped "Blanchard for Gover*ner.*"

5. On April 9, 1983, a Grand Rapids family asked Western Union to send a telegram to their son at the University of Michigan saying, "Dear Son, We love you so much. Mother and Dad, Brothers and Sisters." Instead, according to a lawsuit filed by the family, their son received a message that read, "Dear Son, We love you so much. Mother's dead. Brothers and Sisters."

6. The Canadian Press wire service, in late February 1982, sent out detailed reports to its clients across Canada of a stunning series of wins — from a 1-0 upset over West Germany in their first game to a 1-0 finals upset over the Soviet Union — by their country's junior soccer team at a weeklong world championship tournament at Sydney, Australia.

The Canadian team's stirring triumph, however, came in a tournament that existed only in the mind of a Western Michigan University freshman, who, by temporarily adopting the name of a Canadian soccer coach, phoned the fictitious reports to the wire service from Kalamazoo.

4 DJ MISTAKES
Slipped Discs

1. Years ago, according to a story told by WJR (Detroit) host J.P. McCarthy, he asked, during an interview with entertainer Rosemary Clooney, how her sister Betty, whom he claimed to know quite well, was doing. After a pause, Clooney replied, "Joe — Betty's been dead for six years."

2. At about noon on September 25, 1980, a WTRX (Flint) disc jockey cracked what he thought was an obvious joke: "We have a bulletin. A cement truck and a police van carrying prisoners have just collided on Flint's east side. Be on the lookout for 12 hardened criminals." But about 200 parents and a couple of elementary school principals didn't get the joke and herded pupils into gymnasiums while they and teachers searched their grounds for the escapees.

3. A 34-year-old WQRS-FM (Detroit) disc jockey slipped a classical album on the turntable at 8:18 a.m. on September 5, 1983, stepped out into the studio's lobby, then discovered he had locked his keys inside. For the next 45 minutes — the time it took him to find a freight elevator that got him back into the studio — his listeners heard only the clicking, scratching sound of the phonograph needle that had come to the end of the album.

4. In January 1985, an afternoon disc jockey barricaded himself in a WHYT-FM (Detroit) studio to protest the suspension of a morning colleague who had reportedly been taken off the air for playing a parody song about King Boots, a Birmingham sheepdog accused of killing its owner's mother (see page 43). But when the suspension and take-over generated television and front-page newspaper coverage, the station manager confessed that it was all a publicity stunt and was fired by the station owners.

2 ERRANT TV BROADCASTS

1. JACKSON (November 1982)

A local cable-station broadcast of a cheerleading competition involving squads from 12 Jackson County schools was unexplainedly interrupted for three minutes by a pornographic film showing an explicit sex act.

2. HARRISON (1983)

A couple who had ordered the Walt Disney cable television channel for their sons, ages four 4 and 10, came home from work to discover that the Playboy Channel was coming in instead.

4 BASEBALL BLUNDERS

1. Detroit Tiger Dalton Jones hit a grand slam home run against the Boston Red Sox on July 9, 1970, but was credited with only a single because, in his excitement, he passed another Tiger baserunner between first and second base.

2. Before a June 27, 1976 game against Boston, Tiger manager Ralph Houck handed a lineup card to the umpires that mistakenly listed two players as designated hitters. As a result, the umpires ruled that the Tigers could use *no* designated hitter, and Frank McCormack was forced to become the first Tiger pitcher to bat since October 12, 1972. McCormack went 0-3, but the Tigers won 4-2 in 11 innings.

3. The Detroit Tigers set an American League record for errors by committing 12 in a May 1, 1901 game against the Chicago White Sox.

4. The Detroit Tigers and Chicago White Sox played a game on May 6, 1903, in which they committed an American League record 18 errors — six by Detroit and 12 by Chicago.

5 DETROIT TIGERS
WHO HOLD ERROR RECORDS

1. OWEN BUSH holds the major-league lifetime record for most errors at shortstop with 689. Bush also holds the American League record for most errors in one game by a shortstop, 5, set on August, 25, 1911.

2. BILL GLEASON holds the American League single-season record for most errors at second base, 61, set in 1901.

3. ROY JOHNSON holds the American League record for most errors by an outfielder in one season, 31, set in 1929.

4. OSCAR STRANGE in 1911 set an American League record for most errors in a season by a catcher, 41.

5. GEORGE TEBBETTS, who played for Detroit 1939-42 and 1947-49, led the American League in errors by a catcher a record six seasons.

6 CEREMONIAL MISTAKES

1. DETROIT (November 2, 1983)

When the first domestically built small van rolled off the assembly line, the fanfare was momentarily delayed when none of the four passengers, all high-ranking Chrysler Corporation executives, could figure out how to open the doors which had inadvertently been locked with a child-proof safety device.

2. DETROIT (June 11, 1983)

As 300 children and adults watched, a police helicopter carrying Ronald McDonald to a restaurant appearance crash-landed in a nearby parking lot. The uninjured actor — in full clown costume — hopped out of the the overturned demolished copter, walked to a nearby stage, and, as though nothing out of the ordinary had happened, proceeded with his planned safety show for children.

3. MACKINAW CITY (November 1, 1957)

At the grand opening ceremonies of the Mackinac Bridge, Governor G. Mennen Williams posed for pictures by climbing onto a piece of road equipment with wheels 12 feet high. Williams then, at the urging of the photographers, started the machine to drive it a bit and, as he later said, ". . . put it in reverse and almost went off the bridge."

The governor then had the opportunity to be the first official to drive across the bridge but didn't have a current driver's license so his wife, Nancy, drove across instead.

4. MISSAUKEE COUNTY (1984)

Stephen and Debra Vander Weids beat out 10,000 other U.S. Christmas tree growers to win the right to supply a Christmas tree to the White House only to find they did not have one big enough. Russ Hammond (Lake City) rescued the Vander Weids by donating a 20-foot blue spruce that had grown in his front yard for 25 years.

5. GRAND RAPIDS (June 1981)

A woman who had been married in a ceremony performed by the groom had second thoughts and asked Kent County officials about the validity of her marriage. The officials verified that neither a bride nor groom can perform their own wedding ceremony and declared the marriage invalid.

6. SITKA (1968)

Residents of the tiny village forgot their town was 100 years old and didn't get around to celebrating their centennial for another five years.

2 PUBLIC RELATIONS OVERSIGHTS

1. The Ohio Department of Transportation strenuously objected when a Grand Rapids, Michigan firm absent-mindedly(?) printed at least 50,000 of Ohio's

1974 state road maps with interstate highways colored maize and blue, the University of Michigan's colors.

2. During a 1984 Michigan Department of Commerce radio ad for fall tourism in Michigan, an announcer briefly mentioned Saturday afternoon college football excitement while, in the background, a crowd roared and a band played a school fight song — the Minnesota *Rouser*.

4 LATE LETTERS
The mail must go through.

1. In 1936, the year in which the Red Wings won their first Stanley Cup and Ty Cobb became the first player inducted into baseball's Hall of Fame, Harry Kloska, a Grand Rapids salesman, sent postcards to his six brothers and four sisters to tell them about the fun he was having in the Caribbean Islands. One of his brothers finally received his card — 47 years later.

2. Patricia Grambeau (Ann Arbor), upon graduating from Eastern Michigan University in 1942, requested that her diploma be mailed to her. Though she earned her degree in four years, her diploma didn't arrive for another 35 years.

3. A Christmas card mailed in 1954 arrived in 1981 at the address of a Highland Park man who had been dead for 26 years.

4. In May 1966 a Grand Blanc woman mailed a thank you note and $5 to a friend who lived three miles away. Seven years and four months later, the note arrived.

4 WRONG NUMBERS

1. Because of a typgraphical error in the communications directory used during a practice safety drill at the Fermi II nuclear power plant in February 1982, Detroit Edison Company personnel got a "number not in service" recording while trying to contact Canadian officials. Had a real emergency existed, by the time Canadian officials were finally reached, significant quantities of radiation would have been floating over Ontario.

2. An ad in a 1984 issue of *High Society* magazine listed a 313 (Michigan) area code and a number for callers who wanted to hear sexually graphic conversation. A recorded message at that number then included a second number for callers who wanted to hear more. The message, however, neglected to include a Los Angeles area code, and callers, assuming it was another 313 number, reached a Canton couple who, according to a lawsuit, received more than 50 obscene phone calls in one week.

3. During a March 18, 1985 WXYT (Southfield) radio program on taxes, an incorrect number for further tax information was given on the air. As a result, a

37-year-old Detroit woman, who ironically worked as a telephone operator for AT & T, received more than 200 phone calls before the mistake was corrected.

4. In March 1985, in the first judgment of its kind, a Byron Center man, who claimed that the omission of his towing service's number from the 1979 Grand Rapids telephone directory cost him so much business that he had to close the company, won a $100,000 jury award from Michigan Bell.

4 PHONEY BILLS
Reach out and touched

1. In February 1984, Michigan Bell presented a $320,984.26 bill to the Michigan Association of Governmental Employees (Lansing) for calls charged to credit cards the organization had not yet used. Investigators speculated that credit-card thieves had found out the number of the company's card and, in the biggest telephone credit card fraud in Michigan history, had illegally billed calls to it.

2. Dorothy Willis (Mount Clemens), who never got the new phone charge card she requested, did receive, however, a $18,936.66 bill in February 1984. A phone company investigator told the housewife that it was a mistake and not to worry, but three months later, she received a 121-page-long bill for $249,540.35 that listed calls all over the United States as well as to Iraq, Iran, Australia, and many other countries.

3. Kathleen Vokes (Howell) received more than $60,000 in billings for long-distance telephone calls charged in December 1983 and January 1984 to her credit-card number. One bill listed 4,860 minutes, or more than three days worth of calls during one 24-hour period. On the same day, according to the bill, the Wayne State University commuter student also made 23 calls to six different foreign countries from 10 different locations in the United States — all of them exactly at midnight.

4. When Scott Davison (Canton Township) used his family's telephone credit card to call home after arriving at Fort Sill (Lawton, Oklahoma) in March 1984 for basic training, 44 other recruits who heard him read off the number also used it, and in May, Scott's mother, Dorothy, received a 65-page bill for $1,997.

Two weeks later, with the cooperation of the Army, Mrs. Davison sat in a Fort Sill office as each of the recruits filed in and paid their share of the bill.

2 CREDITABLE MISTAKES

1. In 1970 a Troy man, to settle an argument with his wife that even a dog could get a credit card, sent an application to a department store listing the applicant's name as Tareytown Boyd; age, 2.7 years; occupation, watchdog; income, 0; and social security number, none. A short time later, the Dalmation received a credit card along with a note saying that he was a preferred customer.

2. An eight-year-old Ann Arbor girl, who had received an unsolicited application for a department-store credit card in the mail, filled out and returned the application. Several weeks later, though the girl had stated an annual income of only $1 and had included no social security number or credit references, she received a card.

9 MISTAKEN MONEY DEALINGS

1. MICHIGAN (1981)

A Department of Social Services investigation of Michigan welfare rolls revealed that 92 escaped convicts were getting welfare checks, many without even changing their names. Three months later, after state police, local police, and social services investigators had tried to track down the welfare convicts, only seven were apprehended, 60 were removed from the welfare rolls and, for some reason, 32 still received checks.

2. IONIA (June 12, 1964)

At the close of an open house to celebrate the Ionia County National Bank's 30th anniversary, an employee wound the vault's time clock so tight that the massive door couldn't be opened for 36 hours. As a result, the bank had to start its 31st year by asking customers to bring in some cash and arranging for a 36-hour loan from a competing bank across the street.

3. DETROIT

During contract negotiations in 1982, Chrysler workers turned down a profit-sharing plan — approved by both union and company bargainers — and instead elected to take an hourly raise. In 1984, Chrysler earned a record $2.4 billion profit, which under the rejected proposal, would have garnered each employee an estimated $4,700 bonus.

4. DETROIT (April 21, 1976)

At what was billed as the "world's largest garage sale," the city of Detroit sold $100,000 worth of fire hydrants, old street lamps, typewriters, used police cars, motorcycles, bedpans, old barber chairs, firemen's helmets, and other surplus items to more than 75,000 shoppers.

City officials, however, forgot to collect sales tax and, when informed by the director of the Michigan state sales tax division that they owed more than $4,000, had to take the money out of their profits.

5. DETROIT (April 1984)

The judge presiding over a trial in which a man was suing the city of Detroit for alleged police brutality phoned a message to the city's attorney that the defendant would accept a $25,000 settlement. But either the lawyer's secretary forgot to pass along the message or the attorney forgot to return the judge's call, and as a result, the case went to trial and a jury granted an award of $225,000 plus interest.

6. DEARBORN (September 17, 1984)

During an all-night bargaining session between General Motors and the UAW, a GM executive ordered 10 pizzas to feed the 90 hungry and tired journalists who were covering the sessions. Although GM had made 3.2 billion dollars in the first half of the year and held a AAA credit rating, the driver for the Dearborn pizzeria who delivered the food demanded cash for the $125 bill then waited while the GM executive got the money via a 24-hour bank teller machine.

7. FRANKFORT (June 30, 1979)

The Cuban government sent a bill to a Frankfort aviation club for $41.67 saying one of their aircraft, identified as a Boeing 747, had flown through Cuban airspace. At the time, the club owned only two aircraft — both gliders.

8. SOUTHFIELD (December 1984)

The installation of a new computer system at a federal savings bank delayed payment of property taxes for more than 22,000 mortgage customers, who, as a result, lost $500 to $700 each in deductions on their 1984 income taxes.

9. RENO, NEVADA (April 17, 1984)

A 42-year-old East Lansing judge made national headlines when he was arrested for refusing to pay a cab driver a round-trip fare for a trip to the Mustang Ranch, a legal brothel. The judge, who had been on the bench since 1974, was acquitted of defrauding the driver but was charged with misconduct by the Michigan Judicial Tenure Commission.

3 LOTTERY ERRORS

1. On June 7, 1977, the second day of a new Daily Game, a Lansing TV station interviewed a new lottery agent, who joked that 137 was a good bet since it was his favorite at horse tracks. Hundreds took his advice, and when, incredibly, the number was drawn, the state paid out $25,000 more than was bet.

2. The host on the live May 19, 1981 television lottery drawing misread a number *one* on a ping-pong ball and announced it as a *nine*. Though the man immediately corrected himself, hundreds of callers to the news media and the lottery bureau reported that they had seen the announcer switch balls by, among other things, turning off the lights or falling down.

3. When, at a Lottery Bureau promotion in Grayling, officials released 1,000 helium-filled balloons with 50-cent tickets tied to them, the onlooking crowd rushed the area and started stomping. Not one balloon made it into the air.

2 RECORD-SETTING MISTAKES

1. William Woodfill, owner of the Grand Hotel (Mackinac Island) from 1933 to

1979, told Robert Ripley that, at 880 feet, the Grand's front porch was the longest in the world. Ripley printed the fact in his *Believe It or Not* books, and from that time on, the length of the porch was quoted as 880 feet. But a few years before his death in 1984, Woodfill confessed that, because he generally disliked journalists, who, in his opinion, always confused the facts, he had made up the length. The porch was finally accurately measured in 1982 and found to be not quite 700 feet long.

2. A 39-year Detroit woman who in January 1985 played a piano for 134 hours in an attempt to break a 1958 Guinness Book world record later found out that the category had been eliminated several years ago.

3 MONUMENTAL MISTAKES

1. AUTOMOBILE RECALL

In the largest recall in automobile history by a domestic car company, General Motors called in 5.8 million 1978-81 cars and trucks to replace rear suspension bolts.

2. THE CLINTON-KALAMAZOO CANAL

Amid much fanfare at Mt. Clemens on July 20, 1838, Governor Stevens T. Mason lifted the first shovelful of earth to begin excavation of a proposed canal that was to connect Lake Michigan and Lake St. Clair via the Clinton and Kalamazoo rivers and make it possible to cross southern Michigan by boat. But five years later, only 16 miles of the artificial waterway had been dug, money ran out, and the project was abandoned.

3. ZILWAUKEE BRIDGE

In 1978 a $76.8 million contract was awarded to a Dutch construction company to build a six-lane 1.5-mile span across the Saginaw River near Zilwaukee. Designed to replace a drawbridge that had been an infamous bottleneck on I-75, the new bridge was to be the largest pre-cast concrete-segment bridge in the world.

But on August 28, 1982, a 300-foot section suddenly sagged five feet under the weight of construction equipment and brought to a halt the most expensive highway construction in state history.

For the next two and a half years, blame for the mistake was batted back and forth like a volleyball. At first the state blamed the contractor for overloading the span with equipment. The contractor, in turn, said that the state highway department's design was the cause, then pulled out of the project and threatened to sue. To avoid the costly lawsuit, the state paid the contractor $4.8 million and bought his equipment for another $8 million.

A consultant, hired by the state to review construction operations at the site, also blamed the accident on the contractor's improper placement of a 1,500-ton crane atop the bridge. But an audit by the U.S. General Accounting Office concluded that, in fact, the consultant was mainly to blame because he had miscalculated the stress placed by the crane. The consultant then said that the whole problem was a result of poor communication — that the contractor had not told him what equipment was on the bridge.

Whoever was at fault, the accident delayed the bridge's opening from 1983 until 1987 and increased the cost from $81 million to $121 million.

15 STEPS TO NUCLEAR GLOOM
How the Midland Nuclear Power Plant Came and Went

1. December 17, 1967

Consumers Power Co. and Dow Chemical Co. announced plans to build a twin reactor nuclear power plant to provide electricity and processed steam for Dow and electricity for the utility's other Michigan customers.

SCHEDULED OPENING — 1974

PROJECTED COST — $267 Million

2. January 13, 1969

Consumers filed an application for a construction permit with the U.S. Atomic Energy Commission to build the world's first dual-purpose nuclear plant. Two environmental groups filed official protests.

SCHEDULED OPENING — 1975

PROJECTED COST — $350 Million

3. October 1971

A fairgrounds rally attracted more than 10,000 people to hear comedian Art Linkletter and others endorse the plant.

4. December 15, 1972

Federal **construction** permits were issued.

SCHEDULED OPENING — 1975

PROJECTED COST — $610 Million

5. January 31, 1974

Consumers and Dow signed a steam contract.

6. November 14, 1974

Consumers, short of cash because of a recession and an Arab oil embargo which caused skyrocketing costs, halted construction for nine months.

7. 1975-78

Top Dow officials questioned the wisdom of their contract to buy steam. Consumers threatened to sue Dow if the chemical manufacturer pulled out. Dow sought renegotiation of the steam contract and a new pact was signed.

SCHEDULED OPENING — 1981

PROJECTED COST — $1.6 Billion

8. July 1978

Engineers discovered that a newly constructed diesel generator building had sunk more in a few months that it should have in 40 years.

9. December 6, 1979

Nuclear regulators called a halt to all safety-related construction because of soil-settlement problems.

SCHEDULED OPENING — 1984

PROJECTED COST — $3.1 Billion

10. December 2, 1982

The Nuclear Regulatory Commission (NRC) halted most safety-related construction and later fined Consumers $120,000 for quality assurance violations.

11. April 19, 1983

The NRC ordered a complete reinspection of the project.

SCHEDULED OPENING — 1985

PROJECTED COST — $4.43 Billion

12. July 14, 1983

Dow pulled out of a contract to buy processed steam and filed a lawsuit charging Consumers with "continuing negligence and recklessness" that contributed to cost overruns.

13. November 1983

Consumers delayed completion of the reactor which was to provide steam to Dow and requested a $564 million rate increase to cover partial construction costs of the other reactor.

14. April 10, 1984

SCHEDULED OPENING — 1986

PROJECTED COST — $5.7 Billion

15. July 16, 1984

Consumers halted the project and sought immediate rate boosts to cover the costliest power plant project ever abandoned in the United States — and possibly the world.

16 REN CEN WOES

Detroit's glittering river-front Renaissance Center, a $337-million complex of towers and office buildings, was built to revitalize the city by attracting business and people back to the downtown area. While the Center has at least partially accomplished that purpose, it has not done so without its share of mistakes and problems including:

1. March 1977

Seventeen contractors working on the project were fined more than $30,000 by the state Department of Labor for safety violations.

2. May 1977

Though the Plaza Hotel, the 73-story glass-cylinder centerpiece of the complex, had a sizable around-the-clock security force and closed-circuit television monitors to protect guests, a Pennsylvania woman was raped and robbed by a man who broke into her room.

3. June 1977

Dust stirred up by ongoing construction jammed elevator mechanisms causing them to stop between floors or skip floors.

4. July 1977

Heat sensors placed to close to steam pipes set off two or three false fire alarms a day. Each time an alarm sounded, seven trucks from a nearby station responded at a cost of $125 to taxpayers.

5. July 1977

A three-alarm fire started in a garage and lower floor of a uncompleted 39-story office tower.

6. August 1977

A 20-year-old New Jersey man got out of a stalled elevator, slipped backward though an opening between the bottom of the elevator and the hall floor, and fell 39 floors to his death down the shaft. City investigators, however, absolved the Plaza Hotel in the death after concluding that the man or his friends had deliberately stopped the elevator.

7. July 1978

During a violent thunderstorm, part of a seven-level $4.5-million parking structure under construction collapsed in a heap of rubble under the heavy rain and high winds. During the same storm, 10 windows were blown out of two office structures, and 80 patrons were briefly evacuated from the 73rd-floor Plaza Hotel restaurant and bar as it swayed in the 70-m.p.h. wind gusts.

8. August 1978

An article in the Journal of the *American Institute of Architects* criticized the Ren Cen's "baffling" interior and lack of directions or signs.

9. January 1979

With a loud blast and burst of water, a 64-square-foot chunk of plaster ceiling — waterlogged from a burst pipe — crashed to the floor of one of the four 39-story towers that surround the Plaza Hotel, damaging several shops and eateries. The same problem occurred three times the winter before.

10. August 1980

Because of huge losses, the partnership that owned the Ren Cen could not make mortgage payments and were granted a moratorium for the rest of the year.

11. August 1980

Twenty-four conventioneers who were headed to a hospitality suite on the 67th floor of the Plaza Hotel sweltered and at times panicked when their elevator became stuck above the 40th floor for more than two hours.

12. January 1981

Lenders granted the Ren Cen owners a two-year moratorium on payments on the mortgage principal, allowing them to pay interest only.

13. February 1981

Detroit's Building and Safety Inspection Department cited the Ren Cen for three major building safety-code violations.

14. January 1983

The owners of the complex defaulted on their mortgage debt for the second time in a little more than two years and, under the terms of the renegotiated first mortgage, faced immediate foreclosure. The Center was also delinquent on $2.2 million in school and county property taxes.

15. November 1983

The Center was refinanced and bought by the four insurance companies that held its mortgage.

16. April 24, 1984

An 18-year-old Detroit youth was shot and wounded near a video arcade inside the Ren Cen. Three days before, several youths who had been ejected from the same area fired four or five random shots as they left.

2 MISTAKES BY WELL-KNOWN MICHIGANIANS

1. HENRY FORD (June 4, 1896)

As Ford prepared to test drive his first gasoline-powered "quadricycle," he discovered that he had built the vehicle too wide to fit through his storage shed's door. So Ford grabbed a sledgehammer, broke out part of a brick wall, then drove the vehicle around downtown Detroit's darkened streets in a successful trial run.

2. WILL K. KELLOGG (1894)

While conducting experiments to invent a digestible substitute for bread, Kellogg accidentally left a batch of boiled wheat to stand. Kellogg tried to reboil and compress the mixture, but a thin layer stuck to the rollers of his processing machines. As Kellogg removed the hardened mess with a knife, it fell in small pieces, and flake cereal had just been invented.

9 GERALD FORD BLUNDERS

In his days as the nation's 38th president, Michigan's Gerald Ford established a reputation as an amiable bumbler who meant well but always somehow slipped up as evidenced by:

4 Slips of the Tongue

Four quotes attributed to Ford.

1. "Whenever I can, I always watch the Detroit Tigers on radio."

2. "When a man is asked to give a speech, the first thing he has to decide is what to say."

3. "If Lincoln were alive today, he would be spinning in his grave."

4. In September 1978, while Ford and Ronald Reagan campaigned in Texas for state candidates, Ford said that he and Reagan were in Houston to help GOP candidate Bill Clements get elected "governor of the great state of California."

2 Pratfalls

5. As the president disembarked from a plane at Salzburg, Austria, in June 1975, he slipped, sprawled forward on his hands and one knee, landed practically at the feet of the Austrian Chancellor, then rose quickly and shook the chancellor's hand.

6. While making a ski run down 11,000-foot Vail Mountain in a December 1975 "photo opportunity" session for television, newspaper, and magazine photographers, Ford fell immediately after getting within prime camera range.

3 Errant Golf Shots

7. While playing in a Minneapolis charity golf match in June 1974, Ford sliced his drive off the first tee and hit a 17-year-old spectator in the head. On the 16th hole, Ford's slashing drive hit a golf cart carrying a policeman.

8. On the second shot of the second hole of the first Jerry Ford Invitational Golf tournament at Vail in July 1977, the former president accidentally hit a spectator, who received a bruise on her arm.

9. Ford, who was serving as Arnold Palmer's partner during a Bing Crosby Pro-Am golf tournament at Pebble Beach, California in February 1980, hit a senior-citizen spectator, drawing blood but not seriously injuring the man.

2 MISTAKEN IDENTITIES

1. Terry Dean Rogan (Saginaw), a part-time Delta College student, lost his wallet in the Pontiac area in January 1981. The following year, a man apparently using Rogan's identity cards was linked to two murders and two robberies in Los Angeles, California, and a warrant in Rogan's name was entered into the FBI's National Crime Information Center computer network.

As a result, during the next 14 months, Rogan was mistakenly arrested and jailed five times, usually after being stopped for minor traffic violations. Saginaw police tried without success to have the warrant canceled, and Rogan might have continued to be arrested except for the *Saginaw News*, which traced the man who had been using Rogan's alias to an Alabama prison, where he was serving time under another name.

2. In January 1984, Robert J. Kleine, director of Michigan's Office of Revenue and Tax Analysis, and his good friend Robert J. Cline, who worked for a Washington, D.C. tax-study group, switched jobs. The job swap caused tremendous confusion for people who called Bob Cline or Bob Kleine and couldn't understand why neither man remembered previous conversations or didn't recognize them.

5 WELL KNOWN MICHIGANIANS OMITTED FROM *WHO'S WHO*

The following five prominent Michigan residents were not, for unexplained reasons, included in the 1984-85 edition of *Who's Who in the Midwest*.

1. JAMES BLANCHARD

Governor. Rick Cole, his press secretary, however, was included.

2. WILLIAM LUCAS

Wayne County Executive.

3. AGNES MARY MANSOUR

State Department of Social Services director.

4. TOM MONAGHAN

Detroit Tigers owner.

5. ALFRED TAUBMAN

Detroit-area developer who owned the Michigan Panthers football team.

2 FORGETFUL VIOLINISTS

1. CAROLYN BERT (Interlochen) — February 1967

Bert, the program director at the Interlochen Arts Academy, laid a rare violin, made in 1747 in Italy, on the back seat of her car after playing in a concert then forgot the expensive instrument, which sat overnight in -32-degree temperatures. Bert saved the violin, however, by gradually thawing it — first in a refrigerator, then a cool room, then a warm room.

2. RICHARD LULEY (Detroit) — November 1966

Following a concert, the 20-year-old musician placed a borrowed $16,500 Guadagini violin on top of his car while he said goodbye to a friend, then drove off. When Luley arrived home, he realized that he had forgotten to bring the instrument inside his vehicle and unsuccessfully retraced his route in an attempt to find it. Fortunately for the young violinist, a man driving home from work at 3 a.m. spotted the violin case in the street, picked it up, and after reading a newspaper account of Luley's forgetfulness, returned it to him.

2 INSTANCES OF MISPLACED AMMUNITION

1. JENISON (March 29, 1983)

Chimney sweeps, who stopped to check a strange rattling sound they heard in the vacuum they were using to clean Ed and Jackie Herrmann's fireplace, were startled to find their cleaner full of .22-caliber bullets. When they checked further, they found another 80 sooty .22-caliber rifle bullets and birdshot shells on the chimney's "smoke shelf."

The Herrmanns, who did not own a .22-caliber firearm, had no idea how the ammunition had ended up in their home nor why the bullets had not exploded in the 18 years they had built fires in the fireplace.

2. PETOSKEY (August 24, 1984)

While looking for sunken barrels in an island area used during World War II for gunnery practice, a sheriff's marine patrol accidentally discovered a four-foot-long high-explosive M33 bomb lying on the floor of Lake Michigan. Two weeks later, a team of divers from an Indiana-based naval weapons support center determined that the half-ton bomb was a dud and left it on the lake bottom.

4 STRAY SHOTS

1. In 1976, Madison Heights police mistook Alvin Bowling (Warren) for a robbery suspect and shot him in the shoulder as he left a bowling alley. Seven years later, the manager of a neighborhood Detroit bar was loading a gun in his back office when it accidentally fired, sending a bullet through the thin paneled wall and into the back of 30-year-old Bowling as he sipped a drink. Forty minutes later, Bowling died.

2. As 34-year-old Louella Brown (Saginaw) entered her home at about 9:30 p.m. on May 8, 1982, she saw police talking to a crowd of people at a nearby intersection then heard what she thought were firecrackers. Brown, who didn't

pay much attention to the incident and went to bed, awoke the next morning to discover that she had been shot twice in the abdomen.

3. While demonstrating a wild-west "quick draw" of his handgun, a 24-year-old Ann Arbor man on February 28, 1985, accidentally shot his 19-year-old wife in the head, killing her instantly.

4. On March 9, 1972, three officers from the STRESS (Stop Robberies Enjoy Safe Streets) unit of the Detroit police force followed a man they had observed carry a gun into a west side Detroit apartment building. Moments later, the plainclothed officers burst through the slightly open door of an apartment where several off-duty Wayne County Sheriff's deputies were playing cards, and a gun battle ensued during which more than 40 shots were fired, killing one deputy and wounding two others.

During a lengthy investigation which followed the fight, the sheriff's deputies claimed that the STRESS officers had burst through the door with guns drawn without warning or without identifying themselves as police. The STRESS officers, three of whom were charged with intent to commit murder but found not guilty, said that the deputies opened fire first.

2 BUNGLED BANK ROBBERIES

1. DETROIT (September 16, 1982)

A Detroit man got so excited at his apparent success in robbing a bank that he accidentally dropped his wallet, complete with photos and identification, out of a briefcase while pushing money into it. When the robber returned home about four hours later, he was greeted by police, who arrested him.

2. KALAMAZOO (September 12, 1984)

A 22-year-old man pulled his truck up to the outermost lane of a drive-in bank then, though there were two other vehicles and a bulletproof window between him and the teller, sent a holdup note through a pneumatic-tube system into the bank. The teller, while continuing to process transactions in the other lanes, slipped the note to the manager, who called the sheriff's department. Two minutes later, patrol cars pulled up, and officers arrested the would-be robber as he patiently waited for the tens, twenties, and hundreds he had demanded to be sent to his truck.

5 BOTCHED CRIMES

1. & 2. MICHIGAN STATE FAIR GROUNDS (Detroit) — August 31, 1982

Shortly before midnight, as a worker closed up a pizza booth, an 18-year-old man walked up and offered to trade four marijuana cigarettes for a pizza. The customer, evidently unaware that the booth was run and staffed by Detroit police officers for charity, then pulled the joints out of his pocket and was promptly arrested.

The next night at the same booth, again at closing time, another customer offered to trade three joints for a pizza. The officer who was attending the booth thought the young man was probably a prankster who had read about the first bartering bust so jokingly replied, "Nope, my boss said we gotta have four joints." The young man left, returned about 15 minutes later, slid four joints across the counter, and was arrested.

3. KALAMAZOO (November 21, 1983)

A Detroit bus driver was arrested for hijacking a plane at Kalamazoo and demanding to go to Chicago. The plane was going to Chicago anyway.

4. TAWAS CITY (November 1, 1978)

According to the *Book of Lists III*, Thomas Schimmel went home from work for lunch to discover that someone had entered his home, eaten a bowl of cereal and some chicken, and left. Schimmel called a sheriff's deputy, filed a report, then returned to work.

At 6:30 p.m., Schimmel returned home but immediately fell asleep on the couch. At 11:45 p.m., he awoke and went to his bedroom, where he discovered that the thief had not only returned, but was asleep in his bed. Schimmel again called the police, who woke the intruder and charged him with breaking and entering.

5. DETROIT (May 12, 1970)

Three young bandits boarded a freight train as it pulled into a west-side freight yard, held a conductor at gunpoint, and broke into two freight cars. The bandits, in what was believed to the first train robbery in Detroit's history, then made off with several items of the freight cars' contents — baby strollers, bassinets and rattles.

4 OVEREXPOSURES

1. In June 1982, an unarmed man took $400 from a Lansing pizza parlor and fled. Nine months later, the robber inexplicably allowed his picture and name to be printed in a local newspaper as part of a man-in-the-street interview and, as a result, was recognized, arrested, tried, convicted, and sentenced to 10 to 20 years in prison.

2. A 1982 newspaper photo-story about a 24-year-old Carleton man who had eloped with an 83-year-old woman attracted a great deal of attention, including that of authorities at the Monroe County Probation Office, who noticed that the groom was a prisoner who had escaped from one of their halfway houses two years before.

3. A Flint fireman in 1969 was so proud that his son had shot a bear that he told a local newspaper reporter, who then printed a story about the 11-year-old boy's exploit. Authorities who read the story, however, noted that the lad was three years below Michigan's minimum hunting age and arrested the proud father, who paid an $81 fine after pleading guilty to a charge of aiding and abetting hunting a bear without a license.

4. During an April 1976 *60 Minutes* television interview, two Michigan men, who collected Michigan unemployment compensation while living in Florida, made statements that violated conditions of MESC policies and, as a result, lost their benefits.

APPENDIX A

24 *MICHILLANEOUS* MICHTAKES

Twenty-four major and minor mistakes that arose during the writing and editing of *Michillaneous*.

1. "8 Counties With No Hospitals" (page 6) included an "Alma County," which caused readers to remark:

"In your *Michillaneous* I discovered a lot of things about Michigan; such as we have an Alma County. Could you please tell me the location of Alma County?"

— *Name withheld by request, West Branch* —

"I take it that the county name should be *Gratiot*, not Alma."

— *Scott Rich, Gaylord* —

2. Probably the author's biggest mistake, certainly the one that generated the most response, occurred in the list, "32 Entertainment Personalities Born in Michigan" (page 21). Judy Garland *WAS NOT* born in Grand Rapids, Michigan, but rather Grand Rapids, Minnesota. This error is particularly embarrassing to the author as he was born and raised only 50 miles from Grand Rapids, Minnesota, a place from which a transplanted Michiganian wrote:

"Being a native of Sault Ste. Marie, I naturally am interested in facts about Michigan. But the first thing I read was about entertainment personalities born in Michigan, and number one was Judy Garland, which is in error.

Judy Garland was born here in Grand Rapids, Minnesota, as Francis Gumm. We have a museum here with many things of interest about Judy."

— *Mrs. D.O. Stumpf, Grand Rapids, Minnesota* —

3. *M*A*S*H* is improperly punctuated (page 21).

4. "3 Movies Filmed in Michigan" (page 28), because of a typographical error, has *Anatomy of a Murder* being filmed in 1969, when in fact:

"The movie, *Anatomy of a Murder*, was filmed in Marquette County in 1959, not 1969. I was a young girl at the time growing up in Ishpeming."

— *Susan Collick, Fenton* —

5. "7 Pulitzer Prize Winners" (page 60) was five short, having omitted the following winners.

Royce Howes, *Detroit Free Press* — Editorial, 1955
John Knight — Editorial,1968
Detroit Free Press Staff — Reporting, 1968
Taro M. Yamasaki, *Detroit Free Press* — Feature Photography, 1981
The Detroit News — Meritorious Public Service, 1982

6. In "10 Famous People Born in Michigan" (page 61), the author attempted to make famous Civil War general and Indian fighter George Custer a Monroe, Michigan native when, in fact:

"General Custer was born in New Rumley, Ohio — his wife was a native of Monroe."

— Paul A. Ott Jr., Mt. Clemens —

7. "14 Cabinet Members" (page 64) failed to include two postmaster generals from Michigan.

"The first was Don M. Dickinson, who was Postmaster General in 1888 under President Grover Cleveland. Dickinson was a prominent Democrat in the state and even had a county named after him.

The second was Arthur E. Summerfield, who served as Postmaster General under President Dwight D. Eisenhower from 1953 to 1961. Summerfield, who owned the old Summerfield Chevrolet dealership in Flint, also was Ike's first campaign manager.

— John Lindstrom, Lansing —

8. In "6 Notable Executions" (page 84), Franklin J. House, Instructor of Criminal Justice at the University of Michigan — Flint points out that:

"The last man to be executed under Michigan law was not Mr. Stephen G. Simmons on September 24, 1830, as Michigan did not become a state until January 26, 1837. Also, the crowd which supposedly was revolted by the sight of Simmons' hanging probably was not as revolted as the papers of the day indicate — at least not enough to prevent them from attending subsequent hangings in Canada when the opportunity arose. We like to think that people would be revolted by the sight; however, public execution has never lacked for an audience."

9. Also under "6 Notable Executions" (page 84), the author misplaced the Chemical State Savings Bank.

"The bank was in Midland, not in Bay City. My grandmother's sister was in the bank depositing money from the store she worked at when the robbery took place."

— James Westphal, Midland —

"The robbery occurred in Midland, not Bay City.

The execution was performed by the late Ira Smith, Midland County Sheriff, who was an old friend of our family. He really has received a lot of 'bad press' as a result of the execution."

— *Terry Lake, Flint* —

10. Through another typographical error on page 86, we tried to postpone for two years an interracial riot that occurred at Detroit on June 20, *1943*.

"I remember going to work at the Dodge Plant in Hamtramck on a street car down Forest Avenue behind Army tanks, not even knowing what was going on. I was single at the time and did not marry until 1944, so I believe the year should be 1943, not 1945."

— *Vera Snyder, Royal Oak* —

11. In "5 Earliest Permanent Settlements" (page 97), the author erroneously repeated the claim of many Michiganians that Sault Ste. Marie is the third oldest remaining settlement in the United States. The Sault is probably the oldest remaining midwest settlement, but many east coast cities predate the 1668 founding of Sault Ste. Marie by Father Jacques Marquette.

12. In "6 Ships Named *Michigan*" (page 107), the author pre-commissioned the latest U.S.S. *Michigan* by six years. The Trident missile-carrying submarine was commissioned in 1982, not 1976.

13. Also in "6 Ships Named *Michigan*" (page 107), the author and the editors all took the U.S. Navy's word when they stamped on the back of the photograph of the U.S.S. *Michigan* launched in 1844 that it was "the only national war vessel to ever sail the Great Lakes." However:

"Not many people seem to remember that, during World War II, there were two aircraft carriers stationed on the Great Lakes — the U.S.S. *Sable* and the U.S.S. *Wolverine*. One, at least, was stationed at a navy pier in Chicago and put out to "sea" daily for naval aircraft to practice landings. I think both ships were probably armed for anti-aircraft firing practice as well."

— *Franklin House, Flint* —

14. The title of the first item under "7 National Transportation Firsts" (page 111) should read "First *Mile* of Concrete Highway." As James E. Kliber (Houghton) points out:

"I read with interest that the first concrete road in the United States was Woodward in Detroit. Having been born and raised in the Motor City, I grew up with that myth also, but since I moved to Michigan's Copper Country, I discovered that 'it ain't so.'

In the heyday of Michigan's copper mining boom, the streets of Calumet weren't exactly paved in gold, but they were concrete. Portland Street in Calumet was paved in 1906, three years before Woodward. Not only that, but the original concrete is still in use today, and a plaque commemorating that occasion can still be found there.

However, in all fairness to Detroit, I am sure that if you research it you will find Woodward was the first *mile* of concrete road in the United States. Portland street is considerably shorter than that."

15. In "Michigan in 6 Wars" (page 124), the author did not give Michigan Civil War soldiers as much credit as they deserved in the capture of Confederate President Jefferson Davis.

"The 4th *U.S.* Cavalry was a regular army unit that was recruited from the country as a whole. Although this regiment was in the same general area at the time, it did not take part in the capture of the rebel president.

The 4th *Michigan* Cavalary was recruited in Michigan and performed the capture in question. This unit, however, was an entirely different unit in the U.S. volunteer forces.

Furthermore, they were chasing the remnants of the fleeing Confederate *government*, not army. There were some troops with them, but more in the form of a body guard than combat troops."

— *John G. Schumitsch, Imlay City* —

16. "4 Counties in the Great Lakes State With No Water Acreage" (page 132) included Gratiot and Macomb counties. However:

"According to the Michigan United Conservation Club's *Michigan Mapped Lakes*, Gratiot and Macomb counties do have several lakes."

— *Allen Pienkowski, Detroit* —

17. In "5 Unique Trees" (page 140), the dimension of the giant 300-year-old "Monarch" white pine at Hartwick Pines State Park was listed as being $4^{1}/2$ feet in circumference, when it is, in fact, $4^{1}/2$ feet in diameter.

18. "I was disappointed that you listed Missaukee County as one of the counties with no veterinarians (page 143). Missaukee County has always had a veterinarian — sometimes two. Alpha S. Clark Jr., D.V.M. has been in this area for over 20 years. He has an animal hospital three miles east of McBain — which is in the southern part of Missaukee County — and treated many of the animals with PBB in their systems."

— *Mrs. Ida Vanderwal, McBain* —

19. In "5 Remarkable Multiple Births" (page 152), Pam Pulter is from Redford Township and gave birth to her quadruplets on November 24th.

Also, the name of the Monroe mother of quadruplets is Marilyn, not Sharon, Drozdowicz.

20. Not to be outdone by "5 Memorable Map Omissions (page 65), the author neglected to include a city from his list, "7 Largest Cities" (page 154).

"In listing the seven largest cities in Michigan, you have omitted Sterling Heights, a city which is ranked sixth, according to the Bureau of Census."

— *Georgina Dillon, Librarian, Sterling Heights* —

21. In "3 Relative Professions" (page 206),

" 'John Bezolte' was misspelled — it should be 'John Bezotte.' His daughter Kathy now works out of Gaylord — not Pontiac."

— *Scott Rich, Gaylord* —

22. The mother of one the partipants in "6 Remarkable Feats" (page 222) informed us that we had tried to change her daughter's name.

"When you told about my daughter's seven-hour 1981 swim across the Straits of Mackinac, you printed the wrong first name. My daughter's name is not 'Debbie,' but is actually Catherine Pauline 'Cathy' Daoust."

— *Mrs. Eugene Daoust, Alpena* —

23. In "7 Pennant-Winning Years" (page 232), we unintentionally slighted the Detroit Tigers and at least one Tiger fan.

"Since the Tigers have won only a few pennants it seemed a shame to omit one of them.

My records indicate they won in 1909 then lost to Pittsburgh in the world series, four games to three."

— *Thomas Roberts, Farmington Hills* —

24. Keweenaw, as in the peninsula and county, is consistently misspelled as *Keeweenaw* throughout the book.

APPENDIX B

17 *MICHILLANEOUS* FOLLOW-UPS

Follow-ups to 17 items that appeared in *Michillaneous*.

1. 3 UNUSUAL AUTOPSIES (page 17)

The parents of the young Powers murder victim whose hands and hair were cut off and used for evidence were awarded $20,000 in damages. The verdict, in which a jury found a deputy medical examiner 75% at fault and a funeral home 25% at fault in the secret dismemberment, also prompted the resignation of all three Menominee County medical examiners.

2. 5 UNUSUAL FUNERALS (Page 18)

In an April 9, 1982 judgment, a casket manufacturer was ordered to pay a total of $73,257 to 17 survivors of a man whose body fell from the bottom of a casket while on the way to his grave.

"This event made the national news — Johnny Carson, Paul Harvey, etc. — but the exact location of the funeral was never mentioned. A *Homer, Michigan* dateline was usually mentioned, the deceased man was from Brighton, but the incident took place in a small country cemetery called Whig Center, located in Butler Township (Branch County). I happen to know this because I am the sexton for that cemetery and was there that day.

Incidentally, the man was buried the next day with only a few family members present. Also, the family was awarded about $60,000, which was divided among 14 or more claiments. So after lawyer fees, they received very little."

— Douglas Van Kampen, Litchfield —

3. 10 GUINNESS WORLD RECORD HOLDERS (page 52)

On January 24, 1983, Jim Purol, a 30-year-old Livonia musician, broke his own Guinness record by stuffing 140 cigarettes into his mouth and smoking them for one minute on a Detroit-area television show.

4. 4 MICHIGAN ASTRONAUTS (page 62)

Add a fifth, Brewster Shaw Jr. (Cass City), who in November 1983 piloted the *Columbia* space shuttle around the earth at 17,400 m.p.h. for 10 days in the longest, most ambitious shuttle mission to that time.

5. 11 ALL AMERICAN CITIES (page 68)

In April 1984, Traverse City became the most recent Michigan city to win the National Municipal League's award.

6. 5 MEMORABLE CASES OF PROSTITUTION (page 76)

The attempt to close a Sault Ste. Marie bordello down by adding it to the tax roles, while at first elevating its owner to folk-hero status, ultimately worked. In May 1982 the owner of the house closed because of non-payment of back taxes.

7. 5 SKYJACKINGS (page 79)

Dale Otto Remling, who flew to a few hours of freedom from the yard of Southern Michigan Prison in a hijacked helicopter, was released from prison in 1984 and, according to newspaper reports, now works on a ranch near Paris, Michigan.

8. 2 FAMOUS MISSING PERSONS (page 81)

In August 1980, James Dallas Egbert III committed suicide, and on December 9, 1982, a court declared Jimmy Hoffa legally dead.

9. 4 MUSEUMS THAT WERE ONCE JAILS (page 87)

According to Haslett resident R. Peter Korstanije, the Muskegon County Museum has moved, and the building is being used as a jail once again.

10. 8 OLDEST COUNTY JAILS (page 88)

Both Monroe and Gratiot counties have built new jails.

11. 10 NATURAL LANDMARKS (page 137)

The U.S. Interior Department in January 1985 added an 11th Michigan Natural Landmark, a 47,671-acre tract in Ontonagon and Gogebic counties that includes the Porcupine Mountains and Lake of the Clouds.

12. 2 EXTRAORDINARY DOG LOVERS (page 145)

Pearl Keeley, who was evicted from her rented home because she shared the dwelling with 92 dogs, was befriended by a couple who bought the 70-year-old woman a mobile home on an isolated acre near Potterville, where she now lives with approximately 60 dogs.

13. 7 MEMORABLE PROMOTIONAL CAMPAIGNS (page 193)

In the wake of loud protests after the awarding of the first *Say Yes To Michigan* advertising campaign contract to an out-of-state firm, subsequent bids were only let to Michigan agencies or consortiums which included a state firm.

14. 2 CONSPICUOUS RESIGNATIONS (page 208)

Mary Cunningham, who vigorously denied rumors that she was romantically involved with Bendix Corporation chairman William Agee, married Agee in June 1982.

15. 4 BREWERIES (page 219)

Stroh closed its Detroit plant on May 31, 1985.

16. 3 NBA RECORDS HELD BY DETROIT PISTON KEVIN PORTER (page 240)

On April 12, 1985, Isiah Thomas was credited with 21 assists to push his season total to 1,110, breaking Porter's single-season assists record. Thomas finished the regular season with 1,123 assists.

17. The puppy shown shown with its father, the world's largest dog, on the back cover of *Michillaneous* was, at last report, well on his way to outweighing his father.

APPENDIX C
COUNTY LEADERS

ALCONA

Lowest birth rate (p. 50)

CHIPPEWA

Most inland water area (p. 89)

CLINTON

Least burglarized (p. 10)

CRAWFORD

Highest divorce rate (p.49)
Highest percentage of new homes (p. 56)

EATON

Lowest per-capita recipient of state aid (p. 114)
Winter-wheat production (p. 129)

GENESEE

Highest weekly earnings (p. 106)

GOGEBIC

Highest widow population percentage (p. 45)

GRAND TRAVERSE

Most new oil wells (p. 133)

HOUGHTON

Highest male/female ratio (p. 46)
Lowest marriage rate (p. 48)

HURON

Lowest per-capita income tax paid (p. 113)
Dry-bean production (p. 129)
Barley production (p. 129)

IRON

Lowest motor-vehicle-traffic-fatality rate (p. 36)

ISABELLA

Highest percentage of working women (p. 107)

KALKASKA

Highest motor-vehicle-traffic-fatality rate (p. 35)

KEWEENAW

Highest widower population percentage (p. 45)
Highest death rate (p. 45)
Highest over-age-65 population percentage (p.52)
Highest percentage of old homes (p. 56)
Fewest doctors per capita (p. 65)
Fewest dentists per capita (p. 65)
Least expensive homes (p. 102)
Highest percentage of vacation homes (p. 179)

LAKE

Highest crime rate (p. 2)
Most burglarized (p. 9)
Fastest growing (p. 53)
Lowest percentage of renters (p.55)
Lowest percentage of high school graduates (p. 60)
Cheapest rent (p. 102)
Highest percentage of medicaid recipients (p. 103)
Highest percentage of welfare recipients (p. 103)

LAPEER

Highest ratio of married couples with children to married couples without children (p. 49)

LEELANAU

Lowest crime rate (p. 2)

LENAWEE

Corn production (p. 129)
Most centennial farms (p. 130)

LIVINGSTON

Lowest over-age-65 population percentage (p. 52)
Most trophy bucks (p. 84)
Most-expensive homes (p. 102)

LUCE

Highest per-capita recipient of state aid (p. 114)

MACKINAC

Lowest divorce rate (p. 49)

MANISTEE

Most fast-food establishments per capita (p. 187)

MIDLAND

Highest rate of seat-belt usage (p. 152)

MISSAUKEE

Highest birth rate (p. 49)

MONTMORENCY

Lowest automobile theft-rate (p. 10)

OAKLAND

Highest percentage of air-conditioned homes (p. 91)
Most expensive rent (p. 102)
Highest per-capita income (p. 103)
Most income tax paid per capita (p. 113)
Highest new-car-ownership rate (p. 138)

OGEMAW

Highest marriage rate (p. 48)

ONTONAGON

Most stable (p. 55)

OSCEOLA

Fewest fast-food establishments per capita (p. 187)

OSCODA

Highest Kirtland's Warbler population (p. 80)
Highest percentage of wood-heated homes (p. 92)
Lowest per-capita income (p. 103)
Lowest weekly earnings (p. 106)

OTTAWA

Lowest percentage of medicaid recipients (p. 103)
Lowest percentage of welfare recipients (p. 103)

PRESQUE ISLE

Lowest percentage of working women (p. 107)

ROSCOMMON

Highest ratio of married couples without children to married couples with
children (p. 50)
Highest percentage of social security income (p. 107)
Highest motor vehicle registration rate (p. 143)

SAGINAW

Soybean production (p. 129)
Cash receipts from farm marketings (p. 130)

SANILAC

Least inland water area (p. 89)
Oat production (p. 129)

SCHOOLCRAFT

Highest female/male ratio (p.46)

TUSCOLA

Sugar-beet production (p. 129)

WASHTENAW

Lowest death rate (p. 45)
Highest percentage of renters (p. 54)
Highest percentage of high school graduates (p. 60)
Most doctors per capita (p. 65)
Most dentists per capita (p. 65)
Lowest percentage of social security income (p. 107)

WAYNE

Highest automobile theft-rate (p. 10)
Highest murder rate (p. 40)
Largest population loss (p. 53)
Lowest motor vehicle registration rate (p. 143)

INDEX

THE AUTHOR

Gary W. Barfknecht, 40, was born and raised in Virginia, Minnesota, the *Queen City* of that state's Mesabi Iron Range. After receiving a bachelor of science degree from the University of Minnesota in 1967 and a master of science degree from the University of Washington in 1969, Barfknecht came to Flint, Michigan, as a paint chemist with the E.I. DuPont & deNemours company.

But after only a year on the job, Barfknecht and the chemical giant reached the mutual conclusion that he was not suited for corporate life, and Barfknecht set out on a freelance-writing career. Barfknecht sold the first magazine article he ever wrote, "Robots Join the Assembly Line" (*Science & Mechanics*, October 1971), and, over the next three years, his articles were featured in *Reader's Digest, Science Digest, Lion, Sign, Lutheran Standard, Modern Maturity*, and other magazines. During that time, Barfknecht also was the ghost writer for the book, *A Father, A Son, and a Three Mile Run* (Zondervan, 1974) and authored a local guide book, *33 Hikes From Flint* (Friede Publications, 1975).

While freelancing, Barfknecht also managed a hockey pro shop at a Flint ice arena. That job led to a position as hockey commissioner, and in 1977, when Barfknecht took over the directorship of all amateur hockey programming (youth, adult, and high school) in the Genesee County area, he had to postpone his writing efforts.

In 1981, Barfknecht resigned as hockey commissioner to once again become a full-time author and publisher and, in 1982, wrote and published what became a best-selling collection of Michigan trivia called *Michillaneous*. In 1983, Barfknecht authored *Murder, Michigan*, a book he describes as "the dark side of Michigan history," and in 1984 he wrote *Mich-Again's Day*, a further collection of Michigan trivia arranged in an "on-this-day-in-Michigan-history" format.

After publication of *Michillaneous II*, Barfknecht plans to take a brief sabbatical from writing to devote full-time efforts to his publishing firm, Friede Publications, which will release, within the next year, three titles: *Fish Michigan Vol I: 101 Great Lakes Trips* by Tom Huggler, *Canoe Michigan Vol I: A Comprehensive Guide to 40 Rivers* by Jerry Dennis and Craig Date, and *Natural Michigan*, a guide to Michigan wildlife sanctuaries and nature preserves, by Tom Powers.

Barfknecht currently resides in Davison, Michigan, with his wife, Ann, and their two daughters, Amy, 19, and Heidi, 14.

MICHIGAN